Sacred Wounds

A Path to Healing from Spiritual Trauma

TERESA MATEUS

chalice
PRESS

"So many people have been wounded by religion. So few understand the personal, emotional, and spiritual dimensions of these wounds. As a pastor and a professional therapist, Teresa Mateus is the first person I would go to for help in processing spiritual pain. Now, her gentle wisdom is available widely through *Sacred Wounds*. It is beautifully written and pastorally rich. Highly recommended!"

—**Brian D. McLaren,** author/speaker

"In the changing landscape of faith, there are so many men and women across ages, demographics, and faith traditions lying on the side of the road bleeding. Scarred and hurt from unhealthy systems, many often don't know where to turn or how to find their way toward healing. *Sacred Wounds* is an incredible tool of hope! Teresa Mateus is an amazing guide, tender and wise, and offers her own experiences, other's powerful stories, and practical, gentle, and meaningful exercises for healing. I will be sharing it with the many people I know longing for hope after experiencing religious trauma."

—**Kathy Escobar,** co-pastor of The Refuge and author of *Faith Shift: Finding Your Way Forward When Everything You Believe Is Coming Apart*

"*Sacred Wounds* is a literary liminal adventure into the holy terrain of trauma, healing, brokenness, and openness. In these pages lie a call for us to be wounded healer-warriors in a fearful, trauma-saturated culture. May it be so!"

—**Anthony Smith,** Postmodern Negro blog; pastor, Mission House (Salisbury, NC)

"This is the book you need if you or someone you know has survived religious trauma. A definitive guide to the origins of religious trauma, effects on the body and mind, and most importantly, how to heal, *Sacred Wounds* is written by a sensitive therapist and survivor with a full cache of honest, loving, insightful, and creative ideas for how to feel better. Offering illustrative vignettes, therapeutic guidance, and practical suggestions for healing processes Mateus elegantly illuminates the imminent path to recovery."

—**Michele Rosenthal,** author of *Your Life After Trauma: Powerful Practices to Reclaim Your Identity*

"The author speaks from both personal and professional experience, and her ideas are well grounded in academic theory. Her writing is both compassionate and full of humor. Tying healing from trauma to the twelve steps of addiction recovery is brilliant."

—**Gail Horton,** MSW, Ph.D., Associate Professor, Florida Atlantic University

"*Sacred Wounds* is not merely an academic exposé on church abuse. It is both personal and poignant, reaching deeply into the souls of those who are still haunted by the abyss between what we expect church to be and sometimes what it is. This book offers a balm of healing that's sacred and pure. Teresa Mateus has heard us. She sees us. She knows us. And she offers us the tools we need to rebuild our lives, our hearts, our souls. This is a brilliant and safe guide through our anxiety, our triggers, our panic attacks, and our nightmares. Reading the stories of those whose wounds are still open, I found myself among them. Each one who so generously shares their stories of healing brings light to all our dark places and reveals the God with whom we are safe. Beautifully written."

—**Daisy Rain Martin,** author of *Juxtaposed: Finding Sanctuary on the Outside* and *Hope Givers: Hope is Here*

"Teresa Mateus looks deep within religion's wounded shadows and, like Christ the wounded healer, finds grace and hope there. Her project in *Sacred Wounds* is twofold: to name the traumas in which religion is complicit, and to provide a map of the healing pilgrimage. Among the unique features of this compelling work are: individual stories, including Mateus', of religion's role in perpetuating wounds; a sophisticated awareness of body-mind healing modalities; and an application of the twelve-step recovery tradition to articulate a positive way forward for transformation. Mateus believes the end result of our wounds does not have to be cynical rejection or wounded avoidance of religion, but a maturing ability to 'transcend and include' even the most painful stages of our lives. This compassionate, wise book will help many people."

—**Mark Longhurst,** pastor and writer

"Teresa Mateus takes us on her own brave journey—and ultimately, intimately, into ourselves. The spiritual traumas are most sacred. No more averting our eyes. We are gently challenged to look, see, sense. Teresa teaches us to remember and trust our instincts once again. She gives us hands-on applications we can use in our lives. Her book is our guide. Take this pilgrimage with her and emerge transformed."

—**Sharon Daugherty,** Sexual Assault Outreach/SART co-facilitator; Palm Beach County Victim Services & Certified Rape Crisis Center

"If one of the definitions of trauma is 'any experience less than nurturing,' then life on this planet is daunting, risky business for us frail humans. While the Church can be an agent to bring healing to that trauma, more often than not our religious experiences end up less than nurturing and typically at the hands of well-meaning yet misguided folks. Teresa Mateus shares with brutal and refreshing honesty her journey in spiritual healing. Hers is not just a story of ongoing restoration: it is one demonstrating that in the midst of the pain, the Divine is there weaving all things into the fabric of a new garment designed to give us and others protection, shelter, and life. As a clinician and healer, the insights she presents bring a bright ray of hope where light is more than ever needed. I'm grateful for her voice to those inside and outside of the Church. She is a refreshing change agent who speaks from both clinical expertise and deep, personal experience."

—**Jonathan Benz,** MS, CAP, ICADC, CDWF, author of *The Recovery-Minded Church*

"Teresa Mateus's gentle voice of wisdom has never been more needed than it is today. With clinical expertise amplified by a personal journey from victim to survivor to victor, Teresa is the perfect wounded healer, and her words are exactly the balm that all those with sacred wounds need!"

—**Reba Riley,** author of *Post-Traumatic Church Syndrome: A Memoir of Humor and Healing*

*For all those
who suffer in silence
and all who speak
their truth out loud.
To the broken wings and the mended hearts,
To the painful endings and the grace-filled new starts.
You are brave.
You are beautiful.
You are worthy.*

Copyright © 2025 by Teresa Mateus

All rights reserved. For permission to reuse content, please contact Copyright Clearance Center, 222 Rosewood Drive, Danvers, MA 01923, (978) 750-8400, www.copyright.com.

Print: 9780827235649
EPUB: 9780827235656
EPDF: 9780827235663

ChalicePress.com

Printed in the United States of America.

CONTENTS

Acknowledgments	ix
Preface: Second Edition	xi
Introduction	1
1 The Wounds That Bind	19
2 Inside the Animal	46
3 Through the Looking Glass	77
4 Faith of Origin	93
5 Wisdom Teachers Versus False Gurus	111
6 Peeling the Onion	121
7 The Lotus and the Mud	145
8 Just for Today	169
9 The Voices Out of Darkness	177
10 Extremism & Religious Trauma That Touches Us All	185
11 Contigo, Conmigo: Moving Forward Together	192
Epilogue: The Cracks Are Where the Light Gets In	200
Addendum: Finding a Mental Health Provider	203

"Sorrow prepares you for joy. It violently sweeps everything out of your house, so that new joy can find space to enter. It shakes the yellow leaves from the bough of your heart, so that fresh, green leaves can grow in their place. It pulls up the rotten roots, so that new roots hidden beneath have room to grow. Whatever sorrow shakes from your heart, far better things will take their place."

—Rumi

Acknowledgments

This book is first and foremost for all the hurt, the unheard, the invalidated, and the discarded. It is for the forgotten, the neglected, and the negated souls who have been given a false myth of a vengeful God or a hateful and power-driven manifestation of divinity. It is for everyone who has survived traumatic experiences in spiritual or religious contexts, or who has been harmed in some way by extremist religiosity. It is also for those who shared their stories for this book and were brave enough to vocalize their own suffering for the sake of others finding resonance and, possibly, a hopeful future.

I have a deep gratitude for everyone who has shared with me their experiences of hate, prejudice, oppression, and marginalization in abusive spiritual contexts or at the hands of communities of extremism. Thank you for your many stories of pain, survival, and hope that bravely stand in opposition to hate, neglect, and diminishment. Thank you for living your story, for surviving—and when you can—for thriving, despite the negative myths of religious and spiritual extremism.

My thanks to the teachers and elders who have guided my own spiritual journey and the ancestral traditions of wisdom that have offered me a home among my ancestral peoples. Thanks to the parents who raised me and offered me an expansive and loving view of what a queer-inclusive, women-empowering, deeply mystical version of Catholicism could look like. Thanks to Teresa de Avila, Julian of Norwich, Sir Juana Ines de la Cruz, and many other mystics from the Christian lineage for showing me the history of powerful and potent women leaders, teachers, and healers within that mystical tradition. I give thanks to the lineage of Teresa Urrea, one of the first borderland Curanderas (born on my birthday), who was a radical spiritual teacher and ancestral medicine healer as well as activist in her time. I am thankful for the ancestral wisdoms from my own Andean Mountain spirituality and the teachers in the Apaza Q'ero Paqos in the mountains above Cusco, Peru, as well as my own ancestral spiritual lineage of the Muiscas, who are beginning to rise again in the mountains of the Andes. I am thankful for the daily teachers I find in my life, who continue to evolve my understanding of myself, my work, my calling, and my own spiritual-healer roots and branches.

Thank you to all those who helped bring this book into being—from those who had late-night conversations with me about the content to those whose adept hands helped bring the book into being, from editorial support and investment to cover design and publication. I especially thank the wonderful team at Chalice Press, and most especially to Brad Lyons, who has been a constant champion of this book and is the reason for it being rebirthed into a second edition nearly a decade after its first printing.

Thank you to my friends and family, who have been amazing supporters, readers, and morale boosters during the late-night writing and editing sessions. A special thanks to my mother, Patricia Bennett, always my editor-in-chief and first reader of anything I write.

Finally, an encore of thanks to my own soul mothers, Teresa de Avila and Teresa Urrea, one who found me at birth and one, as I was on my journey to return to my ancestral spiritual roots and have both been the distinct and robust voices in my head, both when I wanted to listen and when I didn't. When I most need to remember, they walk with me and remind me who I am and from whom I come.

Preface

Second Edition

When the first edition of *Sacred Wounds* was published, we lived in a radically different world. This new edition is meant to speak into the evolving (and in some cases devolving) landscape in which we are living, the pitfalls and hopefulness of this new reality, as well as the continuation and evolution of the work born out of the original narratives and concepts introduced in the original edition of the book.

The rise of Christian Nationalism and religious-political extremism across the globe have made visible a new kind of synchronism that merges political and religious zealotry in dangerous ways and with historically significant consequences. Speaking to the elements of religious extremism and cults in our wider social-cultural context is an important growing landscape of the study of religious harm, extremism, and trauma. That, too, I address in this edition.

While the personal stories from the original edition of *Sacred Wounds* lean into the experiences of religious trauma from the Christian tradition—because those stories were the most accessible and visible to me while I was researching for this book over a decade ago. Since then there have been visible examples—in the public domain and in my own continued work with various communities—coming from across a multitude of spiritual and religious traditions. This edition of the book layers in some of those publicly visible examples and anecdotes from my own work and engagement over the last decade (with some elements altered for privacy) from a variety of spiritual spaces and religious traditions.

Moreover, much of the work I have done related to spiritual and religious trauma since writing the original edition has been with communities, leaders, therapists, spiritual care providers, and loved ones of those who have struggled through spiritual/religious trauma. This edition of the book includes a section specifically for those of you looking to provide support and allyship to survivors of spiritual trauma.

The world has certainly changed since the first writing of *Sacred Wounds*, and so have I. When I began to read back through the first edition of the book, much like seeing the pictures in one's high school yearbook I had moments of, "Oh, wow, why did I think that was a thing to wear?" There are also moments when I paused and thought, "Hmm, yeah, that still works." It is amazing to see what parts of yourself, your work, and your ideals are a thread that run throughout your life, and what is still a work in progress.

The period in which I wrote the first edition of this book was a kind of Christian Renaissance for me, a period in which I found some progressive and nurturing spaces and community contexts for myself. That comes through in the book, in places more heavily than I would have liked. Yet harm and imperfection continue to shine through in the human expressions of our spiritual lineages. So, there were moments at which the misogyny (and sexual boundary issues and harm as a result), racial prejudice (or just ethnic isolation in what were structurally dominantly white progressive spaces), and general messiness of the Christian context rose to the top again, in my own lived experience and in those around me. I was prepared for it, having lived through my own past and having written an entire book about how this happens. Still, it also reminded me why the container as a system was not a place I thrived—at least not a place that could guide the core of my spiritual life.

There was also a deep spiritual craving in me, one that is as long as my life, to return home to the spiritual roots of my origins. For me, the barrier to this return was always knowing where to begin. As a Colombian adoptee, throughout my whole life I felt as if I was reconstructing my cultural and ancestral identity backwards—finding clues along the way but with no direct map of where I came from.

I remember completing a two-year program in the Christian mystics, taught by all white teachers, with a very particular point of view and narrow understanding of the tradition. For me, that study deepened the one part of Christianity that always resonated with me—the mystics. That version of learning and perspective on lineage only fed a fraction of me. It felt whitewashed in every possible way. Those threads of misogyny, a kind of proprietary wisdom-bearing that excluded everyone except those at the very top from owning the wisdom role, and a perspective on the mystics that was threaded with elements of capitalism, colonialism, and Western exceptionalism, just sat wrong with me. In the end, after I finished the program, there was a bittersweetness. I was glad that I had gone to what were the living ends of mystic lineage study, but I simultaneously wondered, "If this is the most I can learn in this tradition, I need something more."

Shortly after, I remember sitting in a therapy session with a Jewish student in the Religious Studies program at the University of Chicago, talking about his academic work and his spiritual life. Seemingly as a non sequitur in our session he abruptly said, "Are you kind of a Curandera?" To which I replied, "I mean, yeah, kinda." The truth was that while I had been asking myself the questions about where to find my spiritual and healing roots—even though ancestral traditions and cultural ways were an integral part of my being—I hadn't really been doing the hard work of rediscovering those roots. Why? Partly out of a fear of being rejected, partly as an adoptee who was not sufficiently a cultural part of where I came from, and partly as a result of not knowing where to begin. Something about his question, and almost certainly of my answering "yes," felt like a calling to return to the roots of myself, a part of my true calling that had been languishing. As a result, every other expression of spirituality and healing work in my life would always feel fractional without it.

I began studying with Curanderas and had a beautiful experience learning the lineage and practices. Some of these are still essential to my own practice today, including *limpias* (a spiritual cleansing bath ritual). In that study with Curanderas, I learned to value the return to one's roots, the medicines born from the earth, and the rituals that are so interconnected with the rest of the natural world. There was a way of being that was exposed to me, and a way of practicing spirituality and being a healer that felt more connected and alive to me than the Western versions had, by themselves. As I found more teachers and studied more deeply, I felt there was still something missing. In retrospect, I understand the Curanderismo tradition, rooted as it is in Meso-American ancestry, as being deeply connected to the place and natural landscape of Mexico, but still only as my cousin tradition. It felt near home, but not exactly home. That was obvious both literally in a geographic way, and at an interior level I couldn't quite explain.

So, I continued my search, and through doing that I found my way to the teachers in the high mountains above Cusco, Peru in the Kiko territory of the Q'eros tribal lands of peoples who are descendants of the Incans. The teachers I found there are from the Apaza family line of the Q'ero Paqos (or spiritual healers), and I spent three years studying and being initiated as a Paqo. In the mountain tradition of the Andes, I finally found my way back home. While my own tribal Indigenous roots descend from the Muisca peoples of the Colombian Andes, due to the extreme decimation of people and culture during early colonization (in pursuit of gold), I learned that the spiritual and healing traditions had been almost eradicated. As a result, the remaining Muisca descendants are just now, during what I would call the Colombian Renaissance, beginning to reclaim and restore what was lost. In the Andean sister countries (Bolivia, Ecuador, and Peru), thanks to the even higher elevations of some of the mountain tribes, and for Peru the origins of the Incan Empire, the people preserved more of the culture and spiritual lineage of the Andes, and that is how I found my teachers there. In the spirituality and ritual traditions of the Indigenous Andes I found a spiritual lineage that resonated at a soul level. The practices, rituals, and healing methodologies were so deeply rooted in the sacredness of the mountains, the four directions of the earth so grounded in the elements and wildlife of the terrain, they felt like an anthem for my heart.

On the day of my final initiation, on the back of a Moto-taxi, I climbed to 15,000 feet and into the peaks of Q'ollority—one of the seven sacred mountains surrounding Cusco—with one of the teachers in the Apaza family line of the Q'ero Paqo tradition. There are ceremonial festival grounds at the base of the highest peaks, used annually in the spring for a synchronistic celebration, one rooted in the Q'eros traditions and with the overlapping of Catholicism throughout, which is something elemental to life in the mountains where the religious leaders of colonization realized that to become imbedded into the communities one needed to superimpose the religion of the empire onto the Indigenous communities; one needed to "Westernize" their ways of being and knowing.

While there are many who engage in the ancestral traditions, many also integrate Catholic element to their spirituality, best articulated in the shrine at the center of the festival grounds. In mid-November, when I was there, the grounds were silent, like a ghost town of sorts. The only ones there were a handful of vendors selling iconography and totems of different practices at the entrance of the shrine, hoping to find customers at this sacred place. Inside the shrine is an open area with seating around the edges, and at the front there is an altar with Manuelito, a core figure in the legend of Q'ollority from Inca times, and above that, as if to supersede the root tradition, is a figure of Jesus.

A version of me from years before would have railed against the syncretism and attempted forced supremacy of Christianity over Indigeneity. I would have mourned the ways in which my ancestral traditions had been overwritten by those with the most power and privilege. There are days on which I still do that, but on that day, something settled over me that was new and welcome—specific to that place and time. As I climbed up the hillside above the shrine with my teacher and spent hours in ceremony and initiation—connected to the Andes, to the mountain range of my birth, to the ancestral memory and living practices of a tradition before the imposition of Spanish and Catholic culture—I felt in me a wild and beautiful symbiosis, discovering at last something I had not quite lost but until then had also not yet found. I felt a thread being rewoven in my spiritual story. I felt mended.

In that high place, as I sat during the ritual, feeling the potency of the high-altitude sun beaming down on me, the sensation of mossy terrain beneath me, and noting the appearance of the sacred condor flying above me during my ceremony, in that moment the blessing of the moment was profound. And something else was healed in me. For the sixteen-year-old version of myself, angry at Catholicism, throwing her rosary beads and Catholic tokens out the window of her attic bedroom, I remembered and released her anger. There is plenty about the overwriting of Indigenous spiritual wisdom which is frustrating. The forced synchronization of ancestral traditions with Christianity across the many diasporas of color is dispiriting. That is still true. Yet, in returning to the spiritual roots I had spent my life seeking, I was able to also hold in my heart with less weight and punishment (of self and the tradition) that which had frankly always also nurtured me in the Catholic tradition of my raising. It was in that state of peace that I was able to walk back down the mountainside after my initiation and stop at one of the vendors and buy two roughly-carved rosaries—one for my mother and one for myself. Those rosary beads still have their place on my altar beside my sacred Paqo tools and other items of greatest spiritual meaning to me.

***

I share all this to explain my own evolution of heart and soul and practice in the intervening years between edition one and two of *Sacred Wounds*. Since this book is written not in an academic and sterile way but rather through the practice of storytelling, it felt important to me to tell you some of the stories from the intervening years about my changes in perspective and my embrace of practices and insights. Throughout the book you will encounter references to words and practices from the Andean and Paqo perspective, and fewer references to a Christian point of view. I love both roots of myself and my spiritual life—the one I was taught that was grounded in Catholicism and the Christian mystics, and the one that I found by returning to my ancestral home in the Indigenous Andean lineages and ways of knowing. I hope that that love is evident, along with my love for the places of learning and growth that I found in traditions like Buddhism, Yoga, mystical Judaism and Islam, Curanderismo, and others.

***

I am deeply grateful to everyone who purchased the first edition, and to those who reached out for support or education related to spiritual trauma since then. It is because of each of you that there is even space for a second edition of this book. I have said that once a book is written and published it goes out into the universe and lives a life of its own, one the author can never fully know. What I do know is that *Sacred Wounds* has had a wild and beautiful adventure since its first publication, and I have been grateful to participate in some of that journey alongside it. That journey has taken me across the country to faith communities, mental health organizations, colleges and universities, nonprofits and philanthropic organizations to facilitate space around this spiritual work of healing.

I am also grateful for all the survivors that have persevered—the ones who bravely shared their stories for the book, and who showed resilience as they found their own path to healing. I am grateful to each of you, your stories and your requests at the beginnings of this book project for it to come to life. You are the reason the book exists at all. I thank you most especially.

* I occasionally reference Quechua, the language of the Incas, and the Paqo tradition, which comes from Inca times. However, just as spiritual

traditions of this time were neither representative of nor originated from the empire/political power of the time, so too the Paqos were from Inca times but not part of the Incan Empire. Even though Incas were victims of Western colonization and empire, the Incas themselves were the imperial power, before the Europeans came to the land. The Quechua language has some complexity because, like English or Spanish, for example, it was the language of the empire before English and Spanish (along with Portuguese and French) came to the Americas. I use Quechua because much of the lineage of the spiritual tradition is rooted in Quechua. But I also want to honor the ancestral languages which Quechua erased, much as the Spanish eradicated the root Indigenous tradition of my Colombian Andes ancestors, the Muisca people and the Chibcha language. All history is complicated, and religious and political powers have a role to play in history the world over and across time. I want to honor that here, because we will repeat our histories in newly harmful ways if we hide from them. It doesn't make everything bad, just like everything isn't good, and that is true of our roots before European empire as well as after.

Introduction
The Human Story, *Ad Infinitum*

The sacred wounds infinity symbol illustrates that our wounds are inextricably linked to the sacred, and the sacred is inextricably linked to our wounds. Our hurt is the origin of our transformation. As Rumi reflected, "The wound is where the light enters."

As someone whose life has been peppered with wounds, I can say, quite definitively, that for me hurt has been the birthplace of the greatest and most transformative places of light entering my life. Most of the time, it didn't seem that way to begin with; instead, it always felt like death. But as in my life, so if we study any myth or religious origin story, we see over and over again that death also midwifes new life. Like the infinity symbol, the journey of the spiritual life is not a period or an exclamation point, but a winding figure eight that constantly feeds back into itself, *ad infinitum*.

The cracks are where the light gets in.

The pain and suffering of life at its peak can transition to joy. Much like physical childbirth, only when the pain reaches a crescendo do we burst into a new place of our own possibility, of infinity, and that crack is where the light gets in.

In psychotherapy, I never over-divulged my pains with clients, and in life I don't spend a lot of time ruminating on them. I think part of the benefit of moving through suffering lies in leaving a trail behind, the crumbs of hope and healing, so others can see it is really possible to find their own healing path. There is value in exploring our pain, and in sharing it when it is appropriate, so that others can see there is a trail to follow. By no means do I have it all figured out, but I know from experience that there is a path to wholeness and healing through trauma, through the pain of spiritual disappointment, and across the scope of human imperfection and struggle. This book is a roadmap to that hopeful place. I created that roadmap not only out of my own tales of pain and reconciliation, but also out of the tales of struggle and recovery from a variety of voices of those who have walked their own path of pain and found hope. Let those tales of the path from struggle to hope be a light for our journey of life. May they show us what is possible for us, too.

We are never ending. We are warriors and creators. We are liberators and manifestors. We are sacred and worthy. We—you—are worthy without caveat or exception. Let the story-making and the hope-mongering begin. Welcome to the shared and sacred journey!

***

It has often been at those moments at which pain intrudes that I really listen. I now recognize that at those moments a personal paradigm shift is about to happen.

I had such a moment nearly twenty years ago, standing in the dimly lit basement room of a yoga studio in Hoboken, New Jersey, where I had spent Monday nights for the previous year. Huddled there with a group of eager twenty-and-thirty-somethings seeking enlightenment from our Buddhist teacher, I sought respite from the painful hypocrisy of my Catholic Church youth. It wasn't a conscious thought, but it was something like, *if anyone can avoid absolutes and platitudes, it's got to be the Buddhists.*

Unfortunately, I was headed for a different kind of awakening—one more akin to the "rude" kind. Surprisingly, even that was beneficial in that it freed me from my illusion that only my faith tradition could be hurtful.

I loved my Mondays spent in the candlelight on mats and meditation chairs. The first half of our class time was always an exploration of foundational Buddhist teachings, which we all scribbled in our notebooks as we ravenously devoured our teacher's wisdom. Many of us were also actual yoga students at this studio, and some in their yoga teacher training program. All of us were seekers on a quest, with many of us having left Western spiritual traditions and now seeking something from the Eastern lineages that we felt was missing in the lineages in which we had been raised. The second half of class was always guided meditation practice.

This was where I learned the power of visualization in meditation to calm the chaos of my mind. In that period of time, I was in the early stages of recovering from sexual trauma and headed to years of post-traumatic stress disorder that I wasn't yet aware I was carrying with me. At that point, I merely knew I needed respite from the cloudy and painful places in my mind. The moments on those mats in that candlelit basement were a profound beginning to learning to heal my mind, body, and spirit from those wounds. The practices of Buddhism mindfulness, of non-attachment to my thoughts and feelings, were essential medicine for my own broken heart and spirit. Even in imperfect places with imperfect teachers we can find the most sacred things.

One evening I was excited to chat with my teacher after class. The previous week I had bought a ticket to hear the Dalai Lama speak at Lehigh University. I was nearly a year into my studies with this particular Buddhist nun at the yoga studio, and I envisaged feeling pride in telling her about this purchase, a way, I thought, of asserting my commitment to move into a deeper place of study and investment in Buddhist practice. I remember clearly that we were standing face to face in front of the shoe cubby at the entrance to the studio, and that I was preparing to take my shoes out of the cubby and leave.

I had been absent for a few weeks, so my teacher came up and gave me a hug, saying, "It's so good to see you back. We have been missing you."

Feeling guilty for my absence, I said, "I know. Work has been so busy, but I wanted to tell you, I just bought my ticket to go see the Dalai Lama next week in Pennsylvania."

As I completed my sentence, her brow furrowed and she replied, "We will actually be there, too. We will be protesting him and his actions. Our tradition disagrees with his actions and engagement in politics. Be careful of his teachings."

Yes. She was warning me about the Dalai Lama, the man who was an international symbol of peace. In my young twenty-something brain, and my newly burgeoning Buddhist student mind, I couldn't wrap my head around the multitude of complexities in different strands of Buddhism that might just mirror what I had found and fled from in Christianity.

I am pretty sure I smiled and nodded and said something that appeared like agreement before I stumbled out of the basement and onto the Hoboken sidewalk, spiritually confused. As her words settled into my brain, my internal response was something like, "Damn it!" That thought was quickly followed by, "Seriously? Not again."

I have since learned that there is complexity and dissonance in every spiritual or religious tradition. What I had been seeking in that basement was a gateway to nirvana on earth—the perfect spiritual practice and tradition without differences of opinion, internal politics, and layers of prejudice and problems. Such perfection doesn't exist. We find our own complex and imperfect path. That path might include learnings from more than one place and teachers and elders who speak to our heart and our own path. And we also find the space to critique what we see as flawed while loving and being grateful for what has nurtured us. I have since similarly learned to look below the surface and ask important questions about the tradition or lineage of practice with which I was engaging, such as: Where does this lineage come from? What are its roots? Who were its original teachers, and who are its contemporary wisdom-keepers? What do those teachers think about the things that are the most important to me? What are their politics about different people groups and identities? Sometimes the new and shiny entry points of a particular spiritual tradition can dazzle our sight, keeping from us the important answers to the questions that can change our understanding and engagement with that tradition.

What I also learned in the years that followed my time in the yoga studio is that the tradition with which my fairly innocent group of novice Buddhist and non-Buddhist yogi students was enamored with is a fairly aggressive and revolutionary group. As I probed deeply into that particular lineage of Buddhism, I read an article that detailed the tradition and its extremist political positions and adversarial stance regarding other lineages of Buddhism. For the first time in my life, I felt something akin to a trigger, something that reminded me of the painful spots I was still holding onto from my childhood religion. All this helped me understand both that my own spiritual wounds were still fresh, and that I was still extra sensitive to fundamentalism, albeit of a different color—in this case the saffron of my teacher's robes.

As unexpected as it was to me, the closest I ever came to a full-on cult was in this seemingly benign lecture and practice series in a New York metro-area yoga studio, not the Christianity in which I was raised. I was lucky that I have only ever skimmed the edges of cult environments—often getting into the gateway spaces, often beginning benignly and then turning up the heat slowly—and I have had a quick allergy to the signs and signatures of the extremist teachings. Even so, I had to learn that things are not always as they appear on the surface, and that spiritual and religious contexts are complex. There is no earthly nirvana, and we have to map the path that is the healthiest for our own spiritual path, doing our best to avoid the hazard zones of spiritual extremism and cult-like lineage that often hide in plain sight.

This is not meant to judge Buddhism. It is simply a reminder that we can find both healthy and extremist versions of every tradition on earth. It is a reminder to be inquisitive and intentional in seeking our own spiritual paths. It is also a reminder that even places and religions that are somehow toxic can offer us valuable wisdom. This is often what complicates our relationships with traditions who do us harm. We can learn something valuable even in painful places.

My experience studying with that Buddhist teacher left me sufficiently open to return to explore the mystic dimensions of my childhood Catholic tradition in a new way and to continue to practice the Buddhist ways, carrying the latter teachings into rethinking how I engaged my childhood tradition, and beginning to forgive the imperfection of my roots. With time, this offered me a new entry point to the Christian contemplative practices and mysticism and prompted a layered life journey of exploring spiritual traditions in a more intentional way. Ultimately, it led me back to the spiritual traditions of my Indigenous Andean ancestors.

Two decades of exploration taught me that no religion or spiritual tradition is immune to fundamentalism or extremism. No religious or spiritual community or discipline is without its flaws, imperfections, prejudices, and blind spots. Religion and spiritual tradition is made up of humans, and our humanity can either be the best of us or get the best of us.

My previous learning experience opened my eyes to my own sacred wounds and became one of the most profound and valuable moments in my spiritual journey. It shifted my perspective on my own spiritual roots and created a clarity in my own path of spiritual seeking. It offered me a way to return to a relationship that had ended on bad terms and find some kind of closure. By seeing the imperfection and factions found in a tradition new to me (Buddhism), I could better validate and honor the imperfections and factions within the Catholicism in which I was raised. I knew I would never be Roman Catholic again, but when I went back to it with a compassionate forgiving heart, my changed perspective enabled me to explore the good elements of my tradition, rather than ditching it all. I could see with new eyes what I loved about Catholicism. By returning, I was granted so many amazing gifts, including contemplative practice and rediscovering the mystic after whom I was named, Teresa of Avila. Catholicism continued to be problematic and fractured to me—in new ways—but at least I knew to expect it, and to heal my hurting heart as I went, rather than being burdened unnecessarily by elements of it for years.

I now think of Catholicism much like a great uncle; Catholicism contains some great elder wisdom, and I love it, but we disagree on a lot. We aren't always close, and some of its beliefs are old and outdated, but even from afar it still feels like family. Our disagreements no longer diminish my love, and for that I am grateful to my sacred wounds—both those that pushed me away from the religion and forced me to ask difficult questions of myself and my spirituality, and those that brought me back into relationship with a branch of my spiritual family, which helped me to repair the pieces and begin a healthier relationship with it.

This is not everyone's story. My religious trauma is not as extensive as that of some people. I don't expect everyone to go back to their sect or tradition of origin with love, and for many people I wouldn't expect that to be the healthy choice. We each have our own path to walk, and each one is as sacred as the wounds that might have shaped the path behind us and ahead of us.

We have the chance to heal our wounds of religious trauma when we choose to. Such healing looks different for each person. I hope that in these pages you will find resonance and understanding, and through them that you will find compassion for yourself and others.

The Frontlines of Spirituality: Suffering, Learning, Loving, and Leaving Religion

I hope that this book prompts a larger conversation about religious and spiritual violence, trauma, and healing. Since the first edition of this book, the general public's understanding of trauma and post-traumatic stress disorder (PTSD) has expanded, in part thanks to the rise of the #metoo movement (sexual trauma and violence), in part thanks to the movements arising from the murder of George Floyd and others (racial and intergenerational trauma), and in part thanks to responses to the Unite the Right rally and violence in Charlottesville, Virginia (religious extremism).

As a practicing trauma therapist for nearly two decades, and whose work with individuals and communities in the last decade has centered around BIPOC, LGBTQIA+, and social movement contexts, I have worked with those suffering from the impact of religious or spiritual trauma in a variety of manifestations, across a breadth of sources and impacts. In recent years, some of the more extreme instances of such abuse and violence have been visible in the public sphere—think sexual abuse in the Catholic Church and the Church's systemic silencing and invisibilizing of that abuse over generations.

I intend this book to guide you through understanding religious and spiritual trauma, wherever they are found. The book explores the origins and roots of spiritual abuse and harm, the systemic, cultural and psychological phenomena of spiritual abuse and trauma, their nature, how they grow, and how we work our way back after we have been harmed. For trauma is paradoxically more complicated and simpler than we tend to think. Diminishing the power and control of religious and spiritual trauma requires that we make it visible. It is, unfortunately, too pervasive and must be recognized as trauma which, if unaddressed and treated, can lead to post-traumatic stress disorder (PTSD). To heal ourselves and support others we know struggling to recover from this kind of traumatic harm, we have to understand what it is, how it functions, and how to address it, and find our own path to healing. When we understand what something is and how it works, it is much easier to begin to dismantle it.

Whenever someone tells me it is *easy* for people to leave an unhealthy religious or spiritual context, I think, "You have clearly never met or fully listened to the story of someone wounded by their spiritual or religious community." People don't leave for a lack of caring. Rather, it's usually caring too much that makes many leave. Most leave with broken hearts. Most leave in mourning.

These are my people—the spiritually wounded, the soul warriors.

If you meet someone who has the battle wounds of such spiritual or religious trauma, be gentle with them. If you are one of these warriors, be gentle with yourself.

There is no magic secret to spirituality or belief inside the walls of spiritual institutions. It is quite simple: it is the people who make or break the institution. And sometimes the people in the institution make or break human souls.

The world is sacred and always unfolding, *ad infinitum*. Some days it is excruciatingly difficult to find anything sacred in this heartbreaking world in which religion has become, nationally and globally, a weapon of war and opposition, a tool for power and superiority and, in the United States (among other nations), a weapon of white nationalism, homophobia, transphobia, racism, and more. Ours is a world in which people use religion not merely as a weapon against those inside their circles, but also against any "outsiders," and do so with the bluntness of a hammer and with hatred born of unsubstantiated fear. In this world there are ever-evolving ways in which people perpetrate sacred wounds, and ever-greater need for us to heal ourselves, our communities, and our world from the collective wound of this harm.

All my life I have been ravenous to explore and unfold the sacredness of the world—to understand the sacred in the profane, the mystic inside the mundane. There were times in my life I couldn't eat the bread, and so I ravaged a sunset instead. In the end, I realized that everything we imbibe are cosmic nutrients. In Indigenous philosophies the world over, what Western traditions call *God* is of and from and in everything. Consequently, we are all interconnected with each other and with all the elements of nature and the universe. We are all part of the ecosystem of existence. If we could live into this elemental way of being with each other, with the world around us, through this alone we would be ending an abuse. For if we are all part of the sacred web of being, then everything in that web is essentially divine and valuable. In the Quechua language of the Andean nations, we call that way of being *ayni*, which means "reciprocity": what we give, we receive, and each of us is called to give as much as we are given, in love and gratitude for the abundance of all things. What would it mean to reframe our way of being with each other through this lens of connection and accountability? The walls sustaining hatred crumble under this collective ethos. Is this aspirational? Of course. But if we don't have aspirations, we don't grow. If we don't dream and envision what is as yet impossible, then the imagination at the core of new creation withers. My hope is that this book will birth what might today seem impossible.

I am calling all of us to enter into both the sacred wounds and the orbits of spiritual expression. I am calling for light in shadowed places, for finding beauty in the darkness of night, and for creating unconventional forms of light where broken sources have flamed out.

Let us together learn the curves of religious trauma, the shape of this pain. Whether as abused and abuser, religious and secular, regardless of your angle of receiving this knowledge, let it penetrate your mind and mine your memory. Let such knowledge and truth unearth your own scars, small and large, and trace the outline of their markings to see the world through the lens of this *sacred pain*. Together we can feel our way through that pain and find the path to heal it—because we heal in community. There is no other way.

I hadn't even finished my first book before this book began demanding to be written. I had every intention of writing it, just not yet. Then, the need for it became overwhelmingly obvious. Wherever I went, I encountered people disclosing the stories of their suffering at the hands of spiritual and religious communities, spiritual leaders, and faith institutions. The stories created resonance with one another, like a symphony of suffering. I have studied trauma as a therapist, sometimes with the eye of a sociologist, occasionally through the historical and cultural viewpoint of an anthropologist, and the nuances of each of these stories of wounding that I heard was in tune with the ones before it and after it, until their music built a pattern that scaffolded my understanding of this specific kind of trauma in the ecosystem of traumatic experiences: *Sacred Wounds*.

The sacred Hebrew, Muslim, and Christian texts are full of desert wandering and arid landscapes. These are the places of deep suffering and deprivation_and of the most profound transformations. Moses and Jesus, the rock stars of the Hebrew and Christian scriptures, did some of their most important work in the desert. Desert as the symbol of deprivation, spiritual testing, and excruciating doubt remind me of my darkest moments in spiritual/religious communities. The causes of my own spiritual brokenness were much more palpable in recollection than I expected them to be. I mined them in this book. Surprisingly I found them as palpable as the sexual traumas of my early adulthood (which I explored in first book, *Mending Broken: A Journey Through the Stages of Trauma & Recovery*) and as the pain and grief of loss (which I explored in my third book, *Going Naked: The Camino de Santiago & Life as Pilgrimage*).

Until I mined such experiences, I had forgotten just how painful it was to be without a spiritual family or home during my many seasons of wandering—which can come throughout the stages of life in different ways and manifestations. Once no longer in the desert, I forgot how tired and thirsty the wandering can make a person.

Those of us who have known such exhaustion, thirst, and wandering tend to carry a fortitude and intentionality that runs deep and perseveres. The desire to have spiritual grounding can often withstand even the most painful of experiences. It can also help pave a path, a path of thoughtfulness and intentionality. It can make us develop stronger, deeper roots that find the nutrient-rich soil on which our spiritual foundations can grow.

Sometimes the origin of our searching journey is an acute trauma or suffering, a rejection of self or identity, or the overwhelming pain of many smaller hurts and alienations over time. As spiritual wanderers, we understand that deep in our hearts, in a place we may not fully recognize as we wander, we will one day discover our path, a place in which we can sink our roots deeply and be well grounded once again. As our understanding grows, and after what may be more than once wandering in the desert, we realize that the rhythm of searching and being found, landing and then migrating is an integral part of the lifelong journey of those who are desert wanderers and deep spiritual seekers.

The way forward looks different for everyone. At the edge of each spiritual desert, there are places of spiritual redemption, and places where the hurt makes way for transformation and growth. Tonight, in spiritual deserts around the world, there are travelers finding their way toward their next destination, their next rooting, guided by stars thousands of years old. In the Q'ero tribal tradition of the Andes, we believe that we come from the stars, that we return to the stars when we leave this human life, and that our sacred ancestors and future generations that watch over us from the cosmos above guide us in the meantime. If we can imagine that the stars or spiritual wisdom keepers who guide us are both above us and in our hearts, urging us forward, it can make the journey feel less lonely.

***

Particularly for those established spiritual and faith communities that have dominated Western culture, this book is a call to become well-versed in and empathetic to the experiences, impetuses, depth of seeking, and spiritual call of desert wanderers. Those from the mainstream religious and spiritual traditions also need to acknowledge the ways in which they and their traditions have caused suffering for centuries, even millennia. Such ways include capitalism, hyper-individualism, exceptionalism, Christian and white supremacy, and culturally shaped sexism, racism, and homophobia. These are all systemic forms of power over others.

This book is also an invitation to explore and excavate the landscape of your own tradition and community by asking questions. Questions about who is in leadership, what that means for those that aren't as visible, questions about who is prioritized, invited in, and how you, your tradition, and your community actualize that invitation in the everyday culture and expression of your spiritual landscape. In actual practice, relationships, ethos, and action, do you and yours truly welcome and give space, power, and equity to disabled persons, queer and trans persons, Black folks, Brown folks, AAPI folks, Indigenous folks, and other people of color? How do you and yours give women and femmes space, equity, and power? How about immigrant community members? Activists? In what ways do you and your community actually engage in social change and advocacy for communities that are marginalized in the wider world?

Not all spiritual religious communities, leaders, and institutions are hurting people, but enough are that we need to do something about it. Be particularly on the lookout for the harm that is less obvious, more subtle. I am thinking, for example, of the structural, systemic marginalization of peoples with less power and voice. For example when women are not given voice or power within a spiritual community or where LGBTQIA+ community members are invited in as welcome in a spiritual space but aren't considered beyond an initial invitation in the door in ways that are meaningful to their identities or lived experience. Additionally, this can be true when spiritual communities tout inclusiveness of any kind but then minimize, through their actions or practices, any community group that falls outside their dominant culture whether it is gender, sexuality, ethnicity or ability. These too we must confront in order to heal those systems and institutions.

Ask yourself in what ways you are complicit in such hurt and such harm. Sometimes we harm by our silence, by not hearing or saying the truth. Sometimes it is in blindness, not wanting to see the hurt in others for fear it will touch something that is hurting in ourselves. Sometimes it is in being someone who causes injury because some part of ourselves has brokenness we don't see, and untapped wounds not addressed. Sometimes it is not seeing our own power and privilege that allows our identities and experiences to be prioritized over others. Sometimes it is just complacency.

Whatever our complicity might be, we must be willing to recognize that the story of our spirituality can be expressed and experienced in ways that are harmful to our communities and the wider institutions or systems to which we are connected. We may perceive our particular spiritual ecosystem as healthy. But it is important to periodically evaluate and reassess our belief system, to see where the cracks might be, and to get outside perspective and input as part of that evaluation. Without the checks and balances that come from external input, we can easily develop harmful biases without realizing it. In such cases, it is our duty to change how we are doing things as individuals and communities. It is our responsibility to reconsider the rusty mechanisms that perhaps have been place for so long that they are outdated and no longer serve the needs of an ever-evolving world. It is up to us to address the spiritual hurts we and others perpetrate every day. For our lack of cultural and systemic introspection is leading to others' exodus from traditional religion. Granted, growing pains of evolving spiritual expressions and the necessary change that comes over time is prompting some of that exodus. However, if existing institutions want to have relevance in spirituality into the future, then it is up to us to be self-reflective and responsive to, rather than dismissive of, the valid critiques of contemporary religion expressions.

The answer to the mass exodus of people from existing faith and spiritual institutions into spiritually unaffiliated categories is not better music, marketing, or branding. The answer is deeper than that. The longevity of any spiritual institution depends not on branding but on healing. It also rests on understanding that an expanded understanding of spirituality and religion means much more than checking a box for one particular religion and then living with it as it is, with all its imperfections, for a lifetime. For many people are now more openly critical of the institutions in which they were raised, and they feel empowered to leave when they don't see expressions of themselves within those walls.

Younger generations of BIPOC, QTBIPOC, queer, and trans folks are building new spiritual landscapes that hold all of themselves and allow room for them to hold multiple strands of lineage. One such trend is among people who were raised in Western spiritual traditions from multiple BIPOC diasporas and ancestries who are now rediscovering their ancestral spiritual lineages and are building new syncretistic forms of spirituality that include all the branches of their various roots. Similarly, young folks form multiple Indigenous diasporas are reclaiming their roots in "two spirit" spiritual traditions or in the sacredness of gender and sexual spectrums that colonization and Christianization largely invisibilized. Across the country people are reclaiming the powerful spiritual practices, songs, and rituals of ancestral and faith-based lineages and social movements without holding onto elements of heteronormativity and patriarchy that were threaded through that past. Across the landscape of the global traditions people are reclaiming what is based on a memory that can be held sacred again. And, they are no longer limited by existing or previously esteemed spiritual and religious ways.

The answer to being authentically inclusive and relevant in the evolving world is less expensive than branding, but more taxing. How the existing traditions respond to the harm of the past and the present, own their part in these issues, and activate change in real and tangible ways will determine whether they are a viable and valuable part of spirituality's shape moving forward, or are relegated to the anthropological past.

This moment into which we are entering is one of change and chaos but also one of powerful transformation. Prophecies from many traditions call this a time of renewal, of change, of turning. In some North American Indigenous traditions such a moment is called a seventh-generation moment, and Incan prophecies refer to it as the point between five hundred years of degradation (through colonization) and five hundred years of renewal (and rising of ancestral wisdoms). Points of great change are larger than any one hurt or trauma, but often come with great pain. Yet once that pain is released, such transitions bring new life.

New life means opportunity, invention, imagination, and creativity. It is a place of becoming where the past, present, and future have the possibility to bring forward the best of humanity, reclaim valuable forgotten truths, and compost what needs to be returned to the soil to fertilize the earth on which the future is built. This is also a place where we must let go of what must be released, and where we must discover what that means for us individually as well as collectively, whether in our own existing communities or by building new communities to meet our future needs.

We can recycle the reverberations of pain from the hurts that haunt us. We can transform the despotic "Father God" idea into a healthier expression of divinity. We can transform the bitterness of pain into hope, but we can do so only by swimming through pain's murky waters, facing the pain, and coming out into a new place— of liberation.

This doesn't mean that pain is good. It doesn't mean we would have chosen it for ourselves, our communities, or others. It doesn't mean we deserved to hurt or were destined for this kind of ache. Yet it also doesn't mean that pain is easy to handle. It simply reminds us that we are creatures with an innate capacity for both resilience and hope. We may have generational and intergenerational trauma. But we also have generational and intergenerational resilience—whispered to us by our healthiest and wisest ancestors.

We all have the capacity to find our way to the sacred center of all things. But sometimes those who have experienced extreme spiritual pain and harm have a capacity to see the path towards the depth of sacredness more clearly than those that haven't felt that struggle. Those who have felt immense spiritual pain know what it is like to be deprived of the divine for far too long; they also have access to beauty. These desert wanderers know that water is life in a way that is not as obvious to those with easy access to water every day. If you are reading this book, you are probably a clear-sighted desert wanderer.

We desert wanderers stretch toward the sun with an earnestness that comes from knowing the intensity of long, dark nights. We lean into joy with more urgency because we know the density of a guttural, deep lament. We wanderers are a special kind of people who do not take for granted the power spiritual liberation and rootedness, and who do not stop seeking even when stymied by barriers along the way. We persevere.

A Foundational Practice: Breathing

Yet even for special, tough, desert wanderers, exploring our painful places can be unnerving. In my work with trauma survivors, as well as in my own life experience, I have found that going into those painful and often triggering places requires centering and grounding ourselves. This way, if there are tough moments when I feel I might lose my footing, I can regroup and get my bearings.

This grounding practice is like a compass that points the way out of the difficult feelings and sensations and into the present reality of the moment. Paying attention to our breathing grounds us in our bodies in the present moment and prevents us from being too easily carried away into past thoughts, feelings, and memories. This simple breathing practice is something I offer every person and community with whom I work, regardless of context. It is a universally useful practice, because it begins and ends with breath.

The yoga tradition teaches three-part breathing. Mentioning the tradition from which I am drawing from is to be not only intentional about our connection with a particular practice and its tradition, but also for me to be accountable and not extract from traditions without crediting their source. This breath technique has been an essential part of my own trauma healing.

This practice of three-part breathing is inherent to the way in which we are intended to breathe. As babies, we breathe in a natural way. When we inhale, our lungs fill with air and expand; when we exhale, we pull our stomach muscles in toward our navel, wringing the air out of our lungs. As we grow and become distracted and hurt, we adopt a sort of strangulation and reversal of our breathing process: we inhale and suck our bodies inward, and exhale and push our bellies out. Many of us will flip-flop our practice of breathing at some point in life without realizing it. All the micro-stressors of daily life begin to divert us from our natural way of breathing and into a more constricted one.

For those of us who have experienced severe stress and trauma, this breath reversal is much more acute. We begin to feel breathless in much of life. Specifically, in traumatic stress or when past trauma is re-triggered, we either hold our breath or hyperventilate. To return to a relaxed place we must begin with the baseline of breath, the anchor of our life. Untethered, we float, go to unfriendly places in our minds, or begin to feel as if we are disappearing altogether (technically called dissociation). Tethered, we are grounded and balanced from the inside out. Soothing and calming three-part breath is the simplest way to correct our learned breathing and return us to the grounded breath of infancy.

1. Sit in a chair or lie down on your back, whatever is most comfortable.
2. Place your hands on either side of your belly.
3. Inhale deeply and imagine that you are filling up your belly with air like a balloon.
4. Feel the balloon filling as your abdomen presses into your belly. When your abdomen is full, pause for a moment then exhale out your nose or mouth.
5. After a few deep breaths, move your hands to either side of your rib cage.
6. Take an even deeper breath, filling your lungs as your belly expands, then your rib cage.
7. After a few deep breaths, move your hands to either side of your upper chest with fingers on your collarbone.
8. Take an even deeper breath, filling your lungs, belly, rib cage, and chest like a wave rising until your lungs are full.
9. Release all the air in a sigh through your mouth.
10. Continue slowly for a few minutes, noticing what it feels like to increase the length of your inhaled and exhaled breaths.

Begin this practice of breath when you are not in distress. Use it throughout your day: morning, midday, and evening is a good rhythm. Using it when we are at ease creates a pattern, teaching our brains and the rest of our bodies to use it as a resource, something we can find more easily when we are in the time of distress. When we have made this practice a solid rhythm and practice of our lives, we can more easily access it whenever we feel anxious or triggered.

Preparation for Reading *Sacred Wounds*

A book about trauma is never just a book. Even in words on a page a book can be a place where we feel moments of personal pain. A book can trigger memories of an array of traumas, big or small, from our own lives.

When I write about, teach about, or speak about trauma, I offer this invitation: Take care of yourself as you engage with this material.

Because we can't know what will hit us a certain way until we are in it, I recommend finding a grounding practice (like three-part breathing), a protective space, and personal supports when engaging with anything that might elicit past and present pain.

If you have experienced trauma or abuse, you may be more prone to push through the pain, ignore your feelings and physical warning signs, or feel a need to push past your comfort zone. Instead, take this opportunity to begin to listen to those interior signals that are giving you information.

Is your breath halting or speeding up? Is your pulse and heart racing? Are your hands clammy? Do you feel nauseous or have a sinking feeling in your stomach? Are your muscles clenched—in your jaw, shoulders, fingers, or toes? Are you curling in on yourself in a protective way? Do you feel overly warm or overly cold? Are you re-experiencing or remembering with anxiety-inducing clarity painful moments from your past?

Listen to the signals that your body and mind are giving you. If you are feeling signs of distress, it is OK to put this book down—for a minute, an hour, a day, a week, a season. This is your journey. You get to decide its pace. This marks one of the first steps of taking back the power in your own healing journey. Listen to yourself and practice the art of "the necessary no." When you need to stop, stop. It is OK. It is more than OK. It is a sign of strength and resilience to listen to yourself and take care of yourself. Give yourself love and congratulations when you do it.

As you move through the book, be sure to take care of yourself. Even in writing this book, there were moments at which I returned to painful places in my own life, and I had to pause to take care of myself. Take a bath with aromatherapy oils or enjoy a steam shower. As you move through your own healing process, do the things that can release heavy energy—*hucha* in Quecha. Throughout this book, I suggest practices that you can engage to support this process of release and healing. Please also bring in your own practices from your own traditions or lineages. Do what you need, when you need it.

I give a number of examples in this text that reference specific contexts of spiritual and religious trauma, many of them from Christian traditions, because at the time of writing the first edition of this book that was the iteration of religious trauma that I encountered the most, and because some of my early painful experiences were in

Christian contexts. Translate those phenomena to whatever context you have experienced trauma. Make the examples useful for yourself, and release examples that do not relate to your context or experience.

This second edition of the book also includes examples that come from readers and encounters with others in a variety of traditions who found me because of my work in this area. I hope you will expand the insights of professionals in this field and help other sufferers by sharing your own narratives of religious and spiritual pain. For what you make visible about religious trauma helps everyone understand this phenomenon and become advocates for visibility and change.

Finally, while I am writing from a spiritually-oriented perspective—rather than merely presenting textbook facts or clinical analysis—I am both a specialist in spiritual and religious trauma and a spiritually engaged person. Not every reader will share this perspective, and some might even find it off-putting, particularly if they prefer a purely technical analysis or a secular understanding of this issue. That is not how I write. I credit the BIPOC ancestral lineages of oral traditions and storytelling for my way of offering information in a personal and intimate way. For similar community-oriented and holistic reasons, I understand spirituality as part and parcel of mental health and social-political discourse.

Part of my own healing journey was about reclaiming, without shame or caveat, an integrated way of being that comes from the roots of culture and community in my ancestral lineage. This is something I have done instinctively since I was a child; I was always an unapologetically spiritual being. What that meant for my own spiritually complicated journey was that, even when I was knocked down, I clawed my way back up, to a path of seeking, as will be evident throughout this book.

As a healer, I understand and have worked with people who have returned to spiritual practice and inquiry after spiritual and religious trauma as well as with those for whom re-engaging (even in different traditions or practices than where their harm has happened) isn't their path. I will speak to that through the book as well. But I want to make you aware at the beginning that I will speak, often, about the healing journey as one that engages a healing of body, mind, and spirit. If the word spirit, or soul, or spirituality/spiritual practice doesn't work for you, that is totally fine. You can replace them with words and concepts that match your own truth.

CHAPTER 1

The Wounds That Bind:

The Nature of Trauma, PTSD, and Religious/Spiritual Injury

My creed is Love; Wherever its caravan turns along the way,
That is my belief, My faith.

—Ibn Arabi

I had really wanted to try a zip line. At least that was the reason I remember being so eager to go away to "adventure" camp in Missouri. Zip lines plus whitewater rafting and treetop obstacle courses. Even though I was petrified of heights, I thought this might be a good time to test myself physically—to practice mind over matter.

I should have known (or at least my parents should have known) that when an uber-Evangelical Christian family from Missouri invites your kids to join theirs at adventure camp, there will be more than the whitewater smiles plastered throughout their literatures.

It was not that we weren't an uber-Christian family in our own right. I was raised Catholic, in a long line of devout Catholics. I was an adoptee born in Colombia and raised by orphanage nuns for the first months of my life, named by those same nuns after Teresa de Avila. My mother had a kneeler in her bedroom—and still does. Could you appear to be more Christian? Where I lived, we were the aberration amongst mostly agnostic, sometimes Saturday Synagogue or Sunday Church goers. Maybe that is why this particular family found affinity with my own. If there had been more options, we probably wouldn't have been their theological besties.

For our part, my family hadn't encountered evangelicals in our progressive pocket of the New Jersey suburbs of NYC, and we didn't understand much of anything about their cultural orientation to the term "Christianity." We were blithely unaware that most believers within their stream of Christianity wouldn't believe that Catholicism was a true Christian denomination. We were a bit of an abomination, I would learn much later in life, for reasons that had to do with a debate around literal or figurative blood.

I got a taste of what it meant to be such a (progressive Catholic) aberration from "real America Christianity" when I arrived at Kamp Kiliki and found that from the start of my introduction as a Catholic, my fellow campers considered me Christian only in the most marginal sense. I felt within the first few hours at the camp that primitive tingling you get when your body is telling you that a place is not quite safe, even before your brain knows why. It felt especially vulnerable as I was miles and states away from any kind of escape.

In those first few hours, I began learning a whole new world and culture, like a cultural anthropologist discovering a new kind of people and trying to understand their ways. In this landscape, I—an overly verbal, inwardly philosophical, and always inquisitive teenager—didn't fit. Especially when it came to philosophical questioning, I learned quickly that in this culture questioning anything was a taboo of the highest order.

Even back home, I always stood out because of my "use of big words," as others my age would tell me. But at least they weren't judging my worthiness at a cosmological level—only that I didn't fit the usual fifteen-year-old girl mold. Not knowing who Madonna was (the singer, not the other one) and, conversely, knowing that familiarity with the works of Jane Austen did not qualify me as being "cool" by teen standards, here at "Kamp" (with a K), it turned out I was religiously uncool—not irreparably so, but definitely not hitting the mark by the cultural standards of Missouri-based "Kristianity."

During this particularly sticky summer of 1995, as I fumbled my way through the awkward midpoint of adolescence, my pensive but still-developing brain couldn't fathom how much it didn't know about the world as a whole, much less about the many nuances of this group of people existing under the same umbrella of Christianity as me. Though I had spent my entire life sheltered beneath it in my pocket of Catholicism, I knew remarkably little about Christianity's wide-ranging cultures.

All I really wanted was to face my fear of heights by trying a zip line, my whole summertime aspiration. In pursuit of this simple goal, a sequence of life events unfolded with such potency that they changed the course of my spiritual life.

I had given an enthusiastic "yes" when asked about heading West the summer after eighth grade, and I had boarded a plane at Newark airport with my brother, three years my junior, for the "Show Me State," and what I was sure was a land of plenty—with zip lines and whitewater rafting galore.

On arrival, I felt the whole thing had a tenor of something else. Apart from my innate sensory alert system buzzing in the background, that "something else" was not quite tangible at first, but it became loud as bullhorn within the first day. To be fair, at this stage of my life I wasn't an altogether ideal "joiner." I tried to be kind, and to a nearly pathological extent hated for people to dislike me, but I was shy, clumsy. I didn't know what evangelism was, and I was not much of a girly girl. I probably would have stood out at any camp, especially any adventure camp. Recall that that this was an evangelical Christian camp with a side of adventure sports, and you have the ingredients for my failure.

I was a Jersey girl in the middle of the woods, in the middle of the country, amid seven shades of white people, even more white (if possible) than those who surrounded me, a Brown girl outsider, in my NYC-adjacent suburbia. My fellow campers had a penchant for late night rallies, which to me felt like a demented caricature of a football pep rally—but for God.

I was in a strange new land devoid of my Manhattan skyline views and the sounds of commuter trains, and instead dripping with sweat and crowded with an overabundance of fir trees. This subculture I had stumbled upon had its own rules, codes, linguistics, and strictly defined ethics. The campers dressed in bright colors and were always full of pep. From early in the morning to deep into the night, screeching cheers exploded from the sound system with "praise the Lords" and language I would come to loathe, like "believers" and "saved"—a language I had neither heard nor used in my short life.

I tried my hardest to learn the new cultural mores. Overall, it was irksome, sometimes exhausting, severely lacking in the aforepromised adventure. But it wasn't necessarily harmful: it was strange to me. I watched my fellow campers' movements, language, and mannerisms. Their sweetness, in contrast to my Jersey-frankness, seemed as genuine as a hot-air balloon filling with steam, corpulent and distended, ready to pop. I wanted to believe it was real—the cheering others on, the friendship bracelets exchanged and exchanged again, and again, and the never-ending supply of hugs. I had never had so many hugs from people I had just met.

If you have ever entered a new society, culture, tradition, or religion, it is polite and essential to learn the ropes—all zip line humor aside. I tried to blend in and smile big and accept big hugs. My jaw hurt, my body felt perpetually smooshed, and my arms quickly had no more room for bracelets.

One of the most surreal cultural mores of this new planet on which I found myself was the tradition in which anyone who "accepted Jesus into their heart," any time of day or night, would go with their counselors to the central hub of the camp, around the circle of the communal firepit, and ring a bell. That was a thing. That happened. Regularly. Daily. Hourly.

Even the language confused me immensely. What did it mean to accept Jesus into one's heart? For twelve-, thirteen-, fourteen-, and fifteen-year-old girls to be articulating something like that so definitively, as though it was some absolute commitment—a blood oath rung out in the clangs—and so iron-clad that it would be marked down on a page to the day and time, seemed esoteric to me:

In this book of names Suzy accepted Jesus into her heart, officially and for the divine record, on July 15th, 1995 at 12:00 p.m., right before arts and crafts. No take backs.

I didn't understand it, but if it made them happy, I figured, "What the hell." Except I didn't say "hell," not even in my head while on the camp's grounds. I was pretty sure they had a different bell, maybe something more akin to a boot camp horn or gym whistle, if you got caught swearing. And probably a different book into which your name would be written.

Every night at dusk this new commune of devotion on this new planet called Missouri would make its way down to a large firepit to sing songs around the campfire, next to that Jesus-heart-commitment bell. Every day the sing-along began with "Stand By Me," a song I had once loved but learned to loathe from this prescribed monotony alone. After the sing-along, everyone from the entire camp, hundreds, maybe thousands of children, would gather in a large auditorium, a sea of bright camp shirts painting the room with a swath of over-bright color, eager eyes fixed on the stage for a vigorous evening of megaphone proselytizing.

I say hundreds and maybe thousands because there is a funny thing that happens to memory when it is inflated by pain and time. What might have been ten people becomes a hundred, and what might have been a high school gym can be recalled as the size of Madison Square Garden. That is how our brain absorbs and makes indelible the things that hurt us. Like a drop of ink on a white cloth, the pain of those things spreads and expands quickly with time. We probably numbered at least in the hundreds, but the only recollection I have now is the indelible ink of memory—foggy in places, absurdly clear in others.

One night that remains crystalized in my memory is when this weird culture of humans brought to life a brimming menace of which my buzzing body alarm had been warning me for days. They again revisited their poppy rendition of "Stand By Me." Like the siren song of a Pied Piper's serenade, all the camp kids made their way into the crowded hall, many of them shouting and singing along, and the pitch of energy in the air was right below rabid. The energy was so high in that space—the bodies so boisterous, bouncing in time with the music, clapping (sometimes off-rhythm) with furious enthusiasm—that I could feel the floor rumbling beneath me, a rhythmic mix of the speaker system cranked high and the pounding of many dancing feet.

The night's lesson, of which there was one every evening, was about heaven. This is the moment in the story at which my older me interjects with an all-knowing anticipatory groan, wanting to scream, "Get out of there now!" Because this is where things are about to go off the rails. The barely teenaged version of myself in this replay wasn't prepared for what came next. She didn't understand the culture and nature of it. She wasn't aware of the landmines. She really didn't understand this culture and these people at all.

The camp Patriarch, a middle-aged white man dressed too-cool for his years, stepped up to the microphone and said something I could barely hear, to which the whole crowd responded with a high-pitched "Amen!"

He spoke of worthiness and eternity, of salvation and being saved. He spoke about who would enter heaven at the end of their lives and the end of time—and who wouldn't. Short version: Everyone in the room was in, and probably their parents, but everyone else was by no means a lock. And anyone who didn't believe in the Patriarch's version of how it would all go could forget about even trying to turn the knob of the door. They probably wouldn't even be told where to find the door.

I had never heard anyone talk so absolutely and with such certainty about something that had always seemed to me a determination far above my cosmic pay grade. I didn't get it. I was baffled by the concepts, the certitude, the prejudice, and the exclusion dripping from this criterion. I didn't understand the need for this all to be sorted and clear, right here and now, defined for us by this random bright-shirted dude on stage at a camp lodge. As the crowd surged with applause, I was rocked by the shaking ground, pulsating with the urgency of hundreds or thousands of pounding adolescent feet. Something about the frenetic roar of the moment freaked me out. What had been merely a light buzz of warning when I set foot in the camp had now surged to a frenetic pitch. If the reference had been available to me at that instant, that would have been my "Get Out" moment.

Where was I? What was this all about? Why did I feel further from what I had called God than I ever had in my life? Why did I suddenly feel so far from home?

Inside of that welling fear was adolescent frustration and maybe a tinge of righteous indignation. I was offended on behalf of the God I had grown to know. For I had been coded with a justice-seeking perspective by a mother who had reminded me throughout childhood to speak out against injustice, even when no one else would, and for my own ethical truths when I heard something that violated my own conscience. Also, I was innately and inherently stubborn. I wasn't exactly the ideal candidate for this kind of indoctrination. I questioned everything, even what seemed like the unquestionable.

What about Gandhi? That was the first thought in my mind.

I was marinating in my internal struggle, deeply refuting everything I had just heard at the rally. As I walked back to my Kamp cabin with my two cabin counselors and a gaggle of my cabin-mates, I looked around at each of them with fresh eyes, still incredulous that everyone in the camp could believe so unquestioningly what the Patriarch had said.

Because I was too young and naïve, I blurted out, *"But what about Gandhi"*

Everyone, simultaneously, looked at me with shocked disbelief, almost laughingly identical. For a second that felt suspended in time, everything froze, until counselor #1 responded, "What did you say?"

"What about Gandhi? I mean, if what you are saying is true, what happens to all the good people who aren't Christian?"

The second counselor stared me down, "Didn't you listen tonight? They go to hell."

She said it as a matter of fact. Even the jury of a murderer headed for death row takes longer to dole out a sentence.

"But that doesn't make any sense," I persisted foolishly. "You're saying that if someone is a serial killer and becomes Christian before they die, then they go to heaven, but Gandhi doesn't? Just like that?"

The counselors answered in unison, "Yes."

"I mean, I don't have a problem with the first guy going to heaven, but I can't believe Gandhi wouldn't be there, too."

The silence between our sentences was so acute that you could hear each leaf that rustled and each bit of dirt that was displaced by each and every shoe on the path.

"Teresa, you have to believe this. This is what Christianity means and this is what Jesus said. If you don't believe this, then you aren't a true Christian. If you don't believe this, then you clearly haven't truly allowed Jesus into your heart. You have to believe this. If you don't, well, you can't call yourself Christian."

This was the moment my heart broke. I had never even considered that there were disqualifying factors to my goodness and God-ness. I didn't know there was non-negotiable fine print to spiritual devotion. I didn't know there'd be such cruel criteria—ones that went against everything I believed about love, divinity, and faith. I might be young, but there were things so true to me that they were my non-negotiables. One of them was that unconditional love was the core of any spiritual tradition of which I participated.

I wasn't even sure whether I believed that the ultimatum they were articulating was real or true. But at the moment my heart broke, that possibility—that I could not really be Christian if I didn't believe in this dictate—slipped into my consciousness and couldn't be unwritten.

Even so, I was still a stubborn human. I figured that if I was going down with this ship that was allegedly not headed to any divine final destination, I might as well go down fighting for what I believed, even if that was no longer Christianity.

I wanted to do what felt right in my heart and soul. I didn't realize that this single night in Missouri would lead me in subsequent years to question everything I believed was true about God, faith, and Christianity. It sent me on an unexpected path.

I pushed on.

"Well, I don't believe that. I don't know what that says about me, but I won't believe that good people go to Hell. A God that would let that happen is one I don't want to believe in."

The silences between sentences began to feel eternal, and the distance between me and the others in the group widened with each step, until I felt like the night might swallow me up.

At this point, the gaggle of girls following the counselors began to move further and further away from me, like a slowly receding wave. These girls who had called me friend and sister just a bonfire, a zip-line, and a few friendship bracelets ago, couldn't get far from me fast enough. It was as if I were carrying some virus nobody wanted to catch. It was as if my sense of cosmic inclusivity were contagious and they had no immunity to it, never having encountered it before.

They knew from the tone of the counselors' voices that they did not want to catch whatever I had, unconsciously aware that my stance meant alienation, isolation, and possibly being dispelled forever from God's love and heavenly home. This was no passing cold but a serious plague.

In a matter of half a mile and a few short words, I had unraveled their pep and was slipping into the pit of eternal damnation. I was violating all the norms and creating a serious glitch in this matrix. Things were about to became far worse.

As we reached the cabin doors, the girls all rushed inside and away from me. The counselors instructed them to get ready for bed, letting them know that we (meaning the two counselors and I) would be out on the porch for a while.

For what felt like all night but was certainly a couple of hours or more, they tried to save my soul and pull me back from my dance with damnation. I tried to break through their script of hell for all except "true believers." Both parties refused to budge.

By the end of the night, we all gave up from sheer exhaustion. They felt the defeat of my unrung bell for Jesus, and I felt a tsunami of indecision and confusion crashing into my former understanding of my spirituality, not certain I wanted to have anything to do with such a Jesus and such followers.

I wanted to do what was just, even if it rescinded my all-access pass through the pearly gates. Given their all-night interrogation of me, in the moment it genuinely felt as if those were the only options. Although I didn't know what to call it then, I was truly traumatized by the abusiveness of the coercion on my teenaged self, which bordered on being reportable behavior.

Part of me thought they were all insane, as if I had fallen through the looking-glass and everyone was a Mad Hatter to my Alice. Another part of me felt as if I hadn't understood what Christianity was before; now, it was as if this Kamp had just made visible a secret set of credos that everyone else had hidden until now. While I was glad to have followed my conscience, I felt lonely on that porch as night crept into dawn, and I continued to feel alone and isolated for the rest of my Kamp experience.

Friendship bracelets and hugs kept flowing, but my cabinmates and I knew we were on different sides of a thin line. Under the surface, pity flowed in both directions—theirs for me and my damned soul, mine for them and their idolatry to a belief system that I felt was morally unjustifiable.

After that night, the minutes, hours, and days at Kamp calcified my rage and resentment for every element of the place, its practices, its manic joy below which hid an infrastructure of rejection of anything not like it, a damnation of anything outside of its scope of understanding and belief.

Every moment felt disingenuous. Every practice, every activity, every community-building exercise and hug was, I realized, merely meant to bolster those on the inside of their version of faith, weave them closer together to each other and further away from the rest of the "lesser" and "unsaved" world. Woven into the foundation of love—with limits— was an exclusion for all those (like me) who fell outside of their indoctrination nation.

I never quite believed the Patriarch, the counselors, or the girls who thought I had acquired some kind of cosmic cooties. But I didn't entirely disbelieve them either. I thought if this was truth, then I was outside of it—and even I knew at some level that this was a really young age for an existential crisis.

It made me lonely, but the residual feeling to which I clung above my confusion, hurt, loneliness—was anger. I was angry that the vision I had of God, born somewhere deep inside in unending and experiential love, had been torn open and broken apart. I was angry at the idea that what they were saying wasn't true, about Christianity being this alienating belief system, and that they were perpetuating a lie. I was equally angry that it was a system of alienation, isolation, and bigoted negation of others, and that perhaps that indwelling face of God I had loved since I could remember was just a myth of my own invention and this was truth part of a reality in which I didn't want to participate.

I spent decades festering with that hate. The girl I was became older, more pubescent, and pimply. She turned into a high school graduate and floundering college student, and then a young woman leaving home for the Colorado Rockies to find something in the mountains and the deserts of the West—seeking, always seeking. All the while I carried with me, like a fanny pack survival kit, my festering hate. I hated the campfire girls and their fleeting promises of friendship. I hated the camp counselors who isolated and bullied me for that long, lonely night. I hated the pep rally leaders and the camp Patriarch, and their megaphone chants. I hated the song, "Stand by Me."

I hated. I hated. I hated.

That hate, born on a sticky hot summer night in 1995, fueled me for over a decade. I ran white hot on that rage; I charged at anything that countered my Catholic roots and towards many things I wouldn't want to share in a confessional booth.

I ran. I ran. I ran.

At the end of the line, I was exhausted from all the fighting and running. I knew I finally had to face the demons created that night. I had to stop running, hating, and judging. I had to stop seeking the perfection I had lost when I saw the imperfect underbelly of the spiritual tradition in which I had been immersed.

What I needed to convert was not my "wrong" theology or spiritual ethic, but my broken, bent, and anguished heart. Getting right with the divine, or what I had called God, the cosmological understandings that were intuitive to me but hadn't had a place to land for a long time, and become grounding in myself, trusting and honoring of that teenaged girl that knew what she knew and meant what she meant and was clear on what mattered. It meant going back to the cabin and seeing everything and everyone for what they were in that moment. It took nearly ten years from that night for me to return to the cabin with a new perspective, as a twenty-something emerging adult, with some space and time from the origin of that hurt.

Those girls were scared teens, who like me had been taught their whole lives to abide by an ethic I was betraying. They were taught that there were divine penalties for any aberration from their teachings, ones that were unimaginable and eternal. As girls like me, their fears were proportional to their understanding of the world, and their worldview was limited to the small and insular spaces they inhabited that were filled with other white Christian evangelicals.

Those teen counselors were girls, too; only older than me by a few years, inches, and bra sizes. They were doing what they thought to be right in the way they had been taught was right to do it. They had been taught that there were dire consequences for falling outside of the rules given to them on a platter of fundamentalism as if it were handed down to their leaders directly from God. They believed that the means were proportional to the outcome—they needed to do everything they could to save my soul. It was what their calling was in the world: to preach the truth and make others align with the version of truth they had been given.

I will deal with those camp leaders with their megaphones and catchy songs later in the book. The accountability and clemency on this one is a bit more complex and relates to the larger continuum of this story—the nature of wounding and healing. That's the dynamics of power and supremacy and the elements of indoctrination and indoctrinating. The levels of capacity for reasoning and moral understanding for those in the positions of greatest power and influence. It gets more complicated at the top of the hierarchies of extremism.

The crux of the intention behind returning to the scene of my scarring, back to the cabin years and miles of rage later, is part of a process often used in trauma therapy. We return to the places of our deepest wounds when we are ready, to see the scene with new eyes; in my case, to be able to see all the players of a scene of great pain and transformation through the eyes of the young teens, counselor-aged teens, adults, and even myself.

On the other side of hate, through the eyes of an adult me, I could see the vulnerability in everyone. I could see the fear and the good intentions, despite the fear and harm done to me.

This practice of return and re-viewing doesn't eradicate the need for accountability or eliminate the imprint of hurt it left on my heart. But it does allow me to see the humanity in the whole experience, and through my humanity to let go of my resentments. It allows me to let go of the hold the past had on my present. It allows me to see those involved with the empathy and kindness I wish I had been shown that night.

This practice was the means to me finding my way back from hate and resentment. I stopped running and reacting to the origins of my spiritual fracturing, and I allowed myself to stare my past in the face, unafraid and without bitterness. Though it didn't negate future experiences of harm, rage, and alienation, it did give me a blueprint of how to recover from their impact. Having experienced spiritual harm once does not inoculate us against future harm. But we grow stronger, more capable, more resilient, and more grounded as we deepen our own wisdoms and moral path. We learn from past harms and find our way forward with the fortitude of the desert seeker.

Perhaps this example of pain that fractured my own spiritual path and my recovery from it can help you on your spiritual journey.

We all have the capacity to be so certain of our spiritual or moral truth that we mock and demean anyone who doesn't understand the world the way we do. Instead, we do well to look for the ways in which the spiritual bully can show up in ourselves and check our own power, privilege, and elitism when it does. We also have the capacity to experience the diminishment and negation of the abused or alienated person, being told we are wrong for speaking or being our own truth. We all need the healing and forgiveness for parts of ourselves that can lean into one end of the spectrum or the other at different stages and places in our own life journey.

Having reflected on my adolescent religious experiences and wounding at Kamp does not mean that this experience by itself was responsible for my annexation and isolation from historic and systemic religion or spiritual systems. There were other chips and fractures, disappointments and harms that showed up along the way.

Over time, these spiritual slights, hypocrisies, and inconsistencies added, log by log, to the fire of my own rage and indignation—one that I had to dismantle, log by log, to find my way forward again on a path that had meaning for me, and that wasn't tainted or reduced by these experiences.

The Kamp experience is the one that first set me off on my path of spiritual fragmentation, and it was foundational to freeing my empathy for all those who wander spiritually and all those that have been harmed—many to a much deeper and more violent degree than me. But I also tell the story because it is an all-too-common tale. In the many years of engaging with folks who have been harmed and even traumatized by religion and spirituality, in my many years as a therapist, community-based healing justice practitioner, and teacher-healer of hearing story after story of religious wounding, I have noticed that many stories resonate with my own. Theirs are stories that transcend place and tradition. Such trauma is ubiquitous.

***

The pact I made with myself on my road back to love, hope, and spiritual clarity was this:

- I would never again give an institution the deed to my belief or spiritual understanding.
- I would never again let one human or one community's words or beliefs have tyrannical rule over my soul or hinder my spiritual journey.
- I would always listen to my intuition, knowing that it is an ancient, primal power and worthy of my attention and trust.

I have found that as long as my beliefs and spiritual understanding are not run by any institution or people group, my heart can stay focused on the divine nature in all things, that some people call God. I can take my own and others' human fallibility for what it is—a necessary ingredient in the journey, even when it hurts. As long as I kept these promises to myself, I knew I could exist within spiritual and religious contexts.

With reference to the third part of my pact, I have also found that when we are in active PTSD, intuitions or warning signals can become exaggerated. We register danger even when it doesn't exist.

It is therefore important to assess and analyze our intuitions, to trust them but also to verify them.

The underbelly of acutely hierarchical system of religion (like Kamp), where one isn't permitted to question the dictates or "truths" of those in greatest power, is that they are also prime breeding grounds for other violations of personal autonomy and free thinking, like emotional and sexual abuse.

And this was indeed the case with Kamp Kiliki. A couple of years ago, I got a family text from my younger brother. "Hey," it said. "Did you all see the story online about Kamp Kiliki? Not surprising, but here it is."

The link he shared went to a news story about the decades of sexual abuse adults had perpetrated on minors at the Kamp. Due to the systemic abuse of power, money, and silencing, the use of Non-Disclosure Agreements (NDAs) and payments to the survivors' families, the camp's owners had kept the secret invisible for years. I was sad but completely unsurprised. The revelation made me reflect on the experience of an abused girl at Kamp: what were the signals that girl's primal survival mechanism offered her. Then I realized that it might have been the many layers of unsafety and trauma that place represented.

Trauma, Up Close

To me, trauma is anything that injures the self—the heart, the mind and the soul.

Clinical definitions always remain pale in comparison to the real-life experience. Trauma is the hurt that we feel from the tips of our toes to the top of our head. It hurts everywhere. When we think of traumatic experience in this way, what constitutes trauma is entirely subjective. It is we who define whether something we experience was traumatic or not. It is not up to an observer or someone with or without credentials to determine that for you. You define traumatic stress for yourself. I can give you scales and measures to quantify your hurt, and these can be useful to some extent. But ultimately, hurt is beyond measurement and trauma is beyond scientific calculation.

That said, I will offer some parameters of trauma so that you can discern your own hurt in the context of the concept of traumatic experience. First, I want to pause and validate your hurt. If others' actions or the experiences you had in a religious or spiritual context have harmed you and betrayed your trust, I am deeply sorry. Any institution, community, or belief system that does not value who you are as a person and that creates harmful or abusive circumstances deserves to be scrutinized. When we are violated in places that are meant to reflect absolute love and inclusion, grace and generosity, spiritual wisdom and deep understanding, that violates not only our bodies, minds, and spirits but also our understanding of belief and meaning making. If your experience of religious or spiritual community has negated who you are as a person—be it your gender, your sexuality, your ethnicity, your life choices, your independent thinking, or any other expression of your authentic you—then I hope that I will help you feel seen, heard, and validated. I hurt for the pain you have endured.

While I can't know the particulars of your pain, I know the pain of negation, abuse, and hurt both through my own experiences and through twenty years of working alongside through others' traumatic pain journeys. I feel heaviness in my heart for the weight that you carry. It is a weighty, isolating, and sometimes deadly burden. If you have had to handle it alone until now, I hope you will begin to feel less alone as you move through this book.

Part of my intention for this time together through this book's words, stories, and reflections is to give voice to religious/spiritual hurts and wounds, to explore their nature, and to validate the often silent suffering of so many people. It is also to validate professionally that religious and spiritual trauma is trauma, and to do my best to set you on the road to healing from this hurt.

The DNA of Trauma and PTSD

Trauma is indeed subjective. What is acutely painful to one person does not inherently carry the same weight of suffering for someone else. Besides, we all have different predispositions and propensities for resilience from potentially harmful experiences due to layered and complex factors including race/ethnicity, gender, sexuality, social location, physical ability, and generational factors of stress and harm. This more expansive understanding of traumatic experience, one based on the complex and intersectional dimensions of our own human experience rather than simply diagnostic criteria, allows us to consider the world of trauma through a much wider lens.

Emotional, psychological, and spiritual pain of sacred wounds, spiritual injury, or religious trauma or harm is any painful experience perpetrated by family, friends, communities, organizations, or institutions representing a particular spiritual lineage, orientation, or religious tradition.

Religious harm happens at all levels of human relationship. One's own family, friends, community members, and institutions can perpetrate and perpetuate it, for in spiritual communities your world is often small enough that almost everyone you know is within that context. From sexual abuse to negation of one's own identity, trauma inside of religion/spirituality is often perpetrated simultaneously by one individual *and* by the group as a whole, each one reinforcing the other.

Consider a person who is discovered to be LGBTQIA+ inside a fundamentalist religious tradition that sees queer or trans identity as a flaw, failure, or even a sin. The religious group created the dogma that enforces this belief system and has connected it to core principles of its tradition. After being indoctrinated with the importance of this value, often at the penalty of some cosmic punishment and community-based threats of alienation, the community then perpetuates this belief. The person's own family and friends, often all part of the insular religious community, then enforce this belief in their home and social circle and enforce this shaming ideology in their daily lives, making it clear in their language and actions that anyone who goes against these principles will be unacceptable and unlovable in their eyes and in the eyes of the god or divine figure who is the stated origin of this belief.

The person's loved ones and the community at large who ostracize the person typically believe that punishment is for the best of their victim. The person has generally been indoctrinated to believe that coming out as their whole self would result in their punishment or banishment from everything and everyone they have ever known.

The fact that the perpetrators believe in the righteousness, goodness, and the divinely manifest destiny of their hurtful convictions is perhaps the hardest and most intractable part of religious and spiritual trauma. Like the teens at Kamp, they believe they are doing it to save souls. In their mind there is no greater calling and nothing that is out of bounds in the quest to save a soul.

I gave this example of a person alleged to have queer and trans identity because religiously fundamentalist traditions often have homophobic and transphobic threads running through their dogma. But we can easily apply the principle to other marginalized identities, which such traditions and communities intentionally other.

Oppressive, abusive systems of power and control deliberately vilify and disempower those at the margins. Again and again, we therefore see leaders, more often than not, white cisgendered heterosexual men targeting queer folks, trans folks, women, and racial/ethnic minorities. We have to be clear on not just the mechanics of religious trauma, but the intent. Abuse is perpetrated on purpose and for a purpose. Recognizing this "big picture" view alongside the personal-experiential view of religious and spiritual trauma is important as we begin to unravel the nature of this harm and expand our understanding of the methods and means of this abuse.

In an ideal circumstance, those persons who have been abused and harmed by religious and spiritually traumatic communities are able to see this kind of injury for what it is, namely true trauma that can deepen and over time become post-traumatic stress disorder (PTSD). For any trauma survivor, there is a potential for the traumatic experience to get "stuck" or locked in place as a pattern of behavior that creates grooves in our mind and body responses over time. When this happens, the experience of trauma moves from being a lived experience, happening in real time, into PTSD—a pattern of responses to that traumatic experience that we repeat, and through that repetition solidify, even when the traumatic experience is no longer happening or not currently happening. General study data shows that about 20 percent of people who experience trauma will experience PTSD. Yet experiences of trauma are underreported, so the actual percentage of those with PTSD is probably much higher.

Furthermore, since religious and spiritual trauma and abuse and its vast spectrum of injuries have not been adequately studied or assessed on a large scale, we do not know how many people who experience this kind of harm will develop PTSD. Most of the people I have encountered in my study have experienced some form of traumatic stress, anxiety, and depression related to their trauma. Granted, given that they are seeking out my work and teachings, I am likely seeing a disproportionate number of people who have experienced greater harm and have greater symptoms of stress, but I share my observations of rates of PTSD to give a sense of the scope of the effects of such trauma.

One impetus for this book is to give voice to such people who have been hurting for years, and who are often afraid of alienation, annexation, or doing harm to themselves or their loved ones if they speak up about their traumatic experiences. Another impetus for this book is to make clear to those who have experienced religious trauma and those who have not that this *is* a valid form of traumatization. For reasons we will explore, there are a variety of reasons why this kind of trauma is very complex and deeply devastating. If you have been suffering from this kind of hurt, I know that your hurt is valid and as deeply traumatic as it feels. There is also real potential for a path toward healing from such hurt and a spiritual-moral journey through pain into something like freedom, hope, and joy. Your potential to heal is as real as your pain. Go on that healing journey whenever you are ready for it. We all heal in our own time, and we all also have the autonomy to choose not to go down that path. This book is a journey. It is an option. It is a choice. You decide what to do with it and how it might serve you.

Given psychology's increased understanding of the depth and breadth of trauma and post-traumatic stress disorder, there are a few other concepts that are important to understand at the beginning of this journey. Healing begins with understanding. Empowerment begins with information. I have found that to be true in my own journey from hurt to healing, in my own traumatic experience and PTSD, and of hundreds of clients. To begin this book, I therefore offer you baseline information about trauma, its versatile facets, an overview of religious trauma, and what scientific and therapeutic professionals are beginning to understand about traumatic experience that is providing a wider pathway to healing and wholeness.

The Different Dimensions of Traumatic Experience

Traumatic response is a complex set of responses of the body and brain systems working together with the best of intentions. When they work for us, or as they were intended, our body and mind seek to protect us from danger. For the earliest humans, that danger would have been very real and physically immediate. In this way, the origin of our traumatic response system is much like our mammalian siblings. Think of the response of a prey animal in the wild. Imagine a deer in the forest. It becomes alert when sounds erupt in the distance. Their ears perk up and turn in the direction of the sound. Their bodies freeze in place yet are ready to flee at a moment's notice. In much the same way, our body and brain respond to perceived danger. Our bodies prepare for a variety of survival responses—fight, flight, freeze, or submit. More recently, one additional method of response has become visible, one noted in the body's creation of oxytocin. This hormone has to do with relational connection, but it is particularly known for its production during the birthing process and how it surges when a birthing person first has skin-to-skin contact with their newborn. The term used to represent this hormone engaged in the survival response is called tend-and-befriend. I will detail each of these responses shortly. Crucial to know now is that when activated appropriately and when there is real danger in our lives, these survival responses help us respond in crisis situations.

When this survival response is overstimulated—when it experiences a single or multiple incidents of trauma—it can become stuck, like a light switch that has been turned on and then jams in place. When this happens, the brain and body can't distinguish between an immediate threat and a previous threat because the survival response addresses safety and danger from the same overstimulated stance. We will explore the many ways this response manifests in a person, but simply put, traumatic stress and PTSD are the survival response stuck in place. Part of the process of healing from trauma, religious or otherwise, and part of beginning to rewire the stuck system entails understanding the mechanisms that create trauma and this excessive survival response.

Traumatic Survival Responses: Fight, Flight, Freeze, Submit/Respond

Fight refers to the body and mind responding to danger (or perceived danger) by engaging it with externalized aggression or a battle-ready response. Such a response can be verbal, nonverbal, and/or physical in nature. In working with combat veterans, I often saw this response in overdrive; the outside world often perceived these clients as aggressors. In truth, a person with PTSD often sees danger everywhere, so unconsciously their fight response is simply a response to a perceived threat. Like all trauma responses, this can be worked on, reduced, and even eradicated. Understanding the response and its source is important for a person to be able to begin to rewire the brain/body system. In religious trauma I see this in the pessimistic or aggressive (usually verbal or written) way people react to others in any religion or spirituality. Because they perceive religion/spirituality as the source of danger, they perceive every religion or spirituality as a source of danger; so, they react not only by avoiding those spaces but also by fighting against the idea that anyone would engage with it. Thus, they harbor a feeling of a sense of hatred or dismissal of others still in those systems of belief as foolish or naive. It is a reflexive response to perceived danger.

Understanding this mechanism as a response to perceived threat is crucial to changing this response for a survivor, so that reactions are thoughtful rather than automatic and disproportionate. Essential in responding to the emotionally and spiritually wounded person is understanding and beginning to act from a space of empathy, sensitivity, and patience rather than engaging the survivor's fight response with one's own reactionary fight or defensiveness.

Flight is the body and mind's response to danger (or perceived danger), which manifests as some form of escape from the dangerous stimuli. This could entail literal fleeing, as one would if one were being chased by someone, or a more nuanced and subtle form of flight such as a person emotionally escaping or creating barriers to relationship with others. Flight in religious trauma can manifest in a variety of interpersonal ways. For example, a survivor moves through a large variety of traditions or religions after leaving the religious-spiritual community that hurt them, or they may vacate a new community when there is perceived danger or hurt on the horizon—even when it is a small infraction. Flight can also manifest as a general avoidance of religious-spiritual contexts or in a pattern of leaving or extracting themselves from discussions or persons related to religion or spirituality. The difficulty with this flight process is that a person is not able to stay still long enough to find out whether a place, person, relationship, tradition, or community group has positive and trustworthy qualities. It can result in a constant state of flight, which is both exhausting and doesn't allow for relationship or community to develop.

However, if the survivor understands this phenomenon, then there is a possibility, when that person is ready, to test their threshold for staying still long enough to determine the difference between actual and perceived danger, and to tolerate some level of difference and conflict as a way of learning to build more complex and rich relationships with people and communities (spiritual or general). Those supporting the wounded can be helpful here: rather than minimizing the hurt and regarding the person's avoidance or "bouncing" from relationships and communities as some flaw of superficiality and lack of depth, the support person(s) can understand the wounded person's behavior for what it is—a traumatic pain manifesting in a fear response. The last thing to do with someone's fear response is to invalidate and minimize it. Once support persons learn to approach those fleeing connection differently, dialogue between individuals/communities and the wounded person can become more productive and transformative for both parties.

The *freeze* response as a survival mechanism is often physicalized, but it can be emotional as well. In the wild, we see it in the deer that stops moving when it hears a noise. For a child that has been abused, such a freeze response might entail holding one's breath and staying still when an abusive parent or caregiver is nearby. Freezing is the response often used when fight or flight are inaccessible due either to the proximity or the overwhelming scope of the threat. It can also relate to the process of *dissociation*, which is when someone's body and emotions become numbed and disappear for all intents and purposes. When describing the experience of dissociation, trauma survivors will often say it feels like floating away or floating above their body looking down on what is happening to them, but not experiencing it in a first-person way. In religious trauma contexts, this can be a response people use who feel they cannot leave their religious-spiritual community or their family within that system; so, they freeze or dissociate at some level to "shut off" their mind and body as best they can in the abusive contexts so that they don't experience the full extent of the pain of their experience. The trouble with this response is that when we numb what frightens us, the numbness can begin to infect even the good parts of life until feeling anything is difficult and being connected to body, mind, and the whole life experience is less possible.

The survivor of traumatic experience can diminish this reaction by increasing intention and attention to staying present in moments of safety. This can include practices interacting with the world in a very present-centered way. It helps survivors if persons working or living with them understand their sensitivities to and threshold for stress, sensitivities, and triggers. By offering to partner with survivors to support their practices and plans to stay in the present when they begin to freeze or become not present, helpers both support and empower survivors to create their own ways to counteract this freeze mechanism. The worst thing to do to someone with an activated stress response is to press or pressure them further into their place of discomfort. Building comfort, protection, and support is paramount for a survivor to feel safe enough to stay present in the moment.

The ***submit/appease*** response is an avoidance of any tension or conflict. In this response, the survivor moves with instead of against the dangerous element/person/community to make the pain or suffering less intense. It is a bit like moving with the ocean current rather than against it. Imagine the puppy being scolded who rolls onto its back, exposing its belly to the dominant force in the room—a white flag exhibiting a kind of surrender to appease the more powerful entity. As a stress response, it can be an effective way not to agitate a dangerous force, whether that be a person, system, or community group. Submitting or appeasing can also be a way to stay safe in an unhealthy or extremist group in which being different from the crowd could isolate a person as a threat to the system, and thereby create a dangerous situation for that person. Like most stress responses, submission/appeasement is effective in dangerous situations. But it can also create a pattern of response in daily life that can lead to staying with unhealthy people or groups or to not feeling able to express one's own feelings, state one's discomforts, or stand up for oneself. Submission/appeasement can turn protection into vulnerability because the person hasn't learned to get out of situations that are unhealthy or even dangerous.

Remember that when a survivor moves out of unhealthy relationships, including religious-spiritual communal contexts, that unhealthy way of functioning is what is familiar to them. Like the devil we know or to whom we have become accustomed, it is difficult to leave what we know, even and sometimes especially when it is harming us. We don't mean to repeat those old traumatic patterns, but we do. It is consequently important for us as survivors to be vigilant of relationships after traumatic experience, religious-spiritual or otherwise. This pattern can repeat, and we survivors can easily find ourselves in toxic friendships or romantic relationships, or different but still unhealthy communities.

In such situations, the support of a therapist/healing provider can help survivors assess the information about people or groups with which survivors are engaging and help them form healthy relationships by seeing the signs of toxic relationships. For both the survivor and the helper, this can be hard work, especially when the survivor has become accustomed to appeasing those who might hurt them. But it is possible.

If you are supporting someone through this process, don't pressure them about their own healing or relationship-building. Even when they want to set boundaries, they might find it hard to push back against the threat—and even against your pushiness. Remind them that they have the capacity to say no and to set boundaries. Support their process of empowerment, but don't overpower their burgeoning independence with your pushiness.

The **tend-and-befriend** response is associated with the hormone oxytocin, which has also been called the "bonding hormone," and which creates connection between humans. In the best of circumstances, it builds healthy relationships, contributes to the bond during and after birth between a birthing person and their child, and generally helps us connect with others.

Unfortunately, like all the survival responses, tending and befriending can also be turned against us when we are distressed or, in the case of PTSD, when our distress has become frozen in place. It can lead to feelings of dependency and emotional reliance on potentially hurtful persons, environments, and community groups. Much like in Stockholm Syndrome or in the relational cycle of domestic violence, a person will feel connected and emotionally bound to even the most difficult situations, persons, or people groups and stay with them even at the cost of their own emotional, spiritual, and physical safety. While elements of the submission/appeasement and tend/befriend responses can overlap, the former entails acquiescence but does not necessarily create a relationship bond as part of the response itself; whereas, in the tend/befriend response, the emotional connection with the harmful person/community is what can keep the person in the situation. The relationship and trying to maintain and mollify is at the core of the tend/befriend response.

Persons with the tend/befriend survival mechanism, as with submit/appeasement, may need external help in identifying these patterns of affection and behavior—to see the difference between healthy and unhealthy relationship patterns. Breaking this cycle of unhealthy relationship building takes practice and time, as well as the support of someone from outside of that unhealthy system who can identify the unhealthy patterns from the survivor's past and help that person apply new patterns of behavior and relationship building moving forward. That support person or community group can help the survivor set boundaries, sometimes by pointing out the need for a boundary or by creating those boundaries on their own side of the relationship. Showing the survivor not only love and acceptance but also strength to keep the boundaries once established will help both the survivor and the relationship in the long run.

The Many Mansions of the Heart

To describe the mansions or rooms of the soul, Teresa of Avila, the Spanish mystic, wrote a book titled *The Interior Castle*. She believed that the soul has many layers, and that each layer is a different mansion or room inside the castle of the interior self. She also believed that we enter each of these places through the doorway of suffering. She herself suffered from many medical issues and pain, as well as from the disappointing ache of being an activist and reformer of her monastic tradition during a time (the Crusades) when being such was a potentially deadly endeavor. She discovered that through dying, we are reborn, and through pain, we are given access to a new doorway or mansion to the heart and soul.

The suffering we experience in trauma initially elicits a response— of primal survivalism— from our internal ecosystem. If we can see it as such and move beyond a life of mere survival, our pain can be a doorway to a new mansion in ourselves—a deeper space of heart, mind, and spirit. I wish suffering weren't the doorway to depth, awakening, and transformation, but it often is. It is through the death of something in us that we are reborn into something new. It is through pain that we have access to something to which a superficial life will never give us access. Our heart, body, and soul have many mansions.

When we move through the pain, we continue to wrestle with it, but we do so from this renovated place. That place is one that has been structurally changed by our struggle, and specifically through knowing what it is like to be in and to survive primal suffering. Our lived experience of struggle also gives us the capacity for deep understanding, compassion, empathy, and the perspective to see beyond ourselves. When we experience trauma and pain and find our way through it, into the deeper mansions of ourselves, we join a lineage of a great many mystics, healers, wisdom teachers, and hope-bearers who found their way to deeper knowing through the experience of the worst of the world. This is our lineage. We didn't ask for it, but we can claim it and be empowered by the eternal truth that pain plunges us into the deepest places where experiential wisdom is born.

There is a story of Teresa of Avila wrestling quite literally with her relationship with the divine, whom she called God. One night she set out on a journey by mule. She almost always traveled by mule and by night because she had few funds for her radical monasticism mission, and enemies of her work were more likely to see and harm her by day. On this night, she was traveling over the rolling hills of Spain to a city in which she was establishing a new monastic community by mule during a thunderstorm. The mule mis-stepped, and Teresa went flying. Covered in mud, cold, wet, and seriously pissed off, I imagine she shouted into the sky, "Seriously?! Seriously?! After all that I am doing? Why? Really, why?" To which God is said to have replied, "This is how I treat my friends." Known for her sarcastic cleverness, this fiery mystic allegedly replied, "And that is why you have so few."

And with that, she stood up out of the mud and got back on the mule, as galvanized by her anger and frustration as anything else to continue her journey.

Yes, hurt can derail us, and difficulty can make our road seem impossible and unending. It's stormy, muddy, and exhausting at times. But there is something sacred about the muddy places. It is where we prove who we are—infinite beings, capable of the impossible. You are an infinite being, capable of the impossible.

That the universe seeks to do us harm simply to manufacture adversity is a myth. We don't need divinely inspired harm: the world already gives more than plenty. But we can battle with our belief or understanding of the universe, with the spiritual energies with which we co-exist. In healthy relationships, we get to argue and be frustrated. It is OK to yell at the sky in frustration.

Hope is a relationship—with ourselves, with others, and with whatever grounds us. Belief is a relationship. Believe in yourself, and who knows where that belief can take you. Even in the thundering night, you are still capable of the of pulling yourself out of the mud. Trauma is a muddy, rainy, sacred road. It may at first rile you enough to make you get up out of spite. Once up, hope is the impetus to keep riding that gets us to new places, to new mansions of our heart, mind, and spirit.

So scream into the sky. Rage into the rain. Do what you have to do to get back up on that mule and ride it into the next chapter of your healing.

A HEALING PRACTICE:
Grounding Oneself in the Present Moment

Life in traumatic experience can feel as wild and untethered as trying to ride a tornado: you can't get your bearings; you no longer know where the ground ends and sky begins. Part of healing from what injures us is being able to create a safe distance from the thoughts and feelings that can overwhelm us when we are inside traumatic experience or suffering from traumatic stress. Even the body itself can often feel overloaded, buzzing on a high frequency of sensation.

Breath, as we explored in the Introduction's practice, is the gateway—the beginning—to soothing overstrained nerves and an overtaxed nervous system. Once you have begun to access a slow and steady breathing pattern, like that in the three-part breath practice, you can begin to develop a more robust grounding, so that when you are swept up in the tornado of suffering and crisis you have some way to touch back down on the ground.

The following is a very simple practice for grounding yourself—your mind, body and spirit—in the present moment. Whenever you feel overwhelmed, use this as an extension of the breath practice to help you stay centered in the eye of the storm. If you regularly find yourself in these moments of ungrounding, fear, panic, anger, or aggression, you might want to add an object as your grounding object or point of focus—maybe a smooth rock you keep in your pocket or something that has significance for you, which you can carry without anyone else noticing.

1. Wherever you are, become aware of your surroundings. Where are you sitting or standing in this moment?
2. If it is possible, begin to engage with some part of your three-part breath. Even if this just means breathing in your nose and out of your mouth, begin to engage with a practice of intentional breathing. (And if you need a reminder how, turn back to page 000.)
3. Begin to feel your surroundings. Touch whatever is closest to you. Perhaps it's your cellphone, the fabric of your clothes, or the ground or a nearby plant.

4. Notice the texture and dimensions of this object, as you continue to breathe quite intentionally through the moment of stress. Is the object (your phone, clothing, element of the natural world, etc.) rough or smooth, cold or warm? Notice how it feels. If you have a specific grounding object, pay attention to its dimensions and feel.
5. Memories, thoughts, and feelings will no doubt flutter through your mind. Ideas and concerns will try to crowd your brain and tense your body. This is quite normal. It is part of the human struggle. Your goals are a) not to attach yourself to any one thought, feeling, or sensation; b) to return to breath as a way to ground yourself in the moment; and c) to return to the object you are using as your point of grounding.
6. Feel the breath moving through your lungs and then begin to ground your whole body in the present moment.
7. Continue to breathe and ground yourself with your object of your choice. Be present with how it feels to be wherever you are in that moment. Feel your feet on the ground (if you're standing), your bottom on the seat (if you are seated), your entire body on the bed or couch, and the object you are focused on. Engage with this process for a few minutes, as you are able.
8. Distractions will always be around. Whenever you feel carried away by the chaos of your mind, life, and body, use this practice to help you to return to your breath and to ground yourself in the present moment. Pay attention to the ground beneath you, and to your body where it stands or sits or lies. If you have an object on which to focus, in this moment bring your attention to that object and how it feels—its weight and texture and size.
9. Engage with this process for a few minutes, as you are able. When you are done with your practice, reactivate your body as you are able by shaking out your body—arms, legs, fingers, toes, head from side to side—and return to your day.

Carry this practice with you and engage with it as part of your daily life. Like the breath practice, the more you do this one when you are calm and relaxed, the easier it will be to engage it when you're distressed or overloaded.

CHAPTER 2

Inside the Animal:

Symptoms, Jargon, and Manifestations of Religious and Spiritual Trauma

> *Permanent good can never be the outcome of untruth and violence.*
>
> —Mahatma Gandhi

I opened the first chapter with my own story of adolescent religious hurt. After I wrote the story; therefore, with the memory fresh in my mind, I shared the experience with a fellow therapist. It is not a story I keep in my back pocket; it is not my cocktail party fodder—unless, of course, it is a cocktail party for religious trauma survivors, which, if you spend enough time in spiritual contexts, is more likely than you might imagine!

It was out of the ordinary that I would be telling a friend and colleague about my own childhood experience. That I did was in the context of of explaining this book to her, what it was about, and why I was writing it.

I told her about how the camp and the adventure sports concealed a propaganda-indoctrination underbelly. I told her about the long night of bullying and my intentional movement away from Christianity following the experience. I didn't have a particular expectation for her response.

From our past conversations, I knew that her mother was an atheist, burned by a rigidly conservative and punitive Lutheran church upbringing, and that her father was Jewish. I knew her family, and that she attended a Unitarian Universalist (UU) congregation now, but not with any substantive regularity. I knew that her family celebrated Christmas and Chanukah and were put off by anything smelling of extremist Christianity. I knew that her UU congregation back home was mostly white, mostly progressive (even though multi-tradition, theoretically), that it was mostly Christian-expats, and that the building had a gender-neutral bathroom. Let's be honest, that is the UU vibe.

We had discussed our surface confluence of childhood experience and our spiritual experiences. When I finished my story, I didn't know how she would respond to my experience. She paused for a moment, began to speak. Then something absurdly cosmic and comedic happened.

It turned out that she had also been sent away to adventure camp, which also spelled its name with a cutesy "K" at the beginning and a long "K" name following, sounding eerily similar to my own camp's name. She had gone because friends were going and was lured in by the promising brochure pictures of smiling kids enjoying whitewater rafting, zip lining, and swimming. The only difference from the start was that her camp was in North Carolina and mine in Missouri.

Then she began her own traumatic religious harm story, which put my night of heaven-laden-interrogation to shame.

(If you experience triggering from your own personal traumas with religion, you might want to skip over the next two sections detailing her experience, which I was given permission to share for the purposes of this book.)

She said she had been at camp for a couple of weeks, and she was settling into the rhythms of the days; it seemed pretty benign, with the usual camp fare of subpar food and crammed bunk bed cabins.

She knew that the friends she had followed to camp were Christian, and the fact that it was definitely a Christian camp became clear early on with the arbitrary and constant insertion of Jesus Christ (first name, last name, period) into every activity, community gathering, and meal. Not being brought up in religious home, it was a new cultural way of being for her—not so much bothersome as different.

Then one day she went to an arts and crafts session, and the campers were invited to make lanyard keychains for their parents. For her mother, she made a bouquet of flowers. For her father, she made a series of connected Stars of David. As she was working on her last star, her camp counselor came over and asked what she was making.

"I'm making a keychain for my dad," she said eagerly.

"What are those on your key chain?" the art teacher asked, pointing to her stars.

"They are Stars of David, because he's Jewish."

Nearby, the ears of fellow campers and counselors perked up, as the syllabic makeup of a word seemingly unfamiliar to their ears echoed in the air.

"Your father is Jewish?!" The shrillness of her art teacher's voice frightened her. Even though she could not register why, she knew something had just changed.

Suddenly all the counselors were huddled around her asking questions and shooting statements at her like darts at a target.

"You can't make those stars in this class. Don't you know that?"

"Jewish! You know your daddy is going to Hell, don't you?"

"Um, I, well, ok, I don't know," she stammered, nervously, not sure what to do or say.

After the art room debacle, everything changed. Word spread quickly to all the adults in camp that her father was Jewish, and soon everyone over the age of eighteen on the campgrounds was approaching her throughout each day, telling her the penalties for not being Christian (in life and the hereafter) and ask-telling her, repeatedly, to accept Jesus Christ as her personal Lord and Savior.

She was flustered and increasingly scared. She was only twelve, way too young to ward off such harassment with confidence.

She asked her counselors to call her parents, but she had been put on phone restrictions. Word was out that she was not allowed to make or take calls. So, she started writing letters daily to her parents, telling them what was happening and pleading with them to come and get her.

Days passed that felt like forever in her young conception of time. She couldn't understand why her parents weren't answering her letters, which became increasingly desperate. When she asked questions about her letters, a weak link in the chain told her that all her letters were piled in the camp director's office. Someone had decreed that her letters to her parents were not to be sent.

In desperation, she wrote her grandmother, hoping that maybe the camp authorities wouldn't catch those letters. She was right. Her letter made it to her grandmother, who immediately called her mother and made it clear that if her mother didn't go get her, she was going to drive up to North Carolina from Florida herself.

Her mother was in disbelief. Who in their right mind wouldn't be? What kind of camp would do that to a child?

But before her mother could react, this child, distressed on her own island of "unbeliever" (as they called her) became wise and figured out an action that might get results. She was finally beginning to understand what they wanted, and like a good cult captive, she gave it to them in hopes of some clemency.

Days that had felt like months into this spiritual waterboarding experience she walked up to one of her counselors and said, "You know, I've been thinking about it, and I decided I want to accept Jesus as my personal Lord and Savior."

She was greeted with a strong hug and a collective showering of praise.

"Do you think I might be able to call my mom? I'd really like to tell her."

My friend was no dummy.

The moment the counselor handed her the phone, my friend began rapidly dialing the numbers to her anticipated freedom. When she heard her mother's voice, she started shouting into the phone, "Mom, please come get me! Get me out of here!"

The counselor grabbed the phone away from her, and a few other camp staff began pulling her out of the room. Her counselor got on the phone and told her mother how she had been misbehaving in camp and had become out of control. They told her mother not to believe what she was saying.

An appropriately protective parent, who recognized the sound of fear in her child's voice, her mother flew into a rage.

"You listen to me: My daughter is to be put in a private room, and neither you nor any of the staff at your camp are to talk to her at all! I will be retrieving my daughter immediately and will get there by morning. You keep away from her!"

The stammering counselor agreed—not that my friend's mother could hear her as she continued to shout directives and to protect her daughter like a mama bear.

Help was on the way.

A long ten hours later, my friend's mother arrived, with a trunk full of candy (contraband at the camp) to heal my friend's wounds; as a "screw you" to the camp staff, she began handing out bags of it to any kid with an outstretched hand. While hungry-eyed and sugar-deprived children pillaged her trunk, and my friend was being consoled by her sisters, who had come along on the rescue mission, her mother made sure that all the camp administrators got a good helping of in-person yelling, replete with many a creatively strung expletive that surely made them all blush.

My friend made it out, and due to her mother's emotional stamina and both her parents' smarts, today she is a strong and determined woman. It is surely no big leap to suggest that the camp affirmed all of her mother's atheist values and reinforced her desire not to engage with institutional Christianity or other faith traditions ever again.

With a glint of cleverness in her eye, my therapist friend ended her story, "I should have just gone with my Jewish friends to *their* camp. I could have made all the Stars of David I wanted, and no one would have bothered me about Hell, since we Jews don't even believe in it."

I share her anecdote of camp trauma for those readers who may not have had a similar experience in their lifetimes and might have thought my opening story was an extreme and isolated incident. If you haven't encountered spiritual or religious trauma in your past, I am glad. I can imagine it seems unbelievable that these things occur, that they do so fairly regularly, and even more disconcerting, that these are the most marginal of examples of harm in that they are singular and isolated incidents rather than some of the narratives that will come later in this book, of people stuck in these systems of harm for years of their lives, and some stuck there even now.

For me, it was a bizarre twist of synchronicity that the first person to whom I disclosed my own story after revisiting it and writing it down had a more extreme, but thematically similar, traumatic experience in a nearly identical camp. I am certain that I would have been similarly abused had I begun crafting Stars of David, instead of transgression of "only" questioning the heaven theology. Our camps were twisted sister-sites of fundamentalism, separated at birth but aligned under a distorted heaven. In my sample size of two, my facts are anecdotal, but in the writing of this book and in my years of hearing similar stories, the current sample size is in the hundreds.

In fact, after the first edition of *Sacred Wounds* came out and I went on a book tour around the country, more synchronicities surfaced and did so at an alarming rate. The most acute of these happened when I visited two different communities, both founded on the premise of being spiritual sanctuaries for refugees of spiritually abusive communities. I visited one, located in the heart of Denver, and then two days later, another in the suburban area surrounding the central city. The name I give the camp in this book is a slight alteration of the actual name, but early into my talk with the first group in Denver a member of the audience raised their hand and said, "The camp you're talking about it, it's [insert name], right?"

I was shocked. Besides myself and my brother, I had never met anyone who had heard of that camp.

"Wow, yes, it is," I replied, laughing in shock.

"Yeah, I know them too," yet another person said. "I had to go there as a kid and knew it right away when I started reading that story." There was a murmur of agreement from another two or three people. It was one of those moments in which the world became immensely smaller to me.

Two days later, I was meeting with the founders of the second community, preparing for the evening to be spent in conversation with the people of their community. I asked them what made them decide to create a space that was dedicated to people fleeing religious harm.

The first leader, a woman I had known previously from the speaking and teaching I had been doing on spiritual trauma across the country, said, "I have just always wanted to help those who most needed it and I have met so many people hurt in this way. Also, I have come from that kind of background, Fundamentalist Christian, where most of our community members escaped from, and so I understand at least some of their experience and pain."

The second leader looked at me with a surprising amount of pain and something that hinted at guilt in his eyes. He took a deep breath and began, "I read your book."

Okay, I thought, that was to be expected on a book tour for said book, but it didn't explain his expression or the steeling breath.

He continued, "I read the first story. It was Kamp [insert name], wasn't it?"

Since I had just left a whole group of people who had known the Kamp's name, I wasn't as surprised as I would have been otherwise. The folks at the first community in Denver had been much younger than this second leader, probably the age of campers when I was there, some who were perhaps five to ten years younger than me. In short, the next generation of Kamp hurt kids. This man, on the other hand was middle-aged.

"Oh yeah, I actually just met a handful of other campers at my last talk," I said, still wondering what he was holding back.

"Yeah, I…well, I was one of the leaders of that camp for many years."

Now I was surprised. But it explained the pain and guilt.

"Oh," I began, a surprising amount of own emotion swirling in me. My thoughts flashed to the man on the megaphone and thought that could have been this second leader or at least one of his peers at that time. "So, you were one of the megaphone men?"

"Yes. I don't know if I was that particular guy from your story, but I was one of them. I spent many years being the one who did that harm to others, and when I left I made a commitment to try to repair, in some way, the hurt I had been a part of creating."

We spent an hour that afternoon talking with one another—a hurt camper to a once top-tier propagandist. In many ways the work that had brought us to that place and time and moment was born out of the same point of suffering—just from two different vantage points. I won't ever fully understand how he did what he did, but in that hour I became clear that whereas I had been granted a childhood founded on the principles of free will, a free exchange of ideas and independent thought, his had been shaped by a fundamentalism that prioritized alignment with collective ideas, unquestioning loyalty to those ideas, and the primacy of power and privilege that came only from fealty. If we're being honest, that power and privilege were accessible to him as a white, heterosexual cismale in a way it wouldn't have been to others, even those who followed the same rules. Like the other refugees he now supported, he had to leave behind everything he knew, which took a kind of bravery—especially to someone who had great power in the system in which he had been raised.

By the time I sat in the circle with the community members later that night, a little bit of my own hurt from the time at that Kamp had been healed. To be able to face one of the persons who had had the power to hurt me in my childhood, to see their humanity, their aged humility, and to forgive the brokenness in him that had causes such brokenness in others, lifted a weight for me.

Let me be clear that we have no obligation to forgive such persons. And even if we do forgive, there is no timetable for how or when we do it. There are many others who have been hurt in much greater ways than I was, and they may not have had access to a way through and out of such harm. One of the harmful myths of a weaponized religiosity is that we are obligated to forgive—and that if we can't, or don't, we are somehow spiritually impoverished.

In abusive spiritual and religious contexts, this myth is often manipulated both to avoid consequences for those in power who have done harm and to keep victims silent. We see this in many of the stories in this book. It is a pervasive and consistent aspect of spiritual trauma. Think of the systemic abuse in the Catholic Church and, more recently, the Danny Masters case in Scientology.

Forgiveness should not be weaponized or sanctified as the only way through pain or trauma. Our ability to reclaim our voice and our own independence of thought after spiritual and religious trauma depends on being able to choose whether we heal, whether we forgive, and how we do any of these things. Just because I had an opportunity that afternoon to find some peace from my childhood trauma doesn't mean you will. I can't know your pain or give you a detailed roadmap through it. What I can do is share my experiences, give some insight from my personal journey and professional experience, and hope these resonate for you.

***

As you will see throughout the book, the people, stories, and suffering we explore are merely the tip of an iceberg that could take down the Titanic. If in this metaphor the Titanic is religious/spiritual contexts and the iceberg is religious traumatization, then we'd better have a whole lot more lifeboats. This does not mean that those hurt by religious or spiritual traditions are doomed, only that we must be clear-eyed about the pitfalls and red flags so that we can avoid creating or repeating religious or spiritual harm.

Lifeboats are the issue. In the above Titanic metaphor, the lifeboats are those individuals, communities, and helpers/healers who are willing to lift people from harm to places of protection and healing, and who are willing to do the preventative work to avoid creating new spaces or experiences of harm. As of yet, we don't have enough lifeboats.

Throughout this book, I will add proof of the pervasiveness of this trauma and the many ways this kind of harm manifests and grows in communities. I will explore the trauma of religion and spirituality that is dismantling people's trust and engagement with structured contexts of spirituality and religion. I will also remind that no such ship or context is unsinkable. But I begin by unpacking the process of religious injury, as doing so helps us understand what is needed in order to heal from it.

Overview of Religious Injury and Trauma

The more you understand your brain-body system's response to frequent traumatic experience(s) that led to having your stress response stuck, the easier it is to begin the healing process. That doesn't mean the healing process will be easy: it just means that knowledge is powerful as a first tool of healing. Once you understand why and how your brain-body system reacts, you can begin to change your system's response, and this in turn will change how you experience the world.

Of course, religious and spiritual trauma is commonly a repeated or elongated process of traumatization. Such trauma may be an overtly traumatic experience, more subtle abuse, or it may be neglect or demeaning behavior that accrues distress over time. Whichever is the case for you, your experience and pain are valid, and there are ways to combat that distress. I intend this book—its stories, life parables, and terms and practices—to be a primer for your healing. Your journey of healing will likely include more than this book or its practices. Healing is a communal process, and it can most definitely take a village. My own healing journey from the sexual trauma I experienced in my late adolescence (the subject of my first book, *Mending Broken*) and the years of PTSD that ensued, involved a number of villages or supportive resources. My village included yoga classes, acupuncture sessions, contemplative practices and meditation, as well as writing, reading, and learning everything I could about trauma. All this eventually prompted me to help others heal from traumatic experience.

Your journey is like your fingerprint—uniquely yours. Take with you on your specific journey whatever materials and tools suit you best. I hope this text can equip you to begin your journey by helping you to understand what is going on in religious injury and to learn some beginning practices for your healing from it.

The following is a list of common symptoms of traumatic stress and PTSD, along with examples of how they might manifest in a religious or spiritual context. You may experience some or all these symptoms—or none of them if your stress response has been stuck.

If you are experiencing any of the following issues or other alarming emotional or physical symptoms, seek out and be assessed and cared for by a mental health or medical provider. You *can* find healing with the right coping tools and emotional support.

Triggers

Some readers might be quite familiar with the term *triggers* as it relates to mental health issues and negative experiences; for others, it may be a new concept. Generally, the term refers to anything that instigates a memory, response, or a revisiting of a past emotion or experience that is painful or traumatic. In the language of mental health, this is related to something negative, which can elicit a negative response such as anxiety, anger or, in its most acute presentation, a flashback (a re-experiencing of an initial instance of harm in your mind and/or body).

Examples of Triggers in Religious and Spiritual Trauma

In religious trauma, triggers can be the type of environments, like institutions that represent or remind you of the religious or spiritual organization that initially did you harm. This could include a faith or spiritual institution building (a church, mosque, synagogue, yoga studio, or Buddhist meditation center, for example). It could include certain types of people, like authority figures or clergy from that tradition or lineage (or the attire specific to that tradition). A trigger can be language used in religious settings. In the Christian tradition, such language might be words like: saved, salvation, repentance, sin, chosen, believer/nonbeliever. Or it might be general jargon from the tradition from which the trauma stems, or phrases like "Jesus is my Lord and Savior," and "Hate the sin, love the sinner." There are similarly potent phrases in other traditions. Triggers can also be certain scents, like smoke or incense, or sounds, like church bells or a gong or a meditation chant, that remind a person of the spiritual or religious context of their harm.

Simple Tools to Address Triggers in Religious and Spiritual Trauma

If the traumatic experience or experiences are in your recent past, the safest bet initially is to avoid completely the people, places, and things that will trigger a traumatic response in you. When pain is still raw, it is hard to move through a trigger in a way that does not increase the trauma. After time and emotional distance from the original experience, you may find it possible to address the trigger when you are exposed to it, using simple grounding and breathing practices to center you in your body, mind, and spirit. Many of the practices offered at the end of each chapter, most particularly the *three-part breath*, can be a way to calm yourself when faced with triggering experiences so that you are not taken back to the experience of your harm.

Intrusive Thoughts and Flashbacks

When a person is triggered in some way to remember their traumatic experience, this is *an intrusive thought*. It is a memory from an experience of the past that intrudes on a person's present life. *A flashback* is a more extreme response to a reminder of the past in the present. During flashbacks, people actually feel as if they are returning to a particular traumatic episode from their past. This can last a second or a minute (and longer in extreme cases), but to the person it feels in that moment as if they are right back in that stress. The difference between intrusive thoughts and flashbacks is that with thoughts, the person is still in some way grounded in the present, but with flashbacks the person is mentally taken back to the traumatic incident/s.

Examples of Intrusive Thoughts and Flashbacks in Religious and Spiritual Trauma

In religious trauma, just as in most traumatic experiences, intrusive thoughts or flashbacks take a person back to situations of high distress, because those are the thoughts most prominent in their mind. These thoughts become stuck or lodged in the forefront of the mind, and this is why when triggered the thoughts are easily accessible. The thought may be a specific incident of distress or emotional/physical danger, or it may just bring back the memory of a person or group or setting in which repeated trauma happened—like a religious/spiritual space, a certain religious leader, or a family member who used negative dogma to abuse or diminish someone.

Simple Tools to Address Intrusive Thoughts and Flashbacks in Religious and Spiritual Trauma

The most effective way to deal with an intrusive thought along with its emotional and physical aftereffects is to be able to calm yourself back down. The thoughts can feel overwhelming in all parts of the self, because they engage the hormones and adrenaline responses in the body. When your brain brings you back to the remembered traumatic place, your body and mind in the present respond as if you are in danger now. Our hormones speed up our bodies to try to get them prepared for that danger, so coming out of an intrusive thought or nightmare can feel as if one just jumped out of freezing water. It is a shock that puts one's whole self on high alert. A *grounding practice* like the one in Chapter 2 is often the most effective way to bring a person back to the present and away from the trigger. Simply creating present-centered associations as simple as, "I am sitting in this chair," or "I can feel the floor beneath my feet," can help ground you back into the present.

Nightmares

Nightmares are extensions of intrusive thoughts and flashbacks, which visit a person in their dreams. Because we have more control over our conscious minds when we fall asleep, we are much more sensitive and vulnerable to the traumatic memories, persons, or experiences that our brain retrieves in dreams. Depending on the extent, there may be a few acutely traumatic experiences (or a subconscious version of those experiences) that may show up regularly in our dream state. Sometimes, however, the traumatic experiences appear in nightmares as feelings of being unsafe in our lives—our family home, spiritual or religious space, or elsewhere. So, it is also possible that the nightmares will manifest that feeling of being unsafe as dreams that have nothing to do with traumatic experiences we have had, but that nonetheless create anxiety-based scenarios, which may seem related to no particular memory.

Examples of Nightmares in Religious Trauma

In religious trauma, like with intrusive thoughts and flashbacks, the nightmare can bring a person back to a specific incident of abuse or negation in a person's religious experience. It can even bring into the dream specific persons who were most harmful in the person's negative experiences in religious contexts. It can also, as articulated above, manifest as feelings of lack of control, helplessness, or anxiety. These dreams might have nothing to do with specific instances but manifest in fear-based dream themes, including: the feeling of falling, running from an unknown (or known) source, feeling weighted down or unable to move, being unprepared or underprepared at church or school or for a test or possibly a religious ritual experience, and also just generally being taunted or made fun of and feeling shame or a less-than-good-enough feeling.

Simple Tools to Address Nightmares in Religious Trauma

Often when a person has a trauma-induced nightmare, the fear and even certain imprints from the dream state may leave residual effects right after waking up. That can include still seeing the figures or shapes from the dream like a shadow left over from that acute memory. A person might wake up sweating or with a racing pulse due to that feeling of danger, which is then translated into the dream, and back out again, based on fear felt in a real past-lived experience. In such situations, *grounding* and *breath* practices are both useful to get out of the troubling dream state and center oneself in the present again. If it is an alarming nightmare, it also can be useful to turn the lights on or get a drink of water before returning to bed. Listening to relaxing music or a relaxation CD or Audible book prior to returning to sleep can also set a foundation for safety rather than fear.

Hypervigilance and Exaggerated Startle Response

Hypervigilance is a fancy term for hyper-awareness of your surroundings (sound, smell, sight, or any kind of sensation, including balance) and an *exaggerated startle response* is an extreme stress reaction related to that increased awareness. Both are terms to describe the high-alert status into which the body and mind go when they perceive danger. In normal life this would occur when there was a real crisis or feeling of danger. When the memories and feelings of traumatic experiences become lodged in our bodies and minds, we can be triggered to this level of hypervigilance and over-alertness even when we are safe, but our body and mind believes we are in danger based on old information. Exaggerated startle response is the way in which the body responds to this state of high alert—with an extreme response to a perceived danger.

Examples of Hypervigilance and Exaggerated Startle Response in Religious Trauma

In religious trauma, this kind of hyper-alertness can show up in our lives in the ways we become oversensitive to safe things as if they were dangerous things. Twitching and jumping after being tapped on the shoulder would be an example of that, especially if the traumatic experience involved some kind of bodily assault. Another example would be jumping or twitching at loud noises, like a vehicle backfiring. Other sensitivities could be around all facets of the senses—sensitivity to touch or certain sounds, sights, smells, or tastes that trigger traumatic memories or reminders of traumatic environments.

Simple Tools to Address Hypervigilance and Exaggerated Startle Response

Because this kind of response is an overstimulation of the senses and the body based on memories stored in the body and mind, one typically diminishes the intensity of those feelings by sensitizing oneself in new ways not associated with traumatic experience. Some examples of tools used to do so include a cotton ball or small roller of perfume or natural oils that are contrary to the triggering memory. I often use lavender, because it is soothing to many people, but you could use a favorite scent of any kind. Another example of such a tool is to carry a token or reminder of something positive or grounding with you—perhaps some silly putty, a rock from the beach, or a silver dollar. Anything that is weighty enough to hold in your hand but discrete enough that you can keep in your pocket will work. That way you can hold it when you need to ground yourself, without anyone even seeing it.

Anxiety and Panic Attacks

Anxiety is a natural response to a literal danger or threat, but in traumatic stress this response goes into hyperdrive and can exceed what is necessary for self-protection in certain situations. In its most extreme form, it can induce *panic attacks*, in which the brain-body cannot regulate the level of distress being experienced and the system essentially overloads. It overloads to such an extent that people who are having panic attacks often sincerely believe that they are having a heart attack. Indeed, the symptoms can be almost identical. A person's chest feels acute pain, their muscles contract, their throat can constrict, their palms sweat, and their pulse races. In some cases, panic attacks lead to hyperventilation—which is when the breath speeds up so quickly that one becomes dizzy.

Examples of Anxiety and Panic Attacks in Religious Trauma

In religious trauma, anxiety is rooted in the original spaces and places that induced traumatic response. This could be due to physical or sexual dangers, but it can also be from a general feeling of invalidation by persons or a spiritual/religious community group in response to identity or differences that are taboo to the system/community. Being a woman, LGBTIQIA+, BIPOC, or even disabled could be a reason someone is made to feel less than in a particular community, and that sense of invalidation can lead to anxiety not just in that group but in entering other spaces. There is a constant fear that this new place or space might offer the same painful invalidation. This makes it hard to build intimacy, try new things, or enter new spaces. When this fear becomes acute—due to injury in previous traumatizing environment—just entering a new life experience or environment can lead to a pre-emptive feeling of fear that can become incapacitating.

Simple Tools to Address Anxiety and Panic Attacks in Religious Trauma

Just breathe. As simple or hackneyed as that sounds, regulating breath is the first and greatest antidote to panic. When we panic, we hold or speed up our breath to hyperventilation level. I teach every client, contemplative practice student, and grad social work student breath-regulating practices as a baseline for everything else we work on in their respective contexts. Breath is life—and regulating breath is the first step to regaining life. Breathe again. Breathe fully. Explore practices that help you breathe fully and completely. The three-part breath technique is a starter practice in this book but expand from there. But, please steer clear of any breathing techniques that suggest you hold or speed up your breath; in trauma healing, there is no need for any more of that breathing in your life or your healing practices. Down the road, if you want to use those, you can—but not in the healing process.

Anger and Rage

Anger is the external cousin of anxiety. While on the face of it, people whose traumatic response presents as anxiety and anger may seem on other planes, they are just two primary ways that our brain-body system tries to ward off danger. Anger can present outwardly or inwardly. Anger presented outwardly is regarded as rage and even violence; anger directed inwardly is seen as emotional or even physical masochism and self-hate (the cousin of guilt). They are equally destructive.

Examples of Anger/Anger Outbursts in Religious Trauma

In religious trauma, anger can be a healthy response. But it can also bend toward an emotionally destructive compulsion. It can be empowering, it can be justice-seeking, but it can just as easily be self-destructive as you are telling yourself that it is empowering and justice-seeking. True empowerment that lasts and justice-seeking that has stamina needs to burn away the rage to get to the good stuff; eventually, it has to lead you to let go of hate or be productive in some way, so that you can transform it for your own healing and evolution of your process of recovery.

Anger can destroy us if we get stuck in it for too long. In the process of healing from religious injury, like in the grieving process, there is a season for anger and moments when it is necessary and righteous. But eventually we have to give up raging "against the machine" (a.k.a. religion/spirituality/a person/a community/a system) to transform ourselves into more than just opposition to what we loathe. We want the righteousness to be productive—for ourselves and those around us. What is the outcome our anger is seeking? And how do we get there? Perhaps the outcome is a purpose that is ours alone. Perhaps it has a larger justice-seeking and accountability mission—especially for a community that has done collective harm beyond ourselves.

Our best selves promote what we love. So, ask yourself: How is your anger and rage serving an outcome to preserve, elevate, or evolve towards what or whom you love? How are you effecting change for yourself and for others? And at what point will you have reached something that feels like justice, if not externally, then internally in your own process of healing, so that you can let go of the anger for the long-term?

To burn out the hate is no easy task. But it is an essential part of healing. When anger consumes our thoughts, actions, and our thoughts about the person, persons, or religious system that hurt us, then anger is no longer functional but instead borderline compulsive. We are addictive creatures, and hate is especially addictive. Rage gives us adrenaline and cortisol. That is why we have the term "adrenaline junkie." Hundreds of times I have seen post-trauma rage consume everything good in a person, client, or friend, until nothing is left of life but that anger. This is toxic in religious and spiritual trauma as in all other injuries. It is hard to understand, but getting beyond the hate is essential for healing. Be more than your anger. Use it to help you heal and motivate you, but then let it go. It is the only way to be whole again. Religion and spirituality as an institution cannot consume us to the point of eradicating what makes us unique and whole in our own right—either being immersed in it, or in opposition to it.

Simple Tools to Address Anger/Anger Outbursts in Religious Trauma

Since anger is anxiety's cousin, the same basic rule applies: breathe. Breathe slowly and deeply. This will give you enough time to consider your thoughts, words, and actions before you act driven by anger. You cannot take back what has happened but taking a few breaths before choosing to act is the first step to learning how to change your course and make calm decisions. Given the speed of our culture, and response times between texting or responding to something on social media, stopping to take a breath is a good first response for all of us. Sometimes disengaging and stepping away can be a way to de-escalate our internal responses, instead of allowing them to become hyper-accelerated and quickly turn into anger. This is important for anyone, but especially for someone who is more prone to trauma-induced anger and rage.

Complicated Grief and Loss

Grief and loss are part of every life, but when we are either hurt by or hurt others, the grief can feel overwhelming and unbearable, like a tsunami of pain. Like complex trauma, complex grief typically arises from a web of pain and loss, rather than from a single incident. In religious injury, this pain is very complex. Depending on whether the one hurting is in the community that hurt them or has left that community, the loss can include the loss of family, community, and spiritual or religious tradition. When the place and people who raised us were the ones who hurt us, to lose all those things by walking away is extremely painful. That is a deep layer of grief. If the trauma also includes some version of negation of the self, perhaps in response to one's gender, ethnicity, sexuality, or even personality, that can create a huge amount of grief, a grief which can border on shame. Even when we want to believe the truth about ourselves—that our life is valuable, and that we are good and enough as we are—years of being told the opposite takes its toll. A loss of the person we might have been, without that level of hurt, negation, or abuse, is a great loss and needs to be validated as true grief. Religious trauma includes deep grief and loss. Validate yourself and all you have lost. Give yourself time to feel those wounds, and then, when you are ready, prepare to address the grief, so it doesn't take you down.

Examples of Complicated Grief and Loss in Religious Trauma

Beware of underestimating how much grief you bear from being told you are less than valuable than you actually are. If you are a woman, LGBTQIA+, or BIPOC and in a spiritual or religious tradition that marginalizes those aspects of your self, you have likely felt that pain. It is doubly disappointing when those inside your spiritual or religious community mirror that invalidation and tell you that the source of your insufficiency and inadequacy comes from the ultimate "parent," such as a God figure or a spiritual leader. It takes time to feel valuable as a person again, but the losses from when you felt less-than often persist. Beyond being traumatic, this experience of invalidation, suffering, and pain can manifest into complicated grief—grief that goes deeper and lasts longer than normative grief, which we work through and from so that we are able to move on. Complicated grief, like trauma that turns to PTSD, requires its own healing; we have to mourn when exiting unhealthy belief systems. This loss is often loss of family, friends, and a divine image, and each loss has to be grieved in its own way and its own time. The complexity of the grief can be compounded when the traumatization is not simply invalidation but also sexual, physical, or emotional abuse that occurs. This is particularly the case in spaces where such grief is silenced and concealed by those in power or by loved ones. For, it can make understanding love, family, and community complicated, even baffling, and the grief of not being protected by those relationships is profoundly painful.

Simple Tools to Address Complicated Grief and Loss in Religious Trauma

I find ritual and ceremony to be powerful ways to address grief and loss. Because your pain might be deeply felt and complex, you might find it beneficial to seek the help of a therapist or support professional to move through the process of grief and loss and to fashion ceremonies for release, which can help you move beyond the pain.

Many practices that I describe further can also help you begin this process. Letter writing to a former version of yourself whom you feel is lost is one ritual. Burning your pain in a fire ceremony or using a letting-go ritual with water is another way. Anything that engages us with natural elements or cultural traditions can be great tools to release grief. Without such a release of grief, it is almost impossible to experience trust and intimacy.

Trust and Intimacy Issues

It is no wonder that after experiencing abuse, bullying, or being diminished within an unhealthy faith structure, it is hard to trust and to build intimacy, whether with an individual or a community. Since a community is made up of individuals, and since the people who hurt you are often also friends and family members, it can be excruciatingly hard to rebuild a foundation of trust. If the traumatic experiences or belief systems created negative feelings of shame or guilt in in who you are in the context of a relationship, and particularly as a sexual being, then entering into relationships can make you feel conflicted. Even when you know that what others told you about yourself is not true, it is hard to uproot the triggers to our shame and guilt for loving someone, being intimate, or having a positive relationship to our own bodies. Moreover, it is hard to build trust if the foundational relationships of your early life (family, faith, friends, God) were all abusive. You have to learn to trust all over again. This is no small feat.

Examples of Trust and Intimacy Issues in Religious Trauma

Trust and intimacy, as well as the understanding of love and of being loved that underlie them, are rooted in how we are taught those elements by family and our community systems during childhood. Since many people's religious trauma begins as part of those early systems—the family and the family in the context of the religious community—opportunities to have a healthy model of love can be scarce. In unhealthy religion, all types of love from divine love, the community's love, and to even the family's love is contingent on playing by a set of rules. It doesn't mirror the omniscient love that prevails in healthy religious systems. Instead, it presents love as conditional. This makes love and trust a fragile element, conditional on doing all the right things the right way or else love is withdrawn and acceptance rescinded. This fragility sets up a delicate capacity for trust and an incapacity for deep intimacy, as deep intimacy requires being who we truly are and being loved for our authentic self.

Simple Tools to Address Trust and Intimacy Issues in Religious Trauma

Love and self-acceptance must often be learned from the ground up after religious trauma. So too must trust and acceptance. Begin with practices that make you feel good about yourself or with hobbies that help you connect with who you are and what you love. Once you have a foundation of self-esteem and self-acceptance along with practice accessing your true self, you can begin to explore external love, trust, and intimacy with less fear. It is a slow process, so begin small. Find one thing that you love and dive into that wholeheartedly. With that as a foundation, you can manifest your own safe space from which to being to love and allow yourself to be loved.

Isolation and Avoidance

Though to begin it can be difficult, but allowing yourself to be loved is important. Yet at the start of the process, removing yourself as much as possible from others can seem like a solution. When you feel you aren't, can't be, or aren't allowed to be your true self in your community or family system, such a solution is alluring. But it can only be temporary, and it's worth the effort to press on and, bit by bit, learn to be around others. When a person leaves their religiously wounding community, that instinctive response of withdrawal from the world can be hard to break. When you are struggling with knowing who you are and are fearful about sharing that with others, given your past experience, removing yourself from the world can feel safe. If someone has battered your sense of self-esteem, it can be hard to imagine that other people want the real you in their lives. But withdrawing from others is also lonely. Isolation is a common coping mechanism following trauma, often as a means of keeping away from old people, places, and things from the past, and to avoid being triggered by them. Yet, over time, this response can feed depression, low self-worth, and create even more complex issues of guilt, shame, and trust. So, I urge you to resist the call of withdrawal, isolation, and avoidance.

Examples of Isolation and Avoidance in Response to Religious Trauma

What are some examples of withdrawal in response to religious trauma? Sometimes it takes the form of selective isolation following religious injury and woundedness. A common example is avoiding any faith community and any program, or even a conversation that includes religious words. But because we all need people and companionship, such withdrawal can become emotionally dangerous when it invades all manner of life. It becomes more problematic if you don't have a single person or place with whom or where you feel safe. This is why it is helpful to start small when building back trust. Getting yourself to be around others, even in small ways, dismantles some of the barriers and wards off isolation that can grow into agoraphobia. I have worked with many clients whose fear and anxiety developed into selective isolation, and then into a sense that all interaction is unsafe. Being around others is something we practice each day by investing in something or someone. With the internet, we have the advantage of interacting with others at a distance. That said, real-life interaction is just as important, and arguably much more important, in this age of one-click relationships. So, how does one begin? Let me suggest some ways.

Simple Tools to Address Isolation and Avoidance in Religious Trauma

After being hurt by your religious community, withdrawing from life and the world can seem like a viable and reasonable response. And in some ways, it really is. But it can also create a habit of avoidance that can become as hard to break as any other symptom or traumatic response. All of us, even introverts, are social creatures. Without some human interaction, life is difficult. Without some community of meaning or shared values, life is likewise difficult. People who leave their tradition often most miss the good parts about being part of a community, as well as about having shared experiences and views. Daring to engage in some new friendships and eventually even community groups can heal this dimension of trauma. The process can be as slow as it needs to be. Over time, many people who have been traumatized do return to some kind of spiritual, religious context, or philosophical, shared values community, be that a meditation gathering, a yoga satsang (community meal), a political party network, a professional network, or even some different facet or sect of one's spiritual tradition of origin, and find it to be a healthy thing to do. Testing yourself with one relationship or picking one community group with which to engage—even the most benign, like softball or knitting—is a good way to learn to be in community again in some way, without the unhealthy components.

Guilt and Shame

Religious hurt often includes an element of guilt and shame. Also, the perpetrator of abuse in a religious context frequently abuses the rules or doctrine of the tradition to validate their abuse and maintain silence and secrecy around their violations of others. Guilt and shame can become imbedded in a person like a tattoo of pain, which is difficult and painful to remove. Issues of gender, sexual orientation, and sexuality are dimensions highly laden with guilt in many unhealthy traditions and doctrines. Guilt and shame take time to work through and shake off, layer by layer.

Examples of Guilt and Shame in Religious Trauma

The guilt and shame that are typically part of religious trauma affect a person's ability to feel good enough or valuable. Being who you are—particularly if you have a marginalized identity like being LGBTIA+, BIPOC, a woman—and being negated by your community can be very painful, especially when the community system influences how you understand yourself in relation to your family, your belief system, and the divine. Shame is particularly difficult to shake off when the systems, its leaders and its doctrine tell you that you should be ashamed of who you are based on what the tradition or God(s) of that tradition believe is right or wrong. It creates a sense that you are inherently divined to be wrong or bad because of who you are intrinsically or how you think if it doesn't align with the belief system. Untangling both that flawed belief system and the resulting guilt and shame is not easy. But I have some tools to help you to tackle the job.

Simple Tools to Address Guilt and Shame in Religious Trauma

Building self-worth is a huge component of addressing guilt and shame, as is being involved in conversations and communities who validate you for who and how you are in your most authentic self. For some people, this could include getting involved in justice, advocacy, or volunteer work in the area of their own negation. The important thing is to remain empowered rather than to rage in these contexts. Advocating for and having a voice on issues about a part of yourself that your faith community regards as "wrong" can be empowering. While rage can be a valid place to begin as an emotional response to injustices done against us, we can get stuck in anger. Rage can be an impetus to create change, find our strength, and fight for our own rights, but if we get stuck in the anger phase of reacting to trauma it can become unproductive in the long run. Find ways to empower your true self—and spend your time around those who validate you. Slowly the pain and shame imposed by the outside source—a system, family, and/or a community—will begin to melt away as you realize that you have value and worth.

Emotional Numbing and Dissociation

When we have been battered and bruised, sometimes the only or the most accessible recourse is to shut down. In the mildest form of this, it can be as simple as tuning out what is being said or where you are in any particular moment. That is something all of us have done. In response to a greater sense of danger, manifesting the freeze trauma response becomes more acute and numbness can become more pervasive. The primary coping mechanism for those who experience trauma and can't physically leave their circumstances may be to become numb. This can mean shutting down feelings, but it can also involve completely removing oneself from the situation. When mind and spirit exit an experience entirely, it is called *dissociation*. Dissociation can manifest as the experience of floating above yourself and seeing what is happening. This is common among survivors of sexual trauma and extensive physical abuse. It can also manifest as losing a sense of time passing due to being completely absent or blacking out during an experience. This is the result not to substances but to the brain exiting the situation as a stress response. If dissociation is more severe, mental health treatment should be sought immediately because this process can be a danger to daily life and functioning.

Examples of Emotional Numbing and Dissociation in Religious Trauma

The nature and intensity of the emotional numbing and dissociation will vary from person to person, depending on the type of trauma experienced in a religious context. Acute physical and sexual abuse can lead to more dissociative states in order to self-protect, primarily because being able to leave might not have been an option in the initial trauma, so the brain creates an escape hatch to protect the person from having to be present for the experience. If the pain and suffering wasn't as dangerous physically as it was emotionally, then being able to numb the feeling states—fear, anxiety, anger, etc.—is often how someone deals with being or staying in a religiously hurtful community. As we know, we can't selectively numb or dissociate, so this way of coping often extends to post-religious/spiritual trauma experiences and is harder to manage once the brain is in the habit of dissociating from any kind of discomfort.

Simple Tools to Address Emotional Numbing and Dissociation in Religious Trauma

Grounding, mindfulness, and guided relaxation practices can help teach the brain and body to stay present and focused in the peaceful moments, so it can also access those resources in times of distress. For more severe dissociation, therapy with a trained trauma therapist is necessary to learn ways to contain stress and find safe space in the mind, body, and physical world. Once the brain-body system can integrate a sense of safety, it will begin staying present rather than exiting or disassociating when stressed.

LIFE PARABLES: Triggers

The following "Life Parables" are extracts of stories of persons interviewed about their experience of religious injury and spiritual trauma. Some include the protagonists' real names, and others have been changed to protect those who don't yet feel safe enough to speak out. The Life Parables describe these people's experiences of triggers, those negative and sometimes visceral reminders of their traumatic religious or spiritual experiences, and how they affect them when these people experience them today. The content of these stories remains as they were told to me, although some language has been altered slightly for readability and flow.

DAVE: Some organized religions and their environments, like churches, still trigger me when I see them or go inside them. Even traditions with which I don't have a history can trigger me with the ritual of kneeling or taking Communion or singing a hymn I sang as a kid. It can bring me back to the absolute ideologies I learned from each of my family members, who through them taught me in different and dysfunctional ways that one way of belief is right, and all others are wrong. This was so conflicting when, after my parents' divorce, each part of my family played tug of war with me, my time, and my beliefs. When I was with my dad, I had to be Catholic. When I was with my mom, I had to be Methodist, and when I was with my grandmother, I had to be Southern Baptist. It was so confusing to me, and I ended up feeling that if everyone thought their way was right, then there was probably no right way at all. So even today the sight or rituals of institutional religions remind me of that painful tug of war of family and faith.

BILL: I think a lot of the canned answers that religion tries to offer still trigger me, especially those that blame people who don't want to come to a faith service as if they are less devout or too lazy or whatever. The idea that people care less because they aren't sitting in institutions (where I would see very faithless people sitting week after week) and are somehow less good or valuable to God angers me immensely. It is one of my greatest religious triggers. Also related to that trigger for me, as someone who sits inside a faith community, is when leaders or member of a religion spend time asserting that there is something wrong with people who don't want to come to their institution. To me, such a response seems to be a form of avoidance—that they refuse to look inward to see how they are contributing to that, how they have been uninviting, or how they are or aren't living out faith in their own lives.

Additionally, as a person of color, to hear white men in institutions talking about their issues and difficulties with political correctness (expressing how they are inconvenienced by it) is very hurtful and triggering for me as someone who has been hurt by people of faith before, and as a person who has been marginalized in religious communities because of my racial background. My sisters and brothers of color don't want to be insulted publicly, and with mostly white traditions I have experienced the lack of understanding and empathy for people of color—in talking about and even toward them when they show up in the institution. For me, that is a very hard pill to swallow.

MARG: I am very triggered any time I am in a group of anti-gay Christians (whether five or five thousand); it impacts me to such a great extent it causes me to experience panic symptoms. Nobody even has to say anything. This panic trigger also occurs when I am around those who use the anti-gay smoke screen that states "Love the sinner, hate the sin." Their words give me an inherent feeling of danger. I also have to be very careful to limit my exposure to anti-gay Christians' remarks overheard in person or on TV, or to anti-gay writing. Even moderate exposure causes me to become emotionally overloaded and unable to control my feelings of anxiety, panic, and fear.

KISHA: When I enter Pentecostal churches I am triggered. I hate seeing the elevated pulpit that congregants have to sit below and look "up" at. I believe the subliminal psychology in doing that causes congregants subconsciously to worship and/or deify the people who sit in those elevated seats. I can even be triggered when I see these churches' services and content about their worship on Facebook. I am also triggered and angered when I encounter church people and they ask me where I attend church, assuming that I do. In order to protect myself from such triggers, I usually try to avoid those situations altogether. However, during those times when they are unavoidable, I generally talk them over with my therapist or with friends.

FAY: Writing this, joining a spiritual trauma survivor group on social media, and counseling others (as a therapy provider) with similar stories are all triggers. I find that I can use this [beneficially], at least in my profession, because being aware of my own weaknesses and pain is so important when being a therapist.

DEB: Certain phrases will trigger me, such as, "I was depressed, and I gave it to God and now I am healed." I'm sorry, you may have gone through a period of depression, but when you are diagnosed with depression, generalized anxiety disorder, and have been through the process of ruling out PTSD (I still self-medicate too much to get that diagnosis I guess), it's not as easy as just giving it up to God. We need medical intervention just like anyone who has a visible ailment, and I feel when people use those kinds of phrases, they minimize the pain, suffering, and the healing process. Another phrase that really triggers me is, "God wants us to have riches, those who are still poor are stuck in the mentality of poverty, and they must not have enough faith if they are still in that position." This makes me think, "Spare me!" My grandparents were piss poor and had the most faith of anyone I knew. Normally when I get triggered in these ways. I react with anger (by venting to the trusted people), because I can't believe this kind of stuff comes out of their mouths. I also try to keep in mind that they may mean well but are terribly misinformed.

ANGIE: When people fill their vocabulary with God, blessed, Jesus, etc., it really triggers me. Going to church is a trigger for my nightmares. And the phrase, "God told me to [fill in the blank]," makes me want to choke the people who are saying it.

DEANNA: Purity culture is a big trigger for me. The moment someone suggests that young women need to show less skin so that their husbands can stay righteous makes me go into a rage that blares through my temples; and it makes me want to get drunk and take my clothes off in front of anyone who will look. The pervasive and persistent attitude that my body is not my own, and that just my moving through life is somehow dirty and tempting to someone else reopens many wounds. When someone says that the spiritual but not religious are just wishy-washy people who can't commit and are afraid of admitting they are sinners demonstrates to me that they are tone-deaf and blind to the spiritual temperature of this world. It hurts. I am also triggered when someone says something completely ignorant toward members of other religions. For me, it demonstrates that they don't care and they don't believe that God cares, which is so untrue.

MELINDA: Words that trigger me are: forgiveness, reconciliation, femininity, evangelical. It still upsets me when people say things like: "We are persecuted as Christians here in America. We are at war!" The debate about homosexuals and whether they can worship in the church also triggers me. I am also triggered by the idea that the only way to be a Christian is to be part of a church.

EMMA: My sister and I learned we were safe with the Native Church as Native American women and the people there brought safety and comfort, but [we were also taught that] if you were not within the Native Church (meaning a church on a reservation with Native American people), you were not safe and not accepted. For years I was triggered by walking into a non-Native church, because after leaving the Reservation, the white churches were the places where we were most alienated, ostracized, and meant to feel both othered and lesser than anyone else. It was a very lonely feeling—to go from feeling God and comfort in church on the Reservation to feeling so unsafe and unloved by how we were treated in the white church. For years after being emotionally hurt and threatened by members of the white church (and also by our community when we lived off the Reservation), I was unable to walk into any church at all; it was just too painful, scary, and triggering of my religious wounds at the hands of those in our first non-Native white church.

REFLECTION ON LIFE PARABLES

While the trigger examples Dave, Bill, Marg, Kisha, Fay, Deb, Angie, Deanna, Melinda, and Emma come from a wide variety of perspectives, they all define the ways in which these persons felt negated, lesser than, betrayed, alienated, and ostracized by their spiritual and religious communities. Beyond that, they also describe how the code of their hurts was written across their lives in the form of triggers, which they repeatedly have to encounter and address, always taking them back to the origin of their hurt. We should all pay attention to this roadmap of hurt, for it helps us learn about ourselves, others, and the power of institutional and communal hurt on someone, long after the original pain experience has passed.

Triggers can have a longstanding ripple effect in a person's life. Whether as the person who might be triggered in a religious context or as one in a religious context trying to understand the wounded, it is important to understand that it takes time to see, address, and diminish the impact of hurtful triggers in life. If you yourself are experiencing religious triggers, then understand that it is reasonable to feel triggered in religious contexts if your wounds come from religious sources. With time and work, you can begin to release the hold they have on you. For those of you who are trying to understand people triggered by religious ideologies, languages, places, and spaces, you have to understand the weight of this hurt. You can't diminish or shame the culprits into changing. If you try to do that you will merely prompt a repetition of the abusive behavior that caused the triggering in the first place. Nor must you diminish or shame those who are experiencing the triggers. Love, patience, and complete acceptance can, with time, begin to help sufferers release the pain for themselves and in relationship to others.

The Reframing of Symptoms: Putting the Brain-Body Relationship to Work

The brain and the body can change. And they can change again. The most absurd hope and reality of post-traumatic stress is that the infection of pain can be reversed. In traumatic stress, and the reverberations of response to that stress in the fibers of our being, we are taught that whatever the nature of the brain, body, and spirit, it can be changed. It may be powerful, painful, and excruciating, but the system of our selves can change. What this proves is that Newton's law applies everywhere: every action in the universe has an equal and opposite reaction. For every suffering imposed on us, for every symptom that becomes rooted in the core of our being, there is the potential (and maybe even a mandate) for an equal and opposite reaction. The force that binds us in suffering also offers us a bastion of hope: that we are capable of an equal and opposite response to that traumatic force. We can change. It is not easy or mandatory. But it is possible. And we can reach into that possibility at any time.

Are you ready? If you aren't yet ready to let go of the safety of symptomology, the triggers of trauma and response, that is OK. Those trigger responses have served you well. They protect you from the pain. But remember that they also keep you cornered off from joy. You can change, but you can do it only when you are ready. For if you have experienced religious injury and spiritual abuse, you have been pushed enough for a lifetime. I will only remind you gently that you can heal. I offer you that hope. I also offer you the option to say, "Not today." When you are ready, the tools are here. Community is here to welcome and embrace you into the space of the possible—even when it seems impossible. You decide whether or when you want to enter through the garden gate of hope. That choice, that timing, is yours.

A HEALING PRACTICE: Creating a Safe Space/ Guided Visualization

When we experience trauma, especially in the places meant to be safe—faith or family—it can make it hard to feel safe anywhere else. The safe space visualization allows you to create an internal safe space, one of your own making, which you can carry with you everywhere and all the time. This safe space becomes what we call in therapy a "transitional object"—think Linus's blanket from Charlie Brown. A transitional object is something we can carry with us that brings a feeling of safety into our lives. The hope is that, over time (like poor Linus was meant to do, if he hadn't stayed an eternal child), we create a sense of safety that doesn't require the transitional object.

The following visualization is a version of a transitional object, as described in some of the tips to deal with stress. You may want to carry a physical object that reminds you to calm down and find that internal safe space—like a coin, rock, or something small but with enough heft to hold and keep in your pocket. The physical object can remind you to use your breath or access your internal safe space when you need it. Over time, you can work toward not needing the physical or visual object as much—and being able to feel the inward-oriented safety in life as a whole.

1. Begin by finding a safe and quiet place to practice the safe space visualization. Get comfortable wherever you may be—seated in a chair or on the floor, lying down, or in some other position.

2. Close your eyes or, if that isn't comfortable, look at a fixed point on the ground that won't bring any outside distractions to your practice.
3. Begin with a slow and steady breath to slow you down and ground you. Focus on your slow and steady breathing as long as you need to until you feel ready to move to the next phase of this practice.
4. Imagine a safe place. If you have a reference point of a real place in your life where you once felt safe, "go" there if it is comfortable to do so. If you don't have any real safe place in your memory, imagine a place you have always wanted to go or your ideal environment—perhaps a beach, or the mountains. Perhaps someplace inside. Wherever it is, find your selected space and visualize it.
5. As you visualize your safe space location, begin to look around. Notice the environment. What are the sounds, scents, and sights in that space? Add objects or elements into the environment that remind you of safety—maybe the warmth of a fire, the sound of birds singing, or the feeling of sitting on a cozy blanket. Whatever makes the space safer and more comfortable, add those elements into your safe place.
6. Take your time becoming familiar with your safe space, until everything about the space is vivid in your mind. Remember that in this space you are safe and that you can always return to this place whenever you need it.
7. Return to your safe space daily if you can. Doing so before bed is ideal as it brings positive imagination into your creative brain before sleep, when trauma can work its way into your subconscious.

CHAPTER 3

Through the Looking Glass:

Religious Injury and Traumatic Stress

In the end these things matter most: How well did you love?
How fully did you live? How deeply did you let go?
—Buddha

I tend to use a lot of *Alice in Wonderland* metaphors when I speak about trauma and healing, but *The Matrix* concepts equally apply. Use whichever suits you. Both Alice and Neo struggled to live in the world as it was, each seeking something greater than the sum of its parts, each coming to a crossroads where they had to choose a potion or a pill to move out of the familiar world and into a new reality. Even if it was one in which everything was turned upside down, somehow truth became far more accessible to them there.

It comes down to the choice to see or not. In any unexamined, unexplained way, we can live in the world we have been offered, or we can choose to go deeper and see all the scary things as they really are. But in seeing the scary things, we also experience the world more fully.

As a very small child, I used to look at the world as it was and search for any way to make both the pain and the joy more intense. I would sit in my room, classroom, or at a play date, and create stories that moved beyond my reality into something I thought would be greater. I was always a dreamer. As I grew up, I learned that I didn't need to create a super-reality to experience things acutely. I learned that my hypersensitivity to the world would bring me all the acute joy and pain that any one human life could handle.

Those experiences came in tidal waves and tsunamis, sometimes with excruciating pain and occasionally with excruciating joy. They were always far more powerful than my daydreams. I always thought life would never be enough. But along the way I learned that much of it felt like too much.

Ravaged by identity tectonics in adolescence, a Latine adoptee, born in the Andes, and raised in Jersey suburbia only an express train ride away from Manhattan, and consequently not quite sure who I was by anyone's standards, I remember feeling very alone in a sea of activity. Later adolescence brought sexual trauma, with two assaults by different perpetrators, and the grand mountainous landscape of PTSD to navigate for the better part of a decade—ignoring, facing, fighting, and healing through the years. Then, when the altitude of that suffering subsided, I became someone who didn't know where she came from or where she was going, plagued by the question, "Who am I?"

There followed years of dealing with issues of acute and chronic pain, including endometriosis that led to infertility and, ultimately, divorce and moving across the country. Then came a series of unexpected spinal surgeries and a hysterectomy, amid the tumult of a pandemic and uprising, and I found myself wondering why I had asked life for more feeling. I was throbbing beyond imagination with the authenticity of life. Amidst all that, I experienced the joy of returning to a spiritual homeland of Andean Indigenous lineages, grounding myself in the work of healing care for BIPOC, LGBTQIA+ and activist communities, and living near family again, and so being able to watch my niece and nephews grow and to enjoy weekend lunches with my parents.

I was Alice. I was Neo. I had taken the elixir of true and excruciating life and gotten everything for which I had asked, each pain and joy surmounting the one before it, life deepening both nauseating troughs and ecstatic peaks where everything was visible, and anything was possible. Those moments of excruciating joy and spiritual wonder, of exploration of new terrain and the beauty of relationship with another, were just as essential to the red pill life as the immense pain that unfolded, sometimes right alongside one another.

What I learned from that experience is that:

1. Whatever our expectations of life, we are given much more than we could ever imagine, whether good, bad, or ugly;
2. Life will always surprise us, painfully and beautifully, and often in equal measure;

3. We don't need to create grand machinations and adventures. Life is the greatest and most terrible adventure. There is no need to expand on its script; and
4. We can see what is, take what is given, and grow something greater than the sum of its parts.

In short, after looking at life through the looking glass to see what is, we can be liberated from the cage of what we have been given and reframe it to make it what we want it to be. Initially, however, we must see the pain for what it is. We have to know our dragons, mad hatters, white rabbits, and Agent Smiths before we can battle them adeptly and surmount them. That is why Neo has to take the pill to see the world as it is. Then, and only then, can he battle the opposition in his story.

Deeper In: Many Faces of Trauma

To understand trauma, we have to see where it lives, how it manifests, and to recognize the many ways in which we can describe the traumatic experience. In our future human universe, there will unfortunately likely be more, not fewer, permutations of traumatic experience. The benefit of all these permutations is that they validate the human experience of pain and illustrate that different pains, even different traumas, manifest slightly differently in the human experience. Childhood trauma is going to have distinct impacts on a person, as is the repeated experience of trauma throughout one's lifetime. Recognizing the distinctions between them can help us identify different traumatic experiences and the uniqueness of the intergenerational or historical traumatic experience, as well as how these might be distinguished from an injury to the moral self. We now can see how living with a person who has experienced trauma or working with trauma survivors regularly can traumatize people.

The field of traumatology (the study of trauma and the practice of treating trauma) is only now beginning to explore the field of religious injury or what I call "sacred wounds." It is isolating different issues specific to someone who has experienced trauma in a religious community setting in order to know how best to treat such persons. The need for this is increasing exponentially as more stories come out about this kind of traumatic experience. In this chapter, we will explore such traumatic issues and what traumatic experience looks like in religious contexts and review some examples of the hurt it causes.

Developmental Trauma

While the term *developmental trauma* is not an official diagnosis in the Diagnostic Statistical Manual (DSM), it has become commonly used to define trauma experienced by a person while still in the developmental stage of life (infancy until the early twenties). What science has been able to illustrate about the developing brain is that it is much more malleable than in later stages of life. Therefore, trauma experienced before the brain is fully developed affects not only the emotional and psychological state of a person but the actual structure of the brain. As I will show in the next chapter, religious and spiritual trauma often begins in childhood. As such, it is not only emotionally detrimental but also affects the entire way a person thinks.

Complex Trauma

Complex trauma is trauma experienced repeatedly over a prolonged period of time and is most often mentioned in regard to situations of domestic violence, childhood sexual or physical abuse, and combat trauma. It can also be the result of the compounding of trauma over the life cycle—the revictimization of someone who might have been abused in childhood and then abused or violated in other ways over the course of their life. When a person has a traumatic experience that is emotionally unresolved, there is often a greater tendency for them to be abused or violated again; this is known as re-victimization. Throughout this book, we will explore the nature of complex trauma as a common dimension of religious trauma. It typically affects long periods of life, often childhood (thereby also being an issue of developmental trauma), and can be a precursor to trauma throughout the life cycle. Part of my intention with this book is to provide a way to look at the religious traumatic experience as a means of resolving the pain, suffering, and (in many cases) PTSD of people who have suffered this wound in silence.

Intergenerational Trauma

Intergenerational trauma is traumatic experience that spans more than the lifetime of one single person to affect generations of people. I call intergenerational trauma *sticky trauma*. Thanks to the science of epigenesis we know that while core DNA doesn't change, environmental factors (like war, starvation, and other traumas) attach to our DNA, collecting over time and transferring from one generation to the next. They "stick" to the DNA of a family line. The one hopeful thing about this is that, similar to the brain (which can change and build new patterns and neural pathways over time), anything that becomes attached can, in theory, be detached. I like to think of the flip side of intergenerational trauma as being intergenerational resilience, which means that it is not only our harmful experiences that attach, but also our positive experiences or strengths, and that we can tap into some of those multi-generational strengths to help us, in this lifetime, overcome the habitual patterns of trauma and trauma response we have that are based on our ancestors' experiences. If we do that work in this generation, there is a possibility to un-stick the unhealthy sticky attachments for ourselves and even the following generations of our families and indeed nations.

Part of the difficulty of intergenerational trauma is that it follows the logic of the adage that those who cannot remember the past are doomed to repeat it. In this kind of trauma, the pain, hurt, and suffering have become so ingrained in a person (or a family, ancestral lineage, collective lineage, or country) that it becomes invisible, woven into the fabric of the way things are, and as such no longer apparent enough to address. Common examples of intergenerational trauma are multiple generations of combat veterans with PTSD, a family history of abuse or addiction across multiple generations, and the suffering of generations of marginalized people such as BIPOC communities.

In the case of religious trauma, hurtful belief systems, doctrines, and mores negatively affect people for many generations. Issues of shame or latent anger then become ingrained in the family or community system. If the abuse or marginalization of a gender or sexuality is prominent in a faith culture, then there can be generations being hurt or abused by the same system, generations living together and reflecting self-hate or other-hate into the next generation.

And yet anything that can change, can change again. And in that lies our hope and our call to action.

Secondary Traumatic Stress/Traumatization and Compassion Fatigue

Secondary stress is the traumatic stress experienced by persons who sit with the traumatic pain of others, which can include professionals in the helping field but also those who are the loved ones of trauma survivors. Similarly, compassion fatigue is the emotional, psychological, and spiritual exhaustion of someone who sits with people through their pain. In a religious system, this could be people who are working with a community and the survivors of abuse within that community. There have instances where people who have been called into a religious community's abuse scandal to help end up holding much of the pain and, in extreme scenarios, can even manifest the symptoms of PTSD themselves. Other ways in which secondary stress can be experienced is in the intergenerational trauma situation where a family is experiencing the residual effects of a family member's trauma. It can also be experienced in the support system of a person experiencing trauma and PTSD. In religious trauma, this can be family members, spouse, romantic partners, and friends who are not part of the hurting system. In the process of any traumatic experience, it is important to validate the powerful effects of this secondary stress and to address it with love and kindness, as it, too, requires healing.

Moral Injury/Spiritual Injury

Fairly new to the trauma lexicon is the term *moral injury*, the ramifications of which can be considered spiritual injury. Moral injury is any experience which impacts a person's morality or spiritual value set. Originally, moral injury was considered to be something that one person perpetrated on another that negatively affected or went against Revise as follows "…went against a common or generally accepted sense of morality - either done to someone by someone else or done by someone that goes against their own sense of morality. It is an injury to the moral nature of the world and the sense of morality which could be experienced by the person doing the harm, the person being harmed or both. For example, a solider who was expected to do actions (like killing others) in a combat zone would face the issue of going against their moral system on the home front. As the concept and its treatment has grown to wider recognition, moral injury has been extended to include anything that might negatively affect someone's morality, whether perpetrated against or by that person. In the case of religious hurt, this concept takes on an even deeper meaning—a deeper meaning that so far has not been explored. The morality of the religious system might, at some point of wounding or fragmentation, go against the inner morality or intuition of the individual. This is a complex and confusing experience: something that feels wrong in their intuition and heart the religious system at large might deem to be right. The crux of what makes it difficult for a person to leave their religious system is going against the moral system of one's upbringing. This takes an immense amount of courage (say, to give up one's own desires and follow Jesus). Negatively, the willingness to ignore reality (say, to go along with financial or sexual practices or other abuses of power that one knows to be wrong) is the only other choice. So, leaving is often near impossible for people who have imbedded the system of their upbringing into their adulthood.

The term *sacred wounds* doesn't fit into a technical set of terms; rather, it is a lexicon that I have created to discuss the wounds that touch the personal moral center, the heart and the soul, and the emotional experience of a person. This includes what is defined above, found in a religious system or context. The sacredness of these wounds has a dual meaning: they are wounds in the sacred places of the self (the mind, the body, and the spirit), but they are also sacred in and of themselves. They hurt the most sacred parts of us. But in a healing place, we can find powerful personal transformation—and that is sacred, too.

The Breadth of Religious Trauma

While it is impossible to illuminate every corner of religious wounds and trauma or depict every scenario of religious or spiritual injury, in what follows I offer examples of what these can look like. This is not an exhaustive list but a reference point for those who have experienced trauma in religious or spiritual contexts or for those who are seeking to understand this kind of traumatic experience:

- A person who has been physically or sexually assaulted by a religious figure, leader, or community member *or* whose physical, sexual assault or abuse has been co-opted by a religious, spiritual leader or institution, or deemed as "ok" by that tradition's doctrine.
- A person who has been abused by family or friends within a religious/spiritual culture or institution and has been shamed or guilted by doctrine or harmful interpretations

of sacred texts reinforced by fellow believers into believing that it was his or her fault.

- A person who has been deemed "lesser than" due to their race/ethnicity or gender based on a religious doctrine, text, or spiritual/religious group's history of marginalization of that or any people group.
- A person who has been told, based on doctrine of the tradition or harmful interpretations of sacred texts, that they are wrong, sinful, or going against God/the divine/the tradition because of their sexual orientation.
- A woman (or other marginalized gender) who, based on the tradition's doctrine or harmful interpretation of sacred texts, has been forced into a variety of kinds of submission to a man in ways with which she is not comfortable or in ways harmful to her spiritual, physical, emotional, or psychological health.
- A person who was shamed, marginalized, or punished for asking questions/showing independent thought within a spiritual or religious culture or tradition and told that questioning anything about the group/institution/religion is wrong, or even sinful.
- A person who has been ridiculed, bullied, threatened, harmed, or punished for any reason by a religious or spiritual community—especially for questioning or leaving that group/community.
- A person who has been excommunicated from a religion or spiritual tradition for disagreeing with practices of that community, its leaders, or its members.
- A person who has been made to feel he or she doesn't belong, or is less than or unworthy, based on nothing more than being who they are or communicating feelings.
- A person who has been prevented from leaving a particular religious or spiritual community and threatened, harmed, or punished for trying to leave.
- A person who has been threatened, harmed, or punished for going to (or trying to go to) someone outside of the spiritual or religious community to report harmful or

dangerous behavior or activity going on within the community/organization/institution.

Trauma Refined by the Living of It

Part of this book is dedicated to the voices of spiritual and religious trauma—the brave, the gentle, the angry, and the quiet. Being able to tell your story is a deeply healing experience; although, doing so is not required and is not part of everyone's journey. Telling your story is your choice, and it is just as OK to say you can't or don't want to as to say you will. Hearing and telling our own stories can be empowering. It creates community where once there was isolation. It creates resonance where once there was loneliness. It creates understanding where once there was confusion. It creates knowledge where once there was ignorance or suppression of the truth. We are by nature storytelling and story-receiving creatures. We want to excavate the truth everywhere it exists, and we get chills when we hear a story that resonates with our own, especially the bold and painful truths of pain and healing.

To honor this truth wherever it resides, I collected over a dozen stories from people who have lived through a variety of spiritual and religious wounds and were willing to speak about them out loud. Those people inhabit the spectrum of healing. Some are still in the deeply hurting place, and others have moved through their pain and found light. Each part of this process is valuable, and each story should be told. As we explore the experience of religious trauma and healing in this book, I will share pieces of these stories along the way—the vivid and living lamplight of what is true.

While many of the stories lean into the Christian fundamentalist and Christian-oriented cult experiences, because they were the people to whom I had most access when writing the first edition of this book, in fact these stories have much in common with others I have heard since, stories which span almost every religion, spiritual community and context you could imagine.

Pain is sacred, and in the stories of pain and healing in this book you will find what is true everywhere. For those of you suffering from religious wounds, I hope these stories bring you solace. For those of you seeking to understand this kind of wound, I hope the stories will increase your learning in a powerful way.

LIFE PARABLES: An Introduction to Religious and Spiritual Trauma

BILL: I was part of an emerging community in Colorado with some post-evangelical folks trying to sort out what happened to us growing up. We were in this post-Christian culture where we were all just trying to figure it out. Key words were *relationship* and *community*. I saw so much dysfunction around that. A lot of people in the community had been burnt by megachurch and church celebrities. But in our small community, celebrity was more insidious when it began to form around a microcelebrity, one person in the community who had weight and gravitas. There were different factions in our small faith family that aligned with different personalities and different microcelebrities. Each of these faction-heads had a very different view and take on faith, God, and the community, and it all became very dysfunctional.

The community was free flowing, which meant no hierarchy, but also no oversight. There was no accountability, but rather, personality cults. I realized that for me (and I affirm not being with the institutional church), I need an institution that can have oversight, so that if someone is screwing up, it can be addressed. Of course, with each community of faith there are light/shadow sides. I, personally, appreciate structure and accountability when things get chaotic. There are emerging expressions of church that can be healthy, but that was not my experience in my Emerging Church community. It felt like people without a story trying to make one. They weren't informed by tradition or church in general, but…by the ideas from their painful church pasts that they found wrong or hurtful, and it felt as if they wanted to recreate the whole thing from the ground up.

That is incredibly draining, and there can be so many blind spots. It was total confusion for me, because I couldn't process how different the reality was compared to the intention for that community. In some ways it was more dysfunctional than the Southern Baptist culture I grew up in. In some ways I am still processing what the hell happened. With the lack of tradition to sustain us, it was a… structure built [entirely] on personalities. There were people hurt by faith who built the community, and so many of them came in with conflicting and untrustworthy thoughts about people and faith, which manifested as hurting other people. In some ways it was even more hurtful than splitting from differences over doctrine, because we all came in with an expectation of living deep in a safe community, each coming out of hurting faith, and then this new community ended up hurting people more.

By saying it was safe from the hurt of church past, then replicating hurt in a very intimate way, [our community] ended up betraying people at a deep soul level. The whole community ended up turning on itself and self-destructing as a result. All of it was extremely disappointing and hurtful for me. Creating this emerging expression of church was supposed to be about not being like institutional church, which we all felt had spit us up like a cog in a big wheel, and then we did the same thing all over again.

FAY: I married an abusive man who was bipolar. At eighteen years of age, I did not see the signs, and neither did anyone else who knew him before our marriage. I spent fifteen years in an abusive relationship, and then he left, deserted [me]. We had two small children at that time. This is when the church left me the first time. At that time, I did not recognize how traditional my upbringing had been, but I found out. You should not divorce, and definitely never remarry. Women should be submissive to their husbands and do everything they [can] to keep them happy. So, I was left, single and alone forever, or so the church said.

DAVE: My aunt killed herself in 1997, when I was ten years old. She was a drug addict and a nurse and got fired for stealing drugs; she lay down on the train tracks. I heard someone at the funeral giving "condolences," saying that she was going to burn in hell for all eternity. She was the sweetest person in the entire world. What kind of God would do that? Was it the belief of everyone who was there that she would suffer forever and ever? When I heard that, I remembered someone telling me once that every second you experience on earth is like a million years of pain in one moment in hell. How terrible is that for someone you love?

I always believed in God 110 percent, but for a long time I felt as if he…[picked]on me. Growing up with a terminal illness (cystic fibrosis), I remember thinking it isn't fair that God did this to me and not everyone else. When there was abuse going on in the home, again I would think, "Where is God now? Why would a loving God allow this to happen to me?" It is a hard thing for a kid to comprehend. I would say my wounds didn't actually happen in one establishment. It was the culmination of different sects of religion telling me different people were bad. Catholicism and Southern Baptists said, "Our way is the way, and other traditions are wrong." Whenever I was with one family member or the other, I felt like I had to be the right kind of person for their tradition (my grandmother, Baptist, my mother, Methodist, my father, Catholic). It felt like different religions pulling me apart.

REFLECTION on LIFE PARABLES

Religious trauma can be experienced in a variety of contexts, shades, and levels. Spaces that are a refuge for some people can be a place of hurt for others. For still others, religious trauma might be rejection of any kind found in religious and spiritual spaces into which people enter assuming absolute acceptance that then harm. This harm is then connected by them to rejection by individuals, communities, and expressions of the divine. Sometimes trauma results from absolute laws that don't reflect love but are just law for law's sake; this can create a belief that if law is greater than love in religion, then religion has no value.

There is a wide variety of pain and suffering in religious and spiritual spaces, so one does well to listen to particular people's stories to fully understand their pain. For people hurt by spiritual or religious contexts, that hurt can look like rejection, diminishment, or law, and it is hard for them to believe in anything again. That is totally understandable. That said, hope and love are whatever you make them. You can believe in something or someone again. That belief might or might not be in a spiritual tradition or practice. It could just be finding the ability to trust another person in relationship or a community of any kind.

HEALING PRACTICES

Depending on where you are in your own hurt and healing process, select whichever of the following exercises that is useful to you. It may be too soon or too painful for you to use all of these tools, but they are here and accessible when you are ready. You can always turn back the pages to a practice you passed over or use a tool months or years later when you are in a new place, stage, and phase of healing.

Writing and Creative Expression Practice

PART ONE: On a scale of 1 to 10, measure the depth of your sacred wounds or spiritual pain in your life at present and the status of your relationship to your place of religious or spiritual harm. If you don't know how to calculate this kind of pain, imagine the scoring system in this way:

1. *You feel slightly distracted throughout the day by whatever issue is plaguing you, but you can still focus on daily life.* You are still imbedded in the community group or relationships with people who might have hurt you. Perhaps the hurt isn't that acute at present.

2. *You think about this issue throughout the day and week.* You find yourself thinking multiple times a week about specific scenarios that hurt you.

3. *You find it more difficult to spend great lengths of time with the faith community/person(s) who have hurt you.* It is harder to let things go when you disagree with them.

4. *You are beginning to find increasing differences between how you feel or think about the world and the worldview of your faith community and its members.* It is harder to let things go that inherently feel "wrong" to you—even though your feelings contradict the larger doctrine of your religious group. This is very confusing and part of you feels sadness and anger, but there is also a part of you that feels conflicted and shameful for disagreeing with the larger group and doctrines.

5. *You are beginning to isolate from people, places, or things that remind you of your hurt or the community/people/persons who have hurt you.* You feel slightly lost and are not sure where to go or what to do next in relation to your hurt or in general. You spend a lot of time questioning others but also yourself—as if you are weighing the scales of what is right and are not sure where you'll land.

6. *You are beginning to read books, connect with people or groups on the internet, and are actively seeking insight from your primary faith group.* Most likely you are doing it anonymously or with a pseudonym because you have a lingering fear that people in your faith group might find out what you are doing. You

disagree with a lot of what happens, is said, and/or the doctrine of your faith group, but you don't feel you are in a position to leave it. It is very anxiety-inducing and exhausting to feel as if you are sitting between two worlds, but it feels as if leaving or even thinking about leaving would mean undoing too much.

7. *You may have spoken up or asked a question of your faith community or its leader(s), and the response was suspicious or condescending.* You are beginning to feel depressed or enraged at the idea that you might have to spend the rest of your life in this system, but you are not yet quite sure you want to leave. You begin to think about what and who you might lose if you walked away from your faith community. You feel like a stranger in your own life but are not sure where else you would go if you left.

8. *You might begin to test the boundaries with close family and friends, creating "for instance" examples to see how they might respond if you left your faith group and/or began to speak about the ways in which you have been hurt outside your faith group.* Your exploration is expanding in the world outside your faith community—both virtually and possibly in person at some other local community group.

9. *You are beginning to feel the flicker of a part of you that is more than just what you have been taught.* You feel a little bit of freedom internally but also a lot of fear. To deconstruct everything you have ever known feels as if it could be liberating but also terrifying. It is an existential crisis of sorts. You are questioning your meaning, faith's meaning, religion's and spirituality's meaning, and what you are meant to do with your life—and where you are meant to be. It is a confusing time.

10. *You may have completely removed yourself from the faith community where your sacred wound occurred and are considering what your next life move might be.* You are feeling the loss and grief that someone might feel at the death of a loved one. They feel overwhelming. Yet perhaps a part of it feels exhilarating—as if you are finally able to be the truest version of you, or at least the beginnings of that person.

This practice enables you to see where you might be in your process of hurt or healing. While the above scale is a stage system, it is not a better/worse hierarchy; to be in stage 1 or 10 at any given point or time is equally valid. Some people are hurt by religion and stay, and others leave. Some stay and feel unhappy; some stay and find balance for themselves. Some leave and feel unhappy; some leave and find balance for themselves. Wherever you are on this 1 to 10 spectrum, there is no wrong place. You are where you can be, and that is OK. The scale is only a way to see yourself and others in a compassionate way. The definitions are loose and are just examples: you might define the stages quite differently for yourself. Feel free to recreate the scale or spectrum so that it works for you or relates to your experience.

PART TWO: Once you have selected your present number on the scale at and/or created a spectrum of your own that suits and defines your own journey, find some way to express where you are in your journey of hurt or healing. You can do this by writing a short story, painting a picture, taking a photo, writing a poem, or building a sculpture. Create something—and interpret "create" in whatever way suits you. Create something from your pain so that even in the difficult times you can always have something of beauty to reference, something by which to remember your pain as both deconstructive *and* creative. Make something that means something to you.

Contemplative Practice

You may feel overwhelmed by your own process of healing from your hurts. It can be exhausting and painful. Sometimes it feels as if it is too much to take on. Sometimes it can feel lonely. Use the following practice on days you feel overwhelmed, to clear your head, heart, and spirit space. We all need stamina for our healing journey. This is one way to create space and build stamina for the long road. Sometimes moving forward is also about periods of letting go.

Thought Release Visualization-Clouds:

1. Find a safe and comfortable place to do this practice. You can be sitting in a chair, on the floor, or lying down—whatever is most comfortable for you.
2. Close your eyes or keep them lightly open and focused on a point on the ground that is not distracting.

3. Imagine a bright blue sky across the landscape of your mind, dotted with white clouds. Imagine that each and every cloud represents a single thought in your mind.

4. Begin your slow and steady breath—imagine your breath as a gentle breeze, moving the clouds across the blue skyline.

5. If you feel crowded by the thought clouds, you can move them farther back on the horizon so that they are smaller and farther away from you. This can help with detaching your emotions from your thoughts.

6. Remember: Your thoughts are not you at your deepest and truest self. Your feelings are not you at your deepest and truest self. Say this over in your mind as much as you need to, to help you detach from your thoughts and the associated feelings.

7. Watch the clouds as they move across your mind, carried by the gentle breeze of your breath, one thought at a time. Observe the thought as it passes. Watch it without judgment or criticism, and without blame of self or others.

8. Let each thought pass one at a time, carried by the gentle breeze across the landscape of your mind.

9. Whenever you feel overwhelmed with thoughts and feelings, you can close your eyes and watch those thoughts until the process becomes slower and less chaotic. If you can't close your eyes, look up at the sky and observe the physical clouds and practice thought watching using that natural landscape.

Continue this practice regularly. Build up to ten minutes of practice at a time. You can then build beyond ten minutes up to twenty minutes. The ultimate goal of most meditative or mindfulness practices is to reach a maximum of about twenty minutes. Don't let this prospect frighten you. In the beginning you may only manage one minute or five minutes, but keep working at it. Doing so will decrease stress and increase your ability to have control over your thoughts and your mind.

CHAPTER 4

Faith of Origin:

Religious Roots and Family Issues

All the trials we endure cannot be compared to these interior battles.

—Teresa of Avila

As an international adoptee, born in Colombia, I spent the better part of my childhood and adolescence imagining my origins. This ranged from imagining my birthmother trekking down from a mountain tribe to bring me to the orphanage, then trekking back up to her community, to envisioning a secret affair between my birthmother, a maid, in the home of Pablo Escobar, who had to take her love child to the orphanage in the covert cover of night, before my birthfather, kingpin of the Americas, even knew I existed. I blame the latter story on the fact that being raised in the suburbs of New Jersey, with no cultural reference to the land of my birth. As a child I had a clichéd coffee-and-cocaine concept of Colombia. I share this embarrassing bit of childhood origin story cosplay as a reference to the ways in which we try to make sense of our origins, whether familial or spiritual.

Upon learning that I couldn't have children, I wondered where I began or ended if the genealogy of "me" was a one-person family tree—more like a genealogical stump. I had no beginnings or endings, at least not in the ways we are taught to construct identity and meaning-making for the self, flawed and outdated as those ways might be. Within the limited social constructs in which I had existed, we are where (and whom) we come from and we live on through those whom we leave behind. I never thought it mattered—until it was an absolute in my own life. Then it was all that mattered.

In the depths of my existential crisis, I recalled something that a feminist studies professor who was also a self-professed clairvoyant, and my namesake, Teresa of Avila, told me. Let me explain.

The truth is, I had always been fairly ambivalent about having children, and even more so about getting married, but I fell in love and found myself in a very traditional iteration of marriage, one that turned out to be ill-fitting. For my partner very much wanted children. The societal assumption was that we would have children. But I wasn't sure I wanted to, partly because I thought that if I had a child I would be unable to give everything I had to that adventure, and partly because something in me kept saying that having children wasn't necessarily my life's calling. However, after a couple of unsuccessful years of trying, and after multiple endometriosis surgeries, I was heartbroken to discover that having children was something I couldn't do. Regardless of ambivalence at the start, the grief at the loss of possibility was deeply painful. It was even more so as an adoptee who had never gotten to know the connection of biology on the front end of her life.

At the same time, at the end of my attempts at getting pregnant, I found myself in a kind of desperation—the kind that no longer had anything to do with the original intention (to create life) and everything to do with the forceful perseverance of the truly stubborn. My desperation became entirely about doing the undoable. Somehow I had entangled my identity confusion of my adolescence with this need to have a genetic future. It all awakened the deep yearning I had as someone who had lived a life and experienced a childhood without genetic connection, and I felt a resurgence of confusion. I wasn't merely confused about which direction to go next: I had lost my compass bearing entirely.

I became obsessed with my origins and depressed by my lack of future—in the genetic sense. Then, Teresa came back into my life. About a decade earlier, my quirky undergrad feminist professor had insisted I read *Interior Castle* by Teresa of Avila. Teresa, my name was given to me by the Grey Order nuns a few decades earlier because of the confluence of my birthday and her feast day. I forgot about the famous mystic for a couple of decades until urged to read her manifesto by the self-styled feminist psychic. As soon as I read it, I felt a deep connection with Teresa—as though she were speaking directly to me, across time and space. The intimacy I found in reading her words I can only describe as if being with family.

Years later, Teresa, my namesake in the form of memory, came into my view again when I found myself unable to manifest life in the literal and biological way. I went to a clairvoyant session with a circle of women, in hopes of a miracle.

I hoped, in my fierce desperation, that some psychic transmission would ordain me for biological parenthood—though all biological facts intimated the contrary. Whoever this clairvoyant was and whatever her true talents were, I don't know. But one thing she told me I have carried with me from that point forward. She selected one woman at a time and asked her to whom she wanted to speak, and then she provided a back and forth related to her and their relationship to the person with whom they wanted to speak. I asked to speak to my mother, and the clairvoyant asked which one, which completely surprised me as the usual assumption isn't that a person has more than one. I said I wanted to speak to my birth mother. The message that came through was this:

> *We are manifestors. The both of us. We burn bright and hot, and paired together in this lifetime would have been a disaster, but I passed along [to you] the calling to be a manifestor in this lifetime. We may not, either of us, have been made to be mothers in the traditional sense, but we were meant to give birth and mother in other ways. Whatever way you are meant to do in this world, know you are a manifestor.*

What is truth and what is fiction? What is magic and what is serendipity? What is coincidence and what is synchronicity? Back then, I didn't quite know. Since then, I have realized that truth comes in many shapes and forms; and, when we are open, we can receive all kinds of information we need to hear, and when we need to hear it. In some ways that encounter was the beginning of my relationship with my birth mother. That essence of her has stayed with me and has reminded me, in deeper ways over time, that we are connected and are family in a cosmic way. That conversation began to heal some of the pain and loss I felt at not having genetic links in this lifetime. It reminded me that I came from a place, from people, and from a woman who, though she couldn't mother me in this lifetime, did give me the inheritance of calling.

Even back then I knew that the message I received that night was true, and I realized that biology wasn't essential for birthing. There are many ways we manifest and create in this world. I remembered in that moment my namesake, Teresa of Avila. She never gave birth to a single biological life, but she gave birth over and over again in her lifetime. She was a manifestor, and she was my primogenitor. Out of that moment and a few subsequent encounters with that Teresa of my origin, I realized that we also can be birthed in many ways. My birth mother gave me physical life. The Teresas—Avila and later Urrea—aligned with my name and birthdate. And along the way I met many beings who made me what I was and gave me connection to where I came from.

As I opened myself to the definitions of both family and birthing, as I recalibrated the meaning of those terms and the calling of my life, as I lived into the work of manifesting, I realized that I had an evolving and growing sacred family and birthing practice. Beginning back then and unfolding ever since, I realize that I was given the gift of a new perspective on the terms that felt so finite and rigid. There was a great liberation from a previous script of scarcity that I had been given by the representations of the terms in the world around me and by my own belief in those limitations.

I explain this evolution to illustrate how we box ourselves by the stories we tell ourselves of who we are, who we are supposed to be, and the meaning of it all. When we look outside the limits of what is, we see what is possible, and the fire of that reality is greater than preordained facts, history, or biology. We all have the potential to be something more than the boxes we have been given to fit into.

Yet to be that something more, we have to learn that our life stories, our life scripts are what we make them. The raw and literal material of life scripted to us is often limited and one-dimensional. That material is part of our story—but it doesn't have to be the whole story. We have the latitude to manifest the fullness, depth, and breadth of our truths in whatever way liberates us from the constraints and expectations that culture and society impose on us. When we finally recognize our truth in all its fullness and then create our destiny *that* is the intrinsic story of our healing and manifestation.

Let us begin with the roots. Let us begin with the origins of our familial and spiritual or religious root system, stumps, trees, or vines, and only then rescript our futures based on an expanded understanding of truth. Though what follows imagines a family systems model of religion/spirituality based on a primary deity or deities at the top of the hierarchy of belief, reimagine it in whatever way suits your own context.

Religion, Spirituality and Family Systems

We learn almost everything from our primary caregivers. How does a person know what love is, what it looks like, or how to love another person? They learn it because their primary caregivers teach them about love and how to love. In therapy, the term for the system that raises us is called our "family of origin." The family that raises us is our family of origin, and they also become the place of origin for everything we know, believe, and feel. They set the template for our understanding of the world. The potency of this early life is the reason why trauma experienced in childhood is so devastating and damaging.

This is made even more complex for trauma occurring within a family system that is also surrounded by or enmeshed with a faith system. In my study of religious community systems and trauma, I have come to call this system that encircles the family system the "faith of origin." The faith of origin is the religious system that has "raised" you, for all intents and purposes. It is the system that (usually) surrounds the family system and enforces or reinforces the values taught by the family. When both family and faith systems are healthy, they reflect to a child a value system that can facilitate caring and kindness, love for all others, generosity and graciousness, and a sense of accountability to do good to others. When either system does not reflect those values, it can do immense harm. If the family system is abusive, violent, or unhealthy but the faith system is healthy, children become confused by the dissonance between what is taught in the pews versus what happens behind closed doors at home. This can prompt them to become jaded about one or both systems. If, conversely, the family system projects and enforces a healthy kind of love but the faith system reflects something different, then this, too, can lead to jaded impressions.

The most common hazardous or wounding interaction between the family of origin and the faith of origin systems is one in which the two work together to continuously enforce a negating God image. If we think of the parent figure in a house as the ultimate figurehead of right and wrong, then we can think of the image of God as the ultimate form of parentage. If we consider abuse, rejection, or shaming by a parent as the most damaging traumatic wound (or at least the one with the most extensive impact on a person throughout their lifetime), then imagine how much that is compounded when the "parent" is God. Imagine as well if the family, community, and religious institution creates and then reinforces whatever abuse, rejection, or shaming a person is experiencing—and then tells the traumatized person that God caused the suffering and that it is deserved. Talk about family baggage!

No wonder it is so difficult for people to see their way away from an abusive God and away from these kinds of systems! If my family is the place of my abuse/hurt but my faith community is a place of refuge, then I have some way to reflect goodness into my life and onto myself. Or alternatively, if my faith community is the place of my abuse/hurt but my family is a place of refuge, then I also have some way to reflect goodness into my life and onto myself. But if both my faith community and my family reflect and mutually reinforce the abuse/hurt, then unless I have some other frame of reference, I will see myself *only* as they see me. I have no frame of reference to tell me I am good or should not be ashamed, or that God or the world can love me exactly as I am. I have no one to tell me it is not OK to be hurt or abused by people or systems. This is what makes religious trauma so insidious and why it is so difficult for people to say "No" and get away.

When I meet people in my study of religious trauma, I begin with this question, "What did the God of your childhood look and act like?" How people answer this is often a great reflection of how they see themselves and of the kind of faith community from which they come. If it is healthy, loving, and nurturing, then the God of their childhood will reflect that—and in a healthy family system their parents will look the same. In abusive systems, the lack of love and acceptance will be reflected and the God-father will often look much like the home-father. God is personified and father is deified in the worst and best scenarios according to the love or abuse of that family/faith system.

At this point it is useful to introduce a few more terms. These are therapeutic terms, which offer ways to look at unhealthy relationships. Given that family and faith institutions can be independently or jointly unhealthy systems, it is important to understand unhealthy relationship concepts as well.

Understanding Family Issues
Codependence

Codependence refers to a relationship built on an unhealthy amount of neediness, in which one person is the caretaker and the other is dependent on the caretaker to function, but each is dependent on the other. With addiction disorders, codependence is due to the compulsive nature of the need and the common instance of one or more people in a codependent relationship being addicted to drugs/alcohol—or to something else. In an unhealthy or abusive religious context, codependence can be rampant. Community members are codependent on the institution and the dogma, the institution is dependent on the doctrines, and the abused/traumatized persons often find themselves in the middle of a web of codependence—on the family system, community, institution, doctrines, and more. This is another reason why leaving an unhealthy faith community can be so hard; the system can make one feel weak, unbalanced, incomplete. The believer feels that he or she needs that system to function in their daily life. Understanding the inherent dependence in the unhealthy faith relationship is a valuable first step in beginning to repair the damage.

Enmeshed/Enmeshment

Enmeshment is a function of codependence. It refers to two things or people who are strongly bound together, like a wire fence. Each strand is tightly wound around the other, so that all parts of one overlap with the other. When someone is enmeshed, it is hard to identify personal feelings, thoughts, and aspirations, or to distinguish the "I" from the "we." Unhealthy religious and family systems rely on enmeshment to keep people bound tightly around the center. If I don't know where I end, how can I know what I want or need? If I don't know what is you and what is me, how will I ever know I can say "no" when something seems wrong? Like the overarching tent of codependence, it is important to acknowledge enmeshment in your life to begin untangling yourself from the wires with which you are bound. It is very hard to become unbound from enmeshed religious and family systems that are themselves inside enmeshed religious contexts.

(Family of) Addiction

You may remember Karl Marx saying that religion is the opium of the people. There is certainly an aspect of addiction to unhealthy religious systems. The most detrimental religious systems are often the most seductive in their fundamentalism. Fundamentalism gets a bad rap for good reason, but it makes life so simple. Everything is clear—black and white—and allows no room for difference of opinion. While for some of us that may seem horrifying, for people who have felt lost inside their own life choices or have grown up in a system of fundamentalism, it is independence that can seem terrifying. This is the bread and butter of fundamentalism—to prey on the fear of ambiguity and to promise a sense of peace and ease with their brand of certitude. This kind of simplicity can be addictive. I have seen the alluring way in which it feeds people's need to feel safe. For years I have counseled people in recovery from unhealthy religious systems and substance addiction. Both addictions are hard to kick, and relapse can happen.

Unhealthy Attachment

Attachment describes what the root word implies—how we attach to one another. In psychology, it specifically describes how we attach to other people after our initial experience of relationship with our parent(s), and then is translated or imprinted onto every subsequent relationship. The way in which we attach can be healthy or unhealthy and conditional on that primary relationship (our parent figures in our family and faith) which teaches us all we know of love and loving. In healthy attachment, we know we are loved, but we are not so dependent on what or whom we love that we feel that we can't function without it/them. In healthy attachment, we know how to love and be loved, but we can also be independent beings. In an unhealthy attachment situation, we are overly dependent on our love object (be it a person or a deity or a thing) and we feel we cannot function without being in their presence constantly or having their assistance to do even the basic functions of life. Unhealthy attachment is the sweet spot of a fundamentalist system; it feeds on that need and holds on too tight. Learning to find the balance of love, community, and faith is a learned experience. It can be very difficult to move from unhealthy to healthy attachment, for it entails restructuring the entire way a person functions in all manner of relationships. But, like anything else, it is possible. With work and time, all the dysfunctional learned patterns can be changed. Knowledge enables that process.

Where Religious Wounds Begin

If we go back to the early years of life, we can see the template for everything that follows. Specifically, as it relates to religious wounds, what we learn about life and love from family and faith informs how we see ourselves and the rest of the world.

The following are a few examples of how the God and parent figurehead showed up in the lives of people who experienced childhood (and often continuing into adulthood) religious trauma. These are based on interviews in which these people were asked a specific question about their childhood experience of God and religion or spiritual tradition. Each had articulated experiencing religious trauma and church-hurt and participated in a survey I sent out to collect data on this experience of family of origin and faith of origin wounding.

LIFE PARABLES: Childhood Images of God

DEB: As far as I can remember, God was to be feared, and he was constantly judging you. Jesus was my uncle who dressed up every Easter as Jesus and re-enacted the story of his crucifixion and resurrection. (He was one of the few light-skinned members of the church and had blue eyes. I wondered many times if that was the only reason they chose him.) I didn't have much of a concept of Jesus as our Savior, or of being a part of the Trinity. I just remembered he was the best character in the book. I don't believe we were taught about Heaven as much as we were about going to Hell if you are a sinner. I remember watching movies with beheadings as a young child, and I pretty much concluded that that was my future. I went to mostly Pentecostal and Baptist churches growing up, and we were taught that Catholics and Jehovah's witnesses were Satan worshipers. Oh…and that God favored men over women.

MELINDA: When I was a child, our family went to the local, somewhat large, Presbyterian Church. But my grandmother was charismatic and took me to various charismatic meetings when I was old enough. When I was very young, I believed that [unless I said] the sinner's prayer, asking Jesus into my heart, I would go to hell. I was terrified of the darkness and loneliness of hell. I very much wanted to please God and be found worthy. I was sure, as a small child, that I was a sinner in need of God's love. But frankly, this was highly influenced by my physically punishing dad and emotionally absent mom. As a child, when I pictured Jesus, He was in the clouds or surrounded by children. But looking back, the concept of him being an adult man whom I was supposed to love seems a little creepy.

KATE: I grew up in an Irish Catholic family. My mother is all Irish—the youngest daughter in a family with twenty-two children, all having the same father. Her mother married her father at age nineteen, after his first wife died and left him with six kids. My grandmother went on to have sixteen children of her own. My mom had eight kids, and I was the fourth born and the first daughter.

I say all this to give you some orientation about the circumstances of my early life, but we weren't a stereotypical big, happy family. We were poor, and my parents were overwhelmed and unable to properly care for us. My mother worked full time (in the [1950s], this made her unusual) because she had no choice, and she was an alcoholic for about half the time I was growing up.

We went to Mass every Sunday, made our First Communions at age six, went to confession every other Saturday, got confirmed at age twelve, and went to Catholic schools whenever they let us in for free. Despite all of this, I don't have a single memory of taking the idea of God seriously. It might have to do with being brought to a church where the officiants faced away from the congregation and spoke in Latin, or with the complete absence of girls and women at the altar, or with the rote nature of the Mass itself.

It might just be that I saw no evidence in the faces of the people around me that what was taking place was supposed to have meaning. Everyone seemed tired, bored, and waiting for it to be over, and that's what I was doing, too—for eighteen years.

HOPE: Childhood faith in God was pretty passionate and intense. I loved and wanted to please Him, but I also had a strange relationship with Him due to my home being deeply religious and grounded in faith yet abusive in many ways. As I grew older, my views about God became complex and confused, yet I always still desired and sought a relationship with Him. I longed passionately for His comfort, and once as a preteen, having cried out to Him one night, "God, I wish I could just feel you hug me!" I experienced very distinctly what felt to be a hug. That helped me to hang on. As I matured, I could look back and see that I developed kind of a push-pull relationship with God—desiring Him and His involvement in my life, yet I'm feeling walls and barriers due to the impact of the abuse. I don't remember clear images in my mind about God, Jesus, or Heaven beyond the pictures in storybooks.

DAVID: God looked exactly like my father. I still see an old man sitting on a throne in the clouds. I just don't fight it anymore. I associated God with father. My dad was a strong disciplinarian, and I saw God as strict. Jesus was more like a buddy, so that is how I maintained my spiritual life—through Jesus—but being obedient to God at the same time. It was as if I was afraid of "father" and didn't want to make him mad, so I was very obedient but inwardly screaming.

REFLECTION ON LIFE PARABLES

From these five stories, a few themes emerge in terms of the God-parent who shows up in many of the early religious experiences of those persons wounded by faith. First, God is a man, an angry man. He is an angry, misogynistic man who appears (specifically in Melinda's account) somewhat like a real-life abusive father figure. Second, this God talks an awful lot about sin and hell. He is selling fire and brimstone, and this is understandably terrifying to a child. It's a bit like a belief system built on Grimm's fairy tales, but much more frightening.

Now, not every interviewee gave such an account. There is not an angry God in other people's childhoods, as you will read later in this book. If we remember that what we learn in childhood is expressed throughout our lives; it is understandable that for people who shared their stories earlier, it is going to be harder to avoid being abused by people/entities who look like their original parent and God-figure.

The primary task of this chapter is to establish where religious trauma can, and often does, begin. It is also to offer insight about where the "angry God complex" begins in family and religious upbringing, and to review how damaging that can be in early childhood. In this chapter I ask you to look at faith and God through the lens of your own childhood to see what your faith of origin looked like. Maybe it was healthy and nurturing, maybe it was aggressive and abusive, and possibly it was somewhere between the two. It is important to see what your origin story looks like, and for you to understand through the lens of the origin stories of those who have been abused by religious communities and leaders.

Although this can be even more difficult, it can help us understand motivation to look at religious abusers through the lens of their family of origin and faith of origin belief structures. Outside of truly inborn sociopathy, at the heart of most evil action is someone who was told they weren't good enough. Not that we don't ask for justice for evil done, but knowing such background can help us to understand that perpetrators of evil have often been wounded or have been taught to hurt or hate as part of their faith and/or family of origin. It is rare to find an abuser in a religious context (again, outside of a sociopath—someone who is incapable of any human emotion) who wasn't in some way invalidated or abused by their earthly or divine parent. This is not to give permission let alone absolution for the kinds of heinous crimes perpetrated by those who abuse—as a survivor of trauma I know how hard that forgiveness is to give—but it may help to understand the "becoming" process of abuse and abusers as well as those who have been abused.

Take a moment to look at your own life and those in your midst. From where did you—and they—come? Take just long enough to see the trajectory of that life based on its beginning. Then move forward and change whatever is necessary to have the life of which we are capable, not just the one we have been given.

The Cosmic and Human Parentage: Double the Parentage and the Hurt

In a way that no other experience has before or since, war has taught me to stand up to most of the difficult questions of belief, life, and suffering. By contrast, contemporary branding of many religious and spiritual systems of belief cannot hold up to the scrutiny of suffering. And that's a problem. For many people I have treated over the years, the religion or spirituality they were offered was one in which good things happen to good people and bad things happen to bad people.

Small wonder that people become jaded with belief systems. If the hurt and traumatic experience is from a religious institution, its leaders, or its members who said, "Follow our rules, and you will be safe. Follow our rules, and you will be saved," then people find themselves doubly hurt when they find out that this is not true. The first betrayal is they were given a false worldview, and the very person(s) who violated that worldview were in the same system selling that story.

Does this mean there is no such thing as complex and dimensional spirituality? Of course not. Sadly, however, a robust and complex belief system is not the one most people are offered.

Childhood Belief Systems and Life Development

Developmentally, we are meant to begin life with a concrete understanding of the world. No wonder that many children's early imagery of God or spiritual understanding is facilitated by storytelling and is very concrete and related to the world in which they live. This is also why so many children's early visions of God or any expression of divinity is a cartoonish imagery of a trustworthy figure in the sky. Due to the ways in which Christianity has been shaped in the West to be very white, in the West the God is often imagined as a white-bearded white man floating in the clouds. This image which children are fed is visual, tangible, and easy for a developing child's brain to grasp. Here, God is a friendly grandfather or the Santa Claus they see at the mall. For some people this kind of God image was tainted by abuses in their family system—if Dad was domineering and abusive it was likely that a) he would be feeding a child the image of a similarly abusive God-figure, and that b) a child would latch onto the identifying qualities of their actual father and attribute the same to a divine father or grandfather image.

Especially as children, we can't identify our belief system based on an "it." Whether we are taught to love, hate, or fear the divine in the stories of our spiritual traditions, there is usually a "who" at the core of the tradition to whom our childhood brains connect. How the "who" is formed and what that being looks like may varies by tradition, but for children who cannot yet reason abstractly, the God-figure of childhood typically and necessarily has some human characteristics. Often the divine figurehead is male. For some, he may be a loving grandfather and for others, an abusive tyrant, but either way he takes shape as human in young minds.

In many ways, this is also the origin point of the problems later in life. As we grow into rational creatures with reason and as we experience pain and suffering, we see people living in ways that conflict with what the concrete God-image described to our younger selves. Most of us were taught a child's understanding of God and spirituality, and that is where the dogma stopped. Our spiritual education often stops at doctrine, rules, and mandates inside of religious traditions. Yet the broader world does not match up to the good/bad, black/white absolutes of spiritual kindergarten. The limited teaching of belief and spirituality many people experience, mixed with the human flaws of every person, in religious-spiritual communities or out can lead to some form of existential crisis. If that crisis is not from overt traumatic experience, then it is by the growing capacity of the rational brain in adolescence and early adulthood. We are set up to be jaded if our spiritual teachings and community do not evolve past spiritual kindergarten. If people also experience abuse as their brains develop into adulthood, then the religious system becomes a place of disappointing platitudes and of an infantile notion of the divine. There is no way for this kind of a construct to hold over time. It will fall apart or be burned down, depending on the level of hurt experienced within a person's religious/spiritual community or institution.

LIFE PARABLES: Being Hurt by Families and Faith of Origin

DAVID: For me I think the most disappointing [and wounding] thing…is [being disappointed or hurt by] my leaders or mentors. I have this fantasy of what family should be, but because none of our families live up to the fantasy, we are always disappointed. It is the same with the church; having a fantasy about what church should be, professes to be, promises to be, and experiencing the opposite—entrusting self to leaders or mentor and being hurt or betrayed by them, or experience them doing something shocking—that to me has been the most upsetting. [It is because of my fantasy for what church could be—rather than dealing with reality.]

DEANA: My discomfort first manifested as hunger. As a teenager I started questioning everything. Why am I here? What's the point? How am I supposed to contribute to this world? Does it even matter?

Why does it matter if I believe? If belief is all that matters, why can't I go live on a mountain and be a monk?

I needed a lot more than [being told] "Stay in church, read your Bible, do your devos," which is what I had heard from church my entire life. Even when my youth pastors branched out, it was always with some sneaky version of "No sex, drugs, or rock and roll." These messages all seemed fine and good, but they turned up empty when I was having the existential crisis that is teenagehood.

KISHA: ** *trigger warning: abuse content*** Fortunately, my theology began to evolve into something more positive during the teen years of my spiritual formation, after I experienced trauma at the hands of a couple of female mentors who sexually abused me. They were mentors whom I met at church and who were supposedly intended to be spiritual guides and/or extended family members to me. During that time, I reached out to God in the Charismatic way I had been taught, and eventually believed He met me and responded to me. However, that was not my "rebirthing" experience.

REFLECTION ON LIFE PARABLES

While church-hurt and spiritual abuse is not always about emotional, physical, and sexual trauma, or the negation of a person based on race, sexuality, and gender, there are far too many examples where this has been the case to ignore it as one of the primary sources of religious injury. To be hurt in one or many ways or negated on the basis of one's core identity, is a deep and profound wound; and it should be treated as such. If this is your story, it is valid and valuable. You should never be made to feel "less than" by someone else's mistakes. And you should especially never be hurt in those spaces where you let your guard down the most, where abuse is done by those who are supposed to "represent" divine love on earth. Of course, there is no perfect person—and those who try to be that for others often veer off course fast, some so far that they hurt others out of their own assumed greatness. If you have been hurt by those people, there is no truth, faith, or goodness in it. It is wrong by all standards. The same is true if anyone in a faith context has ever told you that who you are or what you are is wrong: there is no wrong way to be oneself and to live out self and love in the world. Women are equal and good. Likewise, LGBTQIA+ people are equal and good.

People of color are equal and good. If you have been told otherwise, let me assure you that you are beautiful exactly as you are. Believe that truth about yourself. You are inherently valuable, just the way you are. No exceptions. Part of healing is deeply believing this to be true about yourself. Sometimes the hurt perpetrated on us creates a story we believe about ourselves. Don't believe the myth someone else has created about who you are and what you are worth. You are inherently worthy.

A HEALING PRACTICE: Faith of Origin Storytelling

PART ONE: Tell your "faith-of-origin" origin story. Tell it however you need to, whenever you are comfortable to do so. Answer the questions asked of the interviewees in this chapter:

- *What was your childhood belief system?*
- *As a child, how did you learn to understand God or divinity within your spiritual or religious context?*
- *How did you grow up feeling about God, divinity/divine figures, figures of power and leadership of your tradition?*
- *How did you think God or the divine of your tradition felt about you or was in relationship with you?*
- *How did you picture God or the central figures or elements of your belief system?*

Follow up these questions with one more set of questions:

- *What was your family of origin like?*
- *Did your family/parent(s) resemble your God-figure or what you understood to be the divine or deities of your tradition? If so, how? If not, how?*

PART TWO: If your faith of origin story was unhealthy for you, tell the story you wish you had heard about God or the divine. Do the same for your family of origin experience (if unhealthy): how would you want to re-write the story of your family (e.g. as unconditionally loving and representing the ideal principles of healthy belief and support)? Begin the journey toward living the life you want by creating the origin story you would like to have been given at the outset.

PART THREE: Create a collage of images that symbolize positive family and belief/spirituality iconography and imagery. You can use any source materials—newspapers, magazines, book content—to make up your collage. Put the collage in a place you see daily. If space permits and it is comfortable for you, put it in a sacred space you create for yourself. Remember that what we imagine influences what is possible. While you can't go back to the hurtful experiences and change them, you can change your mind set in the present about how they affect you in the present. Take back your power—first in your imagination (which is where you can safely explore freedom) and then in your life.

Life Rescripting

We are given a script at birth from both our family and community. We acknowledge the impression this life experience has on us; but we also realize that once we see what it is and understand what it means, we can move beyond this storyline and craft the story of our future as we intend it. Sometimes we can also rescript what was into a larger narrative of our life as a whole. This is the part of the practices where you can be inventive.

PART ONE: First, you must remember your narrative as it is. For those of us who have lived entrenched narratives, the ones we were given, these are usually very easy to see and manifest. This is the script we play and replay year after year, over and over. This is the one on which we have to loosen the tether long enough to envision something new. But first we must see what already exists and completely own it.

PART TWO: Second, you have to envision beyond what is and what has been to what you want your story to be. Perhaps this will entail releasing the old narrative; perhaps, it will mean embracing but being able to move beyond the old narrative into something new. Either way, the key is imagination. Imagine what you want for yourself in your life, family, or spirituality, and what you want your story to look like—past, present, and future. Begin to tell that story. Write it down in full-color detail. Make sure to imbed all the senses—taste, smell, sight, touch, and hearing—in your story. Write your new script. Then read it out loud to yourself. Reread it as often as necessary. Work this narrative through until it is imbedded in your imagination. Then, read it again.

PART THREE: The goal of this process is to get to a place where you can accept your history—your faith of origin and family of origin—but in such a way that it is not all you are. The goal is to be able to see your past, present, and future as you want to define and imagine them. Repeat the process for as long as necessary until you see your story beyond the narrative you were given and into the narrative you want to manifest. This is the crux of the rescripting process. It doesn't negate what was or is; it just allows for what might be thanks to the freedom of imagination lived out in daily adult life.

CHAPTER 5

Wisdom Teachers versus False Gurus

Save one life, you save the world.
—Torah

The great danger of power-abusing leaders, especially when bound to spirituality, is that they take what we hunger for the most as humans—meaning, belonging, and understanding—and twist it to feed their ego, their need to be important. Like any abuser, such false gurus can see the vulnerabilities in people, hone in on those most in need of support and guidance, and use their vulnerabilities to their advantage.

With its large addiction recovery community, Southeast Florida has become fertile ground not only for AA and NA meetings, talk of Twelve Steps, and palm trees, but also for such power-abusing leaders—predators, abusers, and other power-hungry people who prey on the members of this vulnerable community.

People in early recovery, especially those willing to change their life and give up their will to a power greater than themselves, are especially ready for transformative spirituality and particularly vulnerable to what I call the "false guru." Guru in Sanskrit means an honored teacher, but I use it here in its distorted sense to mean a false teacher. It can be difficult to discern the differences between them when one is in a vulnerable place in life and wanting to belong. For at that point in recovery, one hasn't yet developed the "muscles" of instinct and intuition to recognize the false teachers, who are always more plentiful than the true wisdom teachers. True wisdom takes time and effort. In our fast-food faith nation eager spiritual seekers can be easily conned by the false teachers.

I commonly see two particular kinds of false teachers. The first is the unintentional false teacher—the person who genuinely believes the (hurtful or dysfunctional) dogma they are offering and really believes they are helping people by being an ambassador of their chosen doctrine. Such a person may have been taken in by the snake-oil sales of their own false guru; therefore, they continue to be ignorant about the falsities they are spreading.

The second is more insidious. At some level this teacher knows that what they are offering is more in pursuit of their own power than it is about genuine belief. They are enticed by the prospect of fame or power, and they align themselves with doctrine through which they can sell false wisdom to others at a great spiritual price.

This second kind of false guru is especially dangerous. Such a guru has a clear agenda that he presents to anyone who is vulnerable and seeking. I recall one such guru—ostensibly a yoga teacher. His persona filled the room, but not in a pleasant way. He was confident with a distinct pompousness that immediately made me feel ill at ease. During the class, I noticed him lock eyes with a bunch of the younger women, and at one point even with me. That class was filled with many young, vulnerable women in early recovery seeking spirituality on their mat. I was immediately suspicious of his actions. There was something inherently car salesman-like about him and the ways in which he moved and spoke. Instead of selling a lemon of a car, he was selling spiritual platitudes in a Sanskrit package. Though sounding superficially wise, those platitudes were bumper-sticker shallow. He gave me "the ick." Always trust your "ick," it's your instinct trying to protect you from harm.

When the class ended, I approached this teacher to ask a question; I had a Groupon I was using for the class, and I wanted to stay and see what his version of Yoga Nidra (guided yoga meditation practice) might look like. I had to wait a few minutes because, predictably but disconcertingly, several young women—some of whom I knew to be in recovery—were waiting to speak to him in the same eager fashion you might a rock star. However, a yoga teacher does not necessarily have more insight and wisdom than any other person. There are healthy leaders and wisdom teachers, and there are dysfunctional and abusive leaders and false gurus.

As our yoga teacher talked to these young women, he got uncomfortably close to them, his language full of platitudes and compliments, and his gaze ravishing their bodies. Once the small crowd dissipated, I asked, "Do I need to sign in again for the next session?"

He looked at me uncomfortably long, moved into my personal space and gazed in his unblinking fashion, and asked, "Did you notice that moment during class? We locked eyes and, in the breath, we had *that* moment. Did you feel it?"

Inner Ick! My question was matter of fact and simple. I gave no inclination with my body language or words that I was seeking anything else, but there he was running his game on me.

With my skin crawling, I replied, "So, do I need to sign in again?"

He touched my arm, leaned in, and said, "It was really a powerful moment. No, you don't have to sign in. Get comfortable for the meditation. It is a spiritually powerful experience. People who have done my Yoga Nidra have had some of their greatest dreams and visions come true."

To which my inner reply was a sardonic, "OK."

My outer response was to move my mat into the back, grit my teeth, and try to get through what had become an investigative meditation: I wanted to see how far his false guru nature went. He did not disappoint. His meditation was full of all kinds of spiritual clichés and softly spoken attempts at allure with just enough morsels of actual truth to hook the naive. He promised us great things from his meditation. His was a quintessentially magical genie approach of wish-fulfillment spirituality, completely superficial, and ultimately disappointing to the receiver. It was also full of clever caveats that remind the student that it is their fault if their dream doesn't come true or their transcendence doesn't materialize. It didn't come true because they didn't try hard enough, meditate enough, or want it deeply enough. His approach was to promise everything and have to deliver nothing, leaving all the fault on the recipient when it doesn't work out. He was a false guru to the core, a common predator.

Such false predators come in many guises but are alarmingly similar. They may reference different sacred texts, spout different platitudes and promises, but they all know how to find those who are the most vulnerable and abuse them for their own purposes.

Unmasking the False Guru

What are the quintessential characteristics and methodologies of the false guru?

1. **Certitude and Extreme Confidence**: They are so sure of themselves, their version of teachings, and their brand of wisdom that they never question themselves or engage in any process of self-reflection related to themselves or their beliefs. If there is any humility, it is often performative and dramatic. Within their spiritual context/community/institution there is no accountability for such persons.

2. **Charisma and Charm Overdose**: They are often well-dressed and alluring, not necessarily in a sensual way, but perhaps in a way that feels imbued with intellect or wisdom. Their smile, stare, and smoothness of speech draws you in, making you feel that they are speaking to you and for you.

3. **Promises and Wish Fulfillment**: They insist that their brand of spirituality, religion, or dogma is going to get you everything you want: no more pain, loss, or (literal or emotional) poverty. All your dreams will come true, or if they don't—it is you who is doing something wrong, not them. They have the answers to every question you want answered and they answer it easily and simply.

4. **The Golden Ticket Rule:** Like Willy Wonka, such fake gurus say they have the golden ticket to your happiness, afterlife, and spiritual journey. Typically, not everyone has access to those goods, but if you stick with the guru, he will help you attain them. If you don't, then there is little chance you can access the source of all truth or transcendence.

5. **The Price Tag:** There is often a hefty price tag for their brand of enlightenment, teachings, and wisdom, or an exclusive members-only afterlife. Warning: If it costs a lot to get to Nirvana, then it probably isn't Nirvana.

6. **The Pyramid Scheme and Isolation:** They want you to invite your friends and family to join this community—and it is your obligation to bring as many new people in as possible. At the same time, you mustn't spend much time with those outside the community, apart from recruitment efforts. Your life must revolve around this community, its teachings, its members, and most importantly, its leader. You are taught that if you really love the people in your life, you will bring them in to this exclusive circle of wisdom, and that if they don't follow, then

they aren't the right friends or community for you. It's a form of imposed isolation.

7. **This Way Is the Only Way:** Building on the isolation tactics, the guru teaches that this way, this teacher, this teaching is the only way to get all that you want. Every other way to spiritual wholeness or belief is not as good or even potentially wrong. There is no ambiguity in such communities: we are right and we are best, so why go anywhere else? And if you try, terrible things will happen. That is both a premonition and a threat.

8. **No Room for Open-Ended Questions or Interpretations:** If your question directed to the leader is about what you should do, think, or believe, then that is OK. If you question or disagree with what is said, then you will be made to feel less than or like you don't "get it." With false gurus, there is no room for ambiguity. The false guru wants power and control over you. They respond to questioning with shame or punishment of some kind.

9. **Narcissism or Sociopathic Tendencies:** This kind of a personality has at least some traits of narcissism. Such a person's confidence comes from a delusional place of having bought into their own greatness. This is how they sell it so well: they truly believe their own hype. In more extreme scenarios, they may also have some or all traits of sociopathy—which is beyond pathological selfishness and lack of self-reflection, and is a complete inability to feel feelings themselves or feel any kind of empathy for anyone else. Since sociopathy is an incapacity for human emotion, it means they don't feel the hurts they impose on others and don't fear any consequences. This makes the manipulation they use easy for them to do, as they have no capacity for remorse and aren't worried about repercussions. Not all false guru leaders are sociopaths, but the intentional type of false guru will fall somewhere on the spectrum between narcissism and sociopathy.

10. **They Are Above the World and Its Rules:** Part of the reason that many of these leaders are the ones who end up in the headlines is because their ego is so big and their understanding of reality outside of themselves is so distorted that they believe what they are selling to the point that they think they

are above reproach. It is not simply that they are not worried about the consequences; at a certain point they believe that worldly consequences cannot touch them. Because they often have at least some traits of narcissism (and the most extreme would probably fit on the spectrum for sociopathy), they push the limits of rules, boundaries, and laws, and most act in illegal ways, often repeatedly, believing they are exempt from punishment by the law (Think Trump saying he could shoot someone on 5th Avenue and still not lose any voters). Their infractions can include: stealing or appropriating community funds for their own personal benefit, sexual misconduct or even abuse, being verbally and emotionally abusive of members or leaders below them in their hierarchy, and protecting those behaviors in others who have some level of power over others in the community.

11. This list is not exhaustive, and a false guru might not exhibit all these traits But, it is important to know the signs to discern the differences between healthy spirituality and leadership and that which is destructive and abusive.

If you are a spiritual seeker on a path of self-discovery, you deserve to have teachers who are wise and humble along your journey. You deserve to be nurtured—and false gurus with the aforementioned personality traits don't know how to do that or don't want to expend the energy to do so. In truth, their intention is to improve their own value and esteem, not to help you grow.

Identifying the Wisdom Teacher

With the contrary in mind, what does a true wisdom teacher look like, philosophically and spiritually? If you are looking for such a teacher or teachers, have been hurt before but want to explore the spiritual or philosophical complexities of life, and want to find spirituality that can grow and deepen your journey, then this listing of traits embodied in healthy teachers is a starting point for your journey.

1. **They Prize Humility over Ego:** Wisdom teachers promote humility in others and, most importantly, in themselves. They are part of communities and relationships of accountability for themselves (with other teachers, peers, elders) and offer their teachings as learned lessons along the way rather than as abso-

lutes. Their teachings are not based on being better than others or having attained some kind of peak level of wisdom but rather on being on their own continued journey. In the communities in which they exist, they make sure there are checks and balances to their own ego, understanding that everyone can be vulnerable to excess and poor behavior.

2. **They Prioritize Community over Themselves:** While they may be wisdom teachers with experience and knowledge, they do not think of themselves as most important or most wise. They want to bring the strengths, values, creativity, and wisdom of the community together for a more diverse and stronger whole, rather than create a leader-centric, top-down system of power with themselves at the top or in the center. They are attentive to creating balance and avoiding power and control roles or characteristics. They don't try to hold on to all the power over decision-making for the community or their students; instead, they welcome a variety of perspectives and decision makers who help them craft important decisions for the community.

3. **They Embrace the Tension:** They offer their teachings and life lessons to others but also accept when outside realities or ideas contrast with what they have learned. They can hold the tension between what they know and don't know, between their truth and the truth as seen through others' eyes, and between being wise and needing to learn and grow themselves. They can listen when others give feedback about their own limitations based on their own life experience or social location that might make them unable to see other perspectives fully based on power, privilege or expression of identities they may hold that are different from others (race/ethnicity, gender, sexuality, ability, socioeconomic standing and more). They are open to critique and able to learn and grow from the mistakes they make. The acknowledge that their teaching must evolve based on new information and perspectives.

4. **They Are Comfortable with the Unknown:** They know enough to realize that the universe, cosmos, divinity, and the ineffable can only be partially understood. They understand that even a lifetime of education can only scratch the surface of

understanding that which is greater than ourselves. They realize that they are limited humans with limited understanding, and they live into the understanding that they can't and won't know everything.

5. **They Are Lifelong Students:** They are willing and open to sharing that much of spirituality and understanding is unknown and unknowable, and that they, as teachers, still have much to learn themselves. They constantly engage with the unknown through their own sacred practices and by learning from other wisdom teachers (older or younger than them). They understand that learning, growth, and transformation is a lifelong process, and they are willing to engage with that process for the duration of their own lives.

6. **They Promote Questions and Don't Have All the Answers:** They don't pretend to have all the answers and are willing to ask others for their wisdom. They believe that human curiosity is a gift, and they nurture that curiosity and the art of asking questions in others. They want people to question and explore their spirituality more deeply.

7. **They Offer No-Cost, Low-Cost, and Sliding-Scale Teachings:** Although some elements of their teachings and programming might have a cost, it is not inflated beyond what the teacher needs to make their own living. Furthermore, their cost structure includes a sliding-scale of fees along with scholarships for those who can't afford to pay. Their intention in doing the work they do is not primarily to become rich, and they don't sell wisdom at the highest cost possible.

8. **They Accept That There Are Many Ways to Transformation and Spirituality:** Wisdom teachers don't believe their way, tradition, or understanding of the universe is the only one; they are open to many paths to the same source. They don't see the world as an either-or proposition, but rather as a series of trails, which lead to the same loving source, however it might be defined.

9. **They Value the Beautiful Diversity of Humanity:** They believe that everyone and everything belongs and that we should all have the opportunity to find happiness, love, and understanding. This means that spirituality or religion is more

than an independent personal journey or a journey for one community alone. Rather, it is a journey on which we all walk together, have to care for one another, and open our homes, hearts, and communities to one another. This includes not excluding people from their work or world or valuing them less because of their race/ethnicity, gender, sexuality, socioeconomic status, or global location.

10. **They Model Unconditional Love:** They believe everyone deserves love, and that love is not conditional on any of the above factors being a certain way. Love is love, and everyone gets the same portion—with no strings attached. There are no conditions in their teachings or practices.

11. **They Acknowledge Their Own Flawed Humanity:** They admit they make mistakes, and when they do, they try to be transparent about them, seek help for themselves, and use them to emphasize their shared humanity and to help others learn and grow.

12. **They Value Uniqueness along with Healthy Interdependence:** They believe in the inherent value of community for opportunities to show unconditional love, work through relationship for authentic companionship, and provide accountability for themselves and others. They also value each person and their unique set of talents, history of hurt, and all that makes them who they are; and, they honor that person and all their parts in community.

13. **They are Authentic:** They are who they are, without a hidden agenda. They work toward deeper authenticity and encourage others to do the same. They believe we are all flawed and beautiful, and that living in the truth of who we are as openly as possible is part of our shared spiritual work.

They Cite their Sources: They don't distribute knowledge and wisdom as if it is entirely their own invention. All wisdom has roots and sources in the lives, or traditions, of our ancestors. They are clear about the source of their teachings, their teachers, and they cite the sources of the information they share.

These criteria are not comprehensive, but I hope you will find them a useful guide along your path. Consider your own wisdom teachers. Listen to your own intuition and gut reactions to them.

Don't be afraid to ask questions and get more information. A wisdom teacher won't mind you doing this deeper work to find out if they are the right fit for you, but the false guru will quickly show discomfort.

CHAPTER 6

Peeling the Onion: Religious Injury Subtypes

Humility…is nothing else but a true knowledge and experience of yourself as you are.

—Anonymous, *The Cloud of Unknowing*

The topic of religious wounds continues to evolve. When *Sacred Wounds* was first published in 2015, a growing number of social media support groups and personal stories were being shared in the wider public square and the news media, along with a handful of books and conversations in spiritual and religious contexts. Even ten years after the first edition of this book, the concept is still fairly new in the sphere of trauma studies and has been only minimally assessed, treated, and tested—let alone proven—within the wider field of traumatology.

In the next section, I divide religious trauma into different types of abuse and traumatic experience. This categorization is a means by which to speak into the pain with a few broadly understood concepts. My hope is that through these means those who have been hurt can feel heard and validated, those who hope to support them personally or as a clinical provider can understand the trauma better, and—perhaps the loftiest aspiration—those persons still in spiritual communities can understand why many others have left these contexts and so that the former can find ways to nurture rather than re-traumatize survivors of religious and spiritual trauma.

To change something—in this case, religious trauma—we must first understand what it is and where it lies in our society and ourselves. With that in mind, I explore a few additional terms, including internalized oppression and attachment issues as they relate to religious abuses, and a handful of other relevant topics. I also present several situations and people groups where historic and pervasive abuse and neglect have occurred in religious contexts. In all this, my goal is to bring religious wounds and spiritual trauma out of the darkness of shameful silence and into the light so that we can all see how to validate this trauma—spiritually and psychologically—and how to find a way to move beyond hurt and pain, as individual persons and as communities

Sexual and Physical Abuse

Sexual and physical abuse, primarily by religious leaders, are the most well-known forms of trauma in a religious context. But before we jump to the conclusion, as many have done regarding the Roman Catholic Church, that priests are somehow more dominant sexual predators than any other people group, or that all priests have an inherent dysfunctional and abusive behavior—let me say a word about such conclusions. For people jump to similar conclusions regarding survivors of military sexual trauma—first, that all the victims are female, and second, that the kind of people and training that occurs in a military context creates sexual predators. Neither is inherently true, and the same should be understood for predators in religious contexts or by clergypersons. For healing to be possible, we have a responsibility to see and speak clearly without making assumptions.

Power-seeking predators, sexual or otherwise, look for places where their predatory nature will be most easily disguised and least likely discovered. Predators prefer hierarchical systems, where there are roles of power or authority, for abuse is essentially always abuse of power. But this is quite different than saying that all people who end up in positions of power and authority will be predators. Predators know that they and their behaviors thrive in systems that are structured to protect power and give victims little room for recourse. This is why we see abuses such as these in places like religion and the military; their structure protest persons with more power. This is the dynamic of which we need to be aware, the one which deserves critique, not necessarily the roles of authority in and of themselves. The important thing is to create more transparency in those structures for the safety of all involved.

If we were to compare religious and military systems, we would find many parallels between them as systems of power and authority. In response to recent scandals and focus on sexual assault, the military is doing a better job at transparency and at creating an external system of checks and balances. Though far from perfect, the military may be a few steps ahead of religious institutions and systems in creating methods to correct this systemic protection of predators rather than victims.

People in positions of power are not inherently abusers or sexual predators. If we remember that, then we can explore the systems that protect predators in systems, and specifically in religious systems.

Sexual and physical abuse in a religious context can be particularly damaging because it is a context in which one expects care. Yet religious contexts typically have a systemic hierarchy and combined with the authority of God as the "boss" of those people in power, the control that a predator in religion has over those they victimize is immense—even more than in most systems. The correlating shame and silencing imposed on the victim is multiplied because there a system of power (purportedly) led by God facilitates this abuse. The perpetrators in religious systems are clever enough to make sure that those they are abusing have low self-esteem and believe they have no recourse to speak up. Sometimes the abuser is the "leader" of a household, sometimes a "leader" in the church structure, and often both. Such abuse is a cruel brutalization at all levels and affects everything from a person's sense of worthiness to their lovability, "sinfulness" or (lack of) goodness. Such effect can make it feel as if there is no way out. To exit such an experience in a religious system takes a lot of courage—and makes it understandable why so many people remain stuck in those abusive situations. Hopefully, the more voices that are heard from those speaking out about this issue, the easier it will become for people to exit these abusive systems.

If you have been abused physically and sexually in a religious community, it is not your fault. You didn't ask for or deserve such abuse or any other negative statement or belief your abuser wants you to believe. There are places to which you can escape and sources of help—domestic violence shelters, child protective agencies, therapists and crisis providers outside the community system. You do not deserve any abuse you ever received. Before all else, that is what you should know, whether you are inside or outside of an abuse situation. You did not deserve such treatment. You are inherently good. You can heal from this pain—although in the worst moments such news is hard to believe.

LIFE PARABLES

DEB: I will start with one [instance of abuse] that has plagued me my whole life. My brother's godfather was a deacon in our church. His wife was also our caretaker after school and on the weekends, because my mother had to work extra hours to make up for my father's irresponsible spending. While I was at their house, I was sexually abused by this man and his son on separate occasions. I don't know if the one knew the other was doing it, and his son was probably about twelve when it started. My first memory of it was when I was three years old. I know I was three because my brother was still in a carrier, and I was three when he was born. The abuse may or may not have occurred in the church. My memory is fuzzy on that, and I am undergoing Eye Movement Desensitization and Reprocessing (EMDR) therapy to remedy that. The abuse continued until 1994, when we moved to Florida. I told my mother a few months later, and she informed the Assemblies of God, who did *nothing* but remove him as a deacon. At age seventeen, I confronted him in the church when I was sent back to Connecticut on vacation/punishment to be with my grandmother for the summer. The meeting was between the two abusers, the pastor of the church at the time (who happened to be my mother's ex-boyfriend), my grandmother, and my uncle. The abusers vehemently denied any wrongdoing, and I spent the time being so angry at them while others watched and did nothing.

Other experiences included seeing my mother being stripped of her singing privileges [at church] after an affair she had with another man. This happened even though I knew that my father had many girlfriends, yet he was still [allowed] to play in the band. My mother's beautiful voice was taken away from the congregation.

My father was also very physically abusive, and after EMDR therapy I have finally determined that he was also sexually abusive. I remember going to my aunt with this accusation. She is a minister and always told me I was probably mistaking my father for the other abusers, and that it was just a dream. I just found out several months ago that it was not, in fact, a dream.

KISHA: I experienced trauma at the hands of a couple of my female mentors who sexually abused me. They were mentors whom I met at church who were supposedly intended to be some sort of spiritual guides and extended family members to me. During that time up until approximately a year-and-a-half ago, I carried around deep shame, confusion, insecurity, and inappropriate guilt regarding my sexuality. For many years, I wasn't exactly sure who I was, what I wanted sexually, nor what was OK for me to want. I was confused about the identity of Jesus, because my faith tradition is a "Oneness" tradition that always combined the identities of both God and Jesus as one [and] the same. Therefore, I thought they both hated me in unison. My view of Heaven was merely that it was a place that I would probably never see. I believed that if I were to see it, I would first have to stand in line naked waiting to be judged on Judgment Day. I worried that everybody in line would see my naked body, and that even in Heaven I would have to go around naked with no clothes, no privacy, and no boundaries. I was deeply ashamed of my body.

Secondary Traumatic Stress (from Religious Abuse)

Earlier, I defined secondary stress as stress that comes from someone in relationship with persons who have been abused or those who hear the accounts of abuse. This is an exhausting role and one not often seen or recognized as such. Recently, with the burgeoning use of virtual networks and social media, I am seeing this happen virtually as well. People or community groups built to support survivors of religious injury or abuse are becoming overwhelmed with the sheer number of stories coming into these virtual spaces from facilitators of these intended safe web spaces and other community members. People are getting exhausted—traumatically stressed—by hearing others' hurt.

This doesn't mean we shouldn't confide in loved ones, care providers, or virtual communities. It does mean that if you are someone absorbing the experiences of others' trauma, you have to be aware that this can affect your own well-being. A brief example comes from my early experience as a therapist intern with combat veterans. I had my own history of trauma and my own PTSD healing when I landed my first graduate internship.

I thought that although the experiences of my clients were traumatic, they were so far away from anything to which I could relate that the likelihood of it impacting me was slim. Slowly, in a way I didn't even see at first, by hearing trauma accounts all day I began absorbing the content and emotional dimensions of their stories, and they became a part of me. I began experiencing symptoms that had nothing to do with my own traumatic experience but were related to my clients' trauma. I would swerve when I saw garbage on the side of the road—a typical combat trauma response of Iraq veterans due to the number of improvised explosive devices (IEDs) in the combat zone. I would wake up from night terrors full of bullets flying and explosions—where I would be injured in the middle of a combat zone. I began appropriating an exaggerated startle response, especially when people came up behind me—something I had all but rid myself of in my own trauma recovery. It was a few weeks into this before I saw the connection; I was manifesting the symptoms of PTSD for the combat veterans who were my therapy clients. This is a form of traumatization, and at some point, it can be helpful to get your own support system, support group, or therapy provider to help you address your own secondary traumatic experience.

Since then, I have learned to curate boundaries that diminish the likelihood of that happening—but sometimes a particular story or experience will linger with me. So, if you are a loved one, community member, or helping professional who is seeking to support those who have experienced trauma in a religious context, know that self-care and boundaries are as important for you as for the survivor. The way you help people best is by taking care of yourself enough to have the stamina for the long haul.

This kind of traumatic experience can often lead to the issues mentioned above: appropriating the symptoms of another person, as well as issues of anxiety, anger, or a general sense of being emotionally overwhelmed. Depending on how overwhelming they are such issues can commonly be moderated by emotional numbing to desensitize the self from the pain of others.

Gender Identity Negation

The use of religious texts to validate one set of people and negate another is something religious traditions in their worst forms have been doing forever. Being a woman in a great many versions of religious traditions can be a negative personal trait. It can limit what you can do in a religious community and culture, for example, whether you are allowed to talk and what you are allowed to say or are considered capable of saying. Your station can be low and limited in a way that much of contemporary society might consider to be like the gender dynamics of the 1800s. This is seen again as a theme in issues of historic abuse and colonization, sexual identity negation, and more.

If we go back to the inherent dynamics of power and privilege in hierarchies, we can see abuses of some by others pursuing power. Selecting a "lesser" gender, or at the very least a passive and silent gender, is one way to rule out any fight for power from about half of any community group.

Even though it may not feel healthy or right, even when women leave communities that devalue them just for being a woman, it is hard to overcome the inherent feeling of "not being enough." That also makes it difficult for women to claim all manner of aspects of their lives and selfhood—including their bodies, sexuality, strengths, and abilities. It is a sort of brainwashing and programming which happens throughout the childhood growth and development cycles into adulthood, and which becomes very ingrained. Even when a woman can leave that belief system and begin to gain some sense of autonomy, it takes time and work to deprogram her own inward sense of being less than a man.

This version of traumatic experience can lead to issues of anxiety, shame, guilt, anger (often through self-inflicted harm through cutting or eating disorders), and grief and loss. This is not all, but these are some common manifestations. The anger is usually directed inward at first due to the learned faith community behavior of not expressing opinions, feelings, and selfhood externally.

LIFE PARABLE

KISHA: In addition to carrying deep trauma and shame surrounding my sexuality, I also carried shame regarding my gender. I come from a musical family. I also come from a very Levitical family. In spite of my gifts for singing, playing instruments, and preaching, I was never encouraged, trained, or allowed to use any of them in the church because those opportunities were only given to boys. There existed a glass ceiling for girls and women within the church that was rarely ever spoken about, but always implied and definitely understood. For the few women who were somehow granted opportunities for leadership within the church, there was so much competition that many of them ended up leaving the church and starting their own ministries elsewhere. Meanwhile I was left stuck with no motivation to practice, sharpen, or appreciate my ministry gifts. I saw no point. They would never be [valued] anyway.

Sexual Identity Negation

Sexual identity negation is another powerfully painful way that unhealthy or abusive religious communities and religious doctrine can negate and devalue a person based on who they are as a human being. Due to the extreme doctrinal statements about being LGBTQ (lesbian, gay, bisexual, transgendered, queer) of many extreme forms of many religions, it can also be physically dangerous to be openly LGBTQ in certain communities. There are many people in these traditions who live closeted and in fear as a means of self-preservation. The alternative could mean losing family, friends, and entire community group indefinitely. Since that is a lot to give up, many people function in these communities for as much or as long as they can. There is no wrong choice in these situations; each one is difficult. If people stay closeted in a community, they lose access to an intrinsic part of who they are; if they leave, they may lose everyone they have ever known and loved.

The difficulty unique to LGBTQ people in abusive faith cultures, different from gender issues, is that who the person is while in that community is a secret. A woman is a woman, and that is a visible fact; even when it is diminished or abused by the community, her gender is open. For someone who is LGBTQ, the love of their family and community can feel especially fragile and conditional. They know that if they come out, that love can be rescinded, and their nature touted as wrong or sinful. If you are not LGBTQ, imagine for a moment that who you are is itself considered a sin—as you are when you were born, and as you are when you die. Imagine for a moment that your very life, your very existence is considered sinful. That is an excruciating thing to bear.

It is no wonder that if they leave their faith traditions LGBTQ persons can find it difficult to return to another faith community, ever, fearing the possible lack of acceptance they experienced in their faith of origin. Some of the common issues from religious trauma experienced by LGBTQ persons are an entrenched sense of shame or guilt developed by a negating religious community, anxiety, isolation, and trust/intimacy issues due to fear of rejection.

LIFE PARABLE

MARG: At sixteen years old, I had come to realize I was a lesbian. My best friend from church and I had fallen in love with each other. Our love felt so pure, so tender, and so holy that I knew being gay was not a bad thing. But it was 1979, and you couldn't be both gay and Christian. Yet, there we were. One day, when I was eighteen, I told the youth minister at church that I was gay. I don't know why I thought nothing would change. Maybe because it was I, and it was my church, I had grown up there, and I [had felt] safe there. But I was wrong. I misread him, and I misunderstood the times. The first thing he said was, "Well, you won't be able to work with the children anymore." I had been working with the younger kids for ten years, more than half my life, likely longer than he had. At first, I was stunned. But then an awful realization came over me. Uttering the two words, "I'm gay," had twisted my reality on its axis. The minister would never trust me again. I had changed. In five seconds, I had become a sexual offender, a sinner going to hell. Church was no longer safe for someone like me.

Soon after that day, I left. I left the building, the people, the music, and the memories. I left what I had thought would be the setting for the rest of my life. I left.

LIFE PARABLE

TIM: So, I developed my faith and sexuality along the lines of what I'd been told since there weren't any alternatives presented. For some reason, it was quite easy to "control myself" around girls, but I ended up getting crushes and dated a few times. I was genuinely attracted to a number of my female friends. But the sex drive I'd been warned about seemed easy, or at least possible, to control around women. (In hindsight, this was probably a result of training, morals, and inexperience. And perhaps having other options! One good thing, it kept me out of trouble!)

But I also experienced crushes and "uncontrollable" feelings for the occasional guy. I then ended up in situations in which I was curious, and things went further than I expected. Ironically, the church training about "keeping safe" around women left me woefully unprepared for navigating these experiences. So, there was no one I could talk to, and I felt terribly guilty. I had no role models for healthy homosexual relationships, and people I trusted handled [the news] very badly. So, I felt increasingly guilty, and because of that guilt, kept Jesus a long way away from that part of my life. Then I discovered internet pornography, and it was obvious that I was interested in homosexual pornography. I felt excruciatingly guilty; but, in hindsight, it was mainly driven by curiosity about a world I had never experienced that I didn't even have words for yet was somehow a part of me. It was an outlet for feelings I couldn't talk about, or even name. So, in my public persona, I was straight by default. There just weren't any other viable options socially, intellectually, or biblically. But in private, I was trying to work out how to navigate a world where I had homosexual desires, and I was trying to hide that fact from myself and suppress those desires. I used to feel Jesus could never love me while I continued to make serious errors, whether I wanted to do these things, or whether I avoided them. (Yes, I had an internal hierarchy of sins.) In particular, I felt that Jesus could never love me while I was attracted to men (among many things not ideal, perfect, and complete in my life.) This led me to feel fear, guilt, and rejection at my core. I could certainly never accept myself in this situation, and I could never entirely be at peace, whatever I told myself about God's love. The condemnation of particular aspects of my life was much clearer than Jesus' love for everyone, whatever their circumstances. While there was obvious pressure to change and conform, I did not feel accepted by Jesus, let alone the church. I had also tried very hard to change my sexual orientation over that decade. I'd had several attempts at counseling, online courses, prayer, behavioral modification, confession, spiritual warfare, and almost anything else I could think of. But nothing worked, at least not for more than a year, or so, at a time. It just made it that much harder to process my sexual orientation, as I am not just bisexual, but fluid in my degree of attraction to masculinity and femininity. It was that fluidity that confused the issue, because I would seem to go straight for a while, but it would never last. And I hated tying the success of my faith to my feelings for men. I didn't even have a functional concept of bisexuality until the last few years. Before that, it just wasn't something I could imagine myself being; I had always thought of myself as a straight guy with a "gay problem." These weren't the only issues I thought of during this time (I had a lot of thinking time). I struggled with how the church functioned for the physically disabled; the not stereotypically masculine "men"; the non-neurotypical (whether autistic or more broadly mentally differing);

and, as I have already mentioned, the "not straight." I struggled with my own experiences of each of these, and I felt trapped to hear that I had been part of what were considered to be negative characteristics. I became quite critical, bitter, angry, frustrated, and demanding.

Intergenerational and Historic Trauma

Intergenerational trauma is the traumatic experience that spans more than one generation or one lifetime and whose impact compounds and increases over the generations. It is handed down in memories, in behaviors of elder generations, and possibly even (as we are learning more recently) in genetic attachments to our DNA. Intergenerational trauma has, for example, been clearly documented in families descended from Holocaust survivors, combat veterans, and in the cultural context, in descendants of marginalized or colonized community groups across the BIPOC diasporas.

The ways in which such intergenerational and historic manifest is multifaceted. When we are discussing issues of colonized or marginalized persons, this can express itself in a variety of social and dynamics, as well as with issues of internalized oppression. Internalized oppression happens when people appropriate a sense of internal self from outward cultural and social negatives about themselves and their people group. In many ways all the symptoms of trauma are internalized abuse, in the sense that the abusing system or person(s) provides a framework to devalue and abuse people in a religious context, and the symptoms are often an inward expression of that outward belief imposed on that person by the abusers. Religious trauma is a form of internalized oppression, oppressing people and their human traits, beliefs, and so forth, to increase the power and value of people at the top of a hierarchical system.

Intergenerational trauma often expresses itself as repeating cycles of abuse and being abused, addiction and low self-worth, and potentially rage, anxiety, and guilt. It is especially profound for those who have felt mutually marginalized by society and by religious/spiritual communities, as we shall see.

...And Racial and Cultural Identity Trauma

Racial and cultural identity trauma relates to intergenerational trauma when it is experienced among marginalized communities in the sense that it is the experience of being lesser than the dominant culture of the church system. This can be felt obviously or subtly. As Bill articulates in his story, the experience of having to show up to a church gathering where dressy attire is expected can be a way to demean those without the economic means to dress that way. Insensitive discussions or actions around issues of race or cultural differences can be especially piercing. Even though intellectually we can say that church is made up of people and therefore will inherently include human mistakes and prejudices, we want to expect more of places that articulate a standard of caring for one another, so it is especially painful when those communities let us down.

This kind of trauma can lead to issues of shame and guilt, low self-esteem, anger, rage, and isolation. It can be hard for people who have been marginalized, such as in their church communities, to trust other community groups and personal relationships. It is important to validate this as real traumatic experience and to hold communities accountable for rectifying their behavior and for improving how they raising their own standards for how to care for others.

LIFE PARABLE

EMMA: The intergenerational trauma for me with the church was related to the overall culture of the community's racism. When I was growing up, we kind of accepted the racism in my church and community. It was kind of weird. There was a lot of racism, but I didn't understand just how much until I moved away from home and looked at other communities. In my small town, it was blatant, in your face. You would feel you needed to dress up just to go shopping; whereas, if you were non-Native or not a person of color, you wouldn't feel that need. I knew the feeling of someone following you around in a store. Moving away from my Native Church into a non-Native church definitely tied into my beliefs of Christianity too. We didn't have the church we were comfortable going to, and it was difficult after our warrior mascot protests with the non-Native church in our town. After we had stood up in front of our school and town in protest of a Native American symbol as a mascot it went from just being a minority person to being someone who was unwanted by our community—including and especially our church. You could tell we were not welcome anymore. We got a scholarship from church when we were leaving high school and it felt like they were saying,

"We are doing the right thing, but we don't want to." They gave us the scholarship because we were confirmed, and the non-Native girl who applied for it was not. They made sure to let us know that was the only reason why we got it.

This church alienation was surrounded by all of the cultural, racial, and intergenerational trauma issues. Back in my community in South Dakota there are no resources, and they are just starting to get more with passing the Violence Against Women Act (VAWA). Before that, there wasn't anything—you didn't feel safe. Being a teenager growing up in a racist community where you know nothing will be done for any wrongdoing against you is very sad. With the trauma I have been through, our decision to protest the warrior mascot and the coronation ceremony for four years, doing what we thought was right, was a lot to take on. That same year we started protesting, I was sexually assaulted, and that erased entirely the ability to feel safe in my own town. During the protests, we had a lot of the people who came to help us—people connected to the Lakota Student Alliance and others connected with the American Indian Movement (AIM). They knew how dangerous the community was, but we didn't. A lot of them had been through the Wounded Knee Occupation as children, but we hadn't. We were just trying to do the right thing. They came in to warn us and say you need to smudge with sage (a Native protection practice) before you leave the house and when you come back. They were right because friends were warning us to not go to this party or to that school event because the community was planning to do something to us. One time they told us not to go to a bonfire—as cheerleaders we were supposed to be there—because the community members/students were going to stone us. My hope is that there are always people helping, so people can work on themselves enough to realize there are so many other people who are hurting too. I have seen that a lot in community. We are seeing there are so many people who need healing and don't even realize it. Now that I understand more about my traumas, as well as intergenerational trauma and how trauma can get passed in the DNA, I understand myself much better. No wonder [that] my feelings are so overwhelming to me; they are related to my ancestors too. A lot of times now when things get overwhelming, I can see where it is coming from.

Family (of Religious) Systems Trauma

In therapy, we call the work with and issues of families "family systems" work. In families of unhealthy or abusive religion, as described in the family and trauma chapter, the unhealthy family system bleeds together with the unhealthy religious system to compound the impact on a person. As previously described, if the household "father" and the church "father" come together to injure, marginalize, or diminish a person, and state that this injury is actually a mandate from the holy "father," this is a very difficult system to untangle. It is triple the trauma and triple the hurt. It is hard enough to work through family traumatic experience with someone because it means dismantling everything they learned from their first breaths about love, themselves, and what it means to be safe (or unloved, invalid, and unsafe). When one is dealing with family trauma inside a faith system of trauma and one adds in the dysfunctional image of God created by both systems, it takes a lot of time and work to undo. It is not impossible, but the complexity of it means it takes time.

LIFE PARABLE

ANONYMOUS: The saddest part of my experience is that I didn't realize [until I was in my forties that] my spiritual experiences had created wounds. I was born into an evangelical, charismatic family whose religious affiliation was a group that was cult-like in [its] approach. In other words, the group believed in God, the Divinity, atonement of Jesus, the Resurrection, and ministry of the Holy Spirit… so far, so good (kind of). But then there were layers and sublayers. For example, "established churches," as they called those groups who meet regularly in designated church buildings, were deceived and not "true Christians." Anyone who didn't worship with us, in the format we considered right, was deceived and not really Christian at all. As in most evangelical groups, the concept of the doctrine of original sin was one of the foundational tenets. Everything was based on how bad humans are, and how important it is to subdue their pervasive sin nature and achieve holiness. Holiness was manifested in behavior—right clothing (restrictions were heaviest on females), right appearances (attendance at thrice-weekly, multiple-hour services), right economics (owning very little outright, sharing of all resources communally, not possessing anything "too nice"), right observations (no "pagan" holidays, which basically meant no observing of any date, although birthdays were considered "okay if you must")...and the list went on. Thus, my childhood understanding of God was that He didn't like me very much, even though He loved me (which made no sense to me, so what stuck was that He didn't like me), and the only way to earn His approval was to adhere to the expectations of those "in authority".

Further complicating my experience was the disease of my family life. Both of my parents were raised in horribly dysfunctional families. The marriage of their mutual woundedness created a narcissist-enabler dynamic in which our family life revolved around the emotional status of the narcissist. From earliest memory, I became expert at perceiving unstated expectations, including the expectations contradicting spoken expectations, so that I could "be good enough to be loved." When I was four, our family left our home state to assist at a community farm that was part of our religious group; and thus began our trek away from extended family, getting farther away geographically and more distant emotionally from them. By the time I was twelve, I barely knew anyone from [my] extended family. My grandparents passed away as strangers. My cousins were unknown, other than as names. Aunts and uncles were vague characters in infrequently told stories.

We lived in several "community" situations and finally ended up in a rented house in a small northern community, which was the economic "source" for nine different community farms in our religious group. My family never lived in that home alone. We had a variety of people sharing our home—another family of six, a single mother and her daughter, a newlywed couple eventually joined by an infant, and a constant stream of single adults who would "come to town" over the winter months to earn money, which they then turned over to the leadership of their community. The message to me was that nothing, not even my parents, were "mine," and that to wish otherwise was sin. In other words, boundaries were sinful.

My most vivid memory from childhood was a keen awareness of the presence of the Divine. I remember as a toddler having conversations with God that were as real to me as my conversations with my parents; and, in some ways more real, because I knew God understood me. As a toddler, I had no doubt that I was acceptable to and loved by God. This assurance was eroded by outside messages, so that by adolescence I felt as if there were two Divine beings in my life. There was the private Divine, who was reassuring, comforting, and strengthening. Then, there was the public Divine, who was disapproving and impossible to please, with hidden expectations. He sent Jesus to live the perfect life, which I somehow got to benefit from, but only if I lived as close to the perfect life as I possibly could.

In my early teens, my parents became disillusioned with this group and moved to a nearby town where we lived as a nuclear family for the first time since my preschool years. We attended an "established church" and discovered these "deceived" people actually had real relationships with God. But there were…hidden expectations here as well, reinforced by the expectations woven into my being from the womb. So, while I heard far more often now that God loved me, I still felt the pressure of ever-lengthening lists of expectations. I received a lot of adult admiration for my "maturity" and "responsible behavior," which only intensified my sense of inner striving toward constantly changing goal posts of what a "Godly life" should look like. Woven throughout was the subtext of my parents' narcissism, which was its own source of changeable expectations and uncertainties.

But all of the double-speak felt normal. It never occurred to me there was any other way to exist or relate. Thus, when I ended up at a fundamentalist Christian college in Texas at age of seventeen, the expectations and hidden messages [there] fit right in with what I had known before. I experienced the first romantic attachment of my young life to a narcissistic young man whose dad was also narcissistic. I saw nothing wrong with the way they treated me or those around them. It was in that relationship reinforced by the religious setting that the erosion of my worth as female began its landslide.

At the end of my third year of college, I was given the shining gift of a nine-week student teaching assignment that took me to a tiny northern community. There, I was gifted with nine weeks of spiritual and emotional intensive care. I lived with a dear Mennonite couple and worked in the church-school of which he was principal. This couple, as well as the church pastor and his wife, showed me unconditional love for the first time in my life. What I received there gave me the soul strength to finish my fourth year of college, as well as to call an end to the emotionally abusive romantic relationship. I spent the next eight years trying to return to that place permanently. The two couples continued to support me long distance, and their loving care helped me get through the years that followed.

Cult Trauma

Cult trauma is a specific kind of religious trauma, even though it may be related to a variety of other kinds of religious trauma. We might say there are elements of brainwashing in most systematized belief organizations whose aim is to bring power to a few by diminishing or controlling the many, but cult mentality is specifically highly focused on member having no independent thought. The cult isolates the person(s) in the cult from any outside communities, especially family, and intentionally hones in on their vulnerabilities to break people down.

While there are extreme versions of cults that can include things like mass suicide and mass sexual and physical abuses, there are also the subtler forms of cult behavior that may include many or most of the elements above but in a subtler fashion. As previously illustrated, there are yoga studios with power-driven leaders and self-help programs that might qualify as cult type in nature. The religious content and the doctrine and dogma (which is usually quite different from any traditional use or interpretation of the same texts) is singularly driven by enforcing control and giving power to a small number of leaders or even to only one person. Once someone is inside a cult community, it is very hard to extract them, because if the brainwashing methods are effective, the person will not want to leave.

The symptoms of traumatic response post-cult can be high anxiety, low self-worth and little sense of identity, and guilt for leaving the community. Depending on the extent of abuse in the practices of the community, symptoms can include a variety of intrusive thoughts and nightmares, especially as the person begins to shed the brainwashing and see the practices of the community as dysfunctional and abusive.

LIFE PARABLE

JULIE: My observations of the church led me to be even more suspicious of Christians than of other people. My dad was kicked out of his first church; it was a very difficult experience for my parents. I loved church because of my faith but was cautious. His third church and final year of pastoring left my mother in a state of complete mental breakdown with three kids. A difficult situation in a small, private Christian school left me, at the age of twelve, in a similar mental state. The only teacher at the small school didn't like me and made my life a living hell, and eventually I would have to be dragged into the school every day as I clung, crying, to the railing of the steps. Finally, my parents took me out of the school after a meeting with the teacher and owners, who told my parents I needed to have a nervous breakdown, because I was a perfectionist.

After that, I was terrified of school and authority figures, and when we moved and started going to a large church, I was scared to participate in any of the youth meetings until I made a friend at school who started going with me. Later, I went to Bible College, where I met my husband, and he was a pastor for one year after graduation, so I was a pastor's wife briefly at the age of twenty to twenty-one in Canada, where I'm from. Shortly after, we left that denomination as we didn't agree with a lot of the doctrine, and through a series of events we ended up moving to the United States and got involved with a different group of independent churches that described themselves as reformed charismatic. I would describe them as patriarchal puritans. I now call it a cult, and we spent about nine years there trying to be biblical. That was by far the most damaging church experience I had experienced, as they focused almost solely on indwelling sin and how sinful we all are. Pastors had dictatorial authority over members, and men had the same kind of authority over their wives and children. We had three children while there, and I stayed at home where I belonged and asked myself many times a day as I had been taught, "What would my husband want?" It didn't work out very well, and after a difficult period of questioning, we decided to leave. I was very depressed and suicidal at that point, disdained all women, including myself, and thought I was absolutely worthless.

LIFE PARABLE

GWEN: I am a woman who was raised in Bill Gothard's Advanced Training Institute (ATI) program.

Over the past two years as I have healed from the ravages of abuse, I have found power and healing in telling my story. I remember the first time I told someone I had been sexually abused. I stuttered over the words, cringing in shame, and crushed by guilt. The more I tell my story and people witness the atrocities that happened to me, the more I have healed. Today I tell you my story without shame.

I was very young when my parents first went to a Bill Gothard seminar. They sincerely believed his teachings were biblical and would "turn the heart of the parents to their children, and the hearts of the children to their parents" (Malachi 4:6). When I was going into second grade, Bill Gothard opened a pilot home school program, and my parents enrolled us as a second-year family. I was raised for ten years in the ATI program, and it shaped every part of my being. As a child I was very fearful and craved security. Since that is exactly what the program offered, I embraced it wholeheartedly. I fully accepted every aspect of being under my authority's "umbrella of protection." I believed that if I aligned even my desires (not just my actions) with the desires of my authorities, I would be the most happy. I remember one time a girl from my church made the comment, "Your parents are really strict!" I disagreed. I replied that actually they don't have "rules" for me. Instead, they have trained my heart to want the very things they want for me, so I simply do what they expect without them having to tell me. This was something the ATI program taught parents to build into their children, and I was proud of the fact that I did it so well. As a result, my teen years were calm and peaceful. I never rebelled. It never even crossed my mind to think differently from my parents. If an authority wanted me to be a certain way, then that was God's best for me. By this time, I was completely unable to think independently or (God forbid) ever say "no" to an authority. If my authority's wishes were truly God's will for my life, why should I ever say no?

Ironically, this was exactly the outcome ATI was designed to create, and from the outside I [appeared to be] a complete success. However, in my heart all was not well. I began to live in daydreams and to feel horribly guilty about them. That was the beginning of the dichotomy between my tumultuous inside life and the perfect image I showed everyone on the outside. My family left ATI when I was nearing the end of high school. In the Baptist circles I grew up in, Bill Gothard was seen as too ecumenical. But as far as my life went, after college, the damage had already been done. I looked at all the stuff I was doing to be a successful Christian—daily devotions and prayer, proper dress and music, moral purity, work in the local church, evangelism, discipleship, and being a full-time missionary—but inside I was so desperately empty! Did God love me? Or even accept me?

After three months I was desperate for help but did not know how or whom to ask. So, I made a very loud cry for help, I overdosed on sleeping pills. My coworkers and mission board were shocked. My dichotomy was exposed. Everyone in my world could now see the truth about me: this "successful" Christian was really a great big *failure*.

But I saw hope from one source. My dad had a friend from college, and this friend had a daughter and son-in-law who ministered to broken Christians. Because they were family friends, I was happy to hear from them; and, when they started emailing me, I was amazed. They helped me see that God loved and accepted me unconditionally. I was so desperate for this truth after my suicide attempt, I decided to move back to the States and receive counseling from this couple.

The problem was that they were not Baptists, nor did they live a lifestyle separated from "the world," as I had been taught to live. All my authorities (my parents, pastor, Bible College) were adamant that I not go to this couple for counseling. They tried hard to warn me that I was too vulnerable and would compromise my higher standards by being around them. But for the first time in my life, I had resonated with their message of unconditional love, so I disagreed with my authorities and directly "disobeyed" them. I was twenty-five years old.

I did not learn to think for myself overnight, however. While I soaked up my counselors' love and acceptance, trying hard to believe that God really loved me that way, I also became very codependent on them. I was trained to be dependent on others my entire life, and one solitary act of independence could not immediately change that.

As it turned out, my counselor took full advantage of my trained submissiveness and began grooming me for sex. As my counselor, he controlled me emotionally, molding me to the place where I believed I could not survive without him. Over three long years he used my body. I would ask him to stop, but he said God was OK with it, and that when the time came, it would stop naturally. Over the years I was receiving "counseling" from this couple, I learned to self-injure, made multiple suicide attempts, ended up in a psychiatric unit four times, and developed an eating disorder. Finally, I had the courage to ask the counselor's wife for help, and I told her everything. She and her husband had a "reconciliation" meeting with me, in which we were each to apologize. However, they had [already decided on the wording of] my apology. I was to ask them to forgive me for seducing him. I was stunned because I had no clue how I had seduced him. But being submissive, as I had been trained to do, I confessed to seduction. As a result, I believed I was a whore and an adulteress, and I could never tell anyone my horrible secret. The sexual abuse stopped for a while, but because I never asked anyone on the outside for help, it eventually started all over again, and I still felt powerless to stop it.

Mercifully, God rescued me from the cycle of abuse. A man on their Board of Directors (who had been told of the abuse by the couple after our mutual apology session but had been sworn to secrecy by them) suggested I move away. I had gone back to school since my return to the States and had become certified as a sign language interpreter, so for the first time in my life I had the means to be independent and self-supporting.

At the age of thirty-two, I began the journey to find a home and a job out of state. I was so excited that I had the ability to be independent! While Bill Gothard's ATI program seemed like a thing of the past for me, my parents still lived in that mindset and lifestyle. I remember the day my parents helped me move. We were up early to load everything and make the drive across the country to my new home. When we arrived, I excitedly showed them around, proud of my newfound independence. But my mom was horrified. She began to lecture me, saying I had done all of this outside of my father's authority, and wasn't I afraid of the judgment of God?

The next day as we were eating lunch, my mom tried again. She said, "Who you used to be is who you really are, and the way you are now is because you are deluded." It hurt deeply, but I was tasting freedom and wanted it too badly to give it up. With a great desire to heal, I found an eating disorder treatment hospital and made an appointment, as this had become a primary way my pain and suffering manifested—in my body. I still believed that my counselor's sexual relationship with me was all my fault and that I had seduced him and was a whore. I felt intense shame. But that day in the nutritionist's office, I heard for the first time that what I experienced was sexual abuse, and that my counselor had violated professional ethics in using his position of authority to rape me.

After nine weeks of treatment in the hospital, I had the courage to tell my parents about my sexual abuse. They were heartbroken and very supportive of my healing. But after a few days, my mom asked me if I felt God's "conviction" against me for my sins. At first, I wasn't sure what she was talking about, but she explained. It was obvious to her that since I had chosen to go against all my authorities' wishes when I chose this counselor, I had sinned, and the sexual abuse was the natural consequence of that sin. I was crushed. Why, when I was already drowning in shame, did Gothard's principle of authority have to be used to pile on even more? It was this very principle that had held me hostage by causing an inability to say "no" strongly or loudly enough to those in authority abusing me.

Being in treatment gave me the strength to contact a couple of other members of the Board of Directors and tell them what my counselor had done. The text I received that day in June from my abuser was his last effort to get me to withdraw my accusations before the Board of Directors met. Thankfully, by then I had the skills to calm down and stand firm. In their meeting, the Board mandated that he stop counseling, and later that year they voted to close his nonprofit organization. More details have come out since, and I've learned [that] I was not the only woman he abused.

Spiritual and Moral Injury Trauma

Spiritual and moral injury can be an included part of any of the above traumatic situations but also stands independently and may not always happen directly inside of religious contexts. As discussed earlier under the general categories of trauma, it is important to list this kind of trauma here as it can occur in religious contexts and affect the spirit. This kind of injury comes from being engaged in practices, a situation, or community group that utilizes practices against a person's moral values. Sometimes the ability to see the difference of values may not appear immediately. Often it is only after leaving a religiously harmful community that people begin to see more of the ways the system's beliefs do not match their own.

This process of realization can lead most prominently to feelings of guilt and shame, but also to issues of trust and intimacy with the self and others. The inner trust issues come from a realization that parts of the community or even one's own actions in the community were against their beliefs and morals, and this can lead to guilt and shame that must be processed to be healed.

Other Related Religious Traumas

The traumatic experiences listed above are by no means a comprehensive list of all methods of traumatization in a religious context. This list is a way to begin a cultural and communal dialogue about how unhealthy, destructive, and abusive religions can hurt people and begin to validate those hurting experiences as traumas. My hope is that this list continues to expand and become more detailed as people feel more comfortable and safer to share their stories and journeys toward healing.

LIFE PARABLE

DEANNA: I was in a theater group in early high school that was my first exposure to good people who weren't also Christians. They were loving, warm, always excited when I was around, and wanted me for me, no strings attached. This was different than my faith community, which expected me to dress a certain way, talk about Jesus a certain way, watch the right movies and listen to the right music, and have correct political opinions. I didn't realize just how much pressure there was until I was in a different environment. I was an assistant director of a play, and at the time I knew I couldn't invite my friends because it had a few swear words, a kiss, and an allusion to sex. It was very lonely. The second thing was that I ran into a guy from a community theater production I had been in years before. He was my first love, with dark eyes, brown curls, and an infinitely young spirit. He wrote me letters and was always creating things by hand like leather-bound notebooks and silver rings. I was entranced. The only problem was that my church friends didn't like him. He made too many innuendos, swore occasionally, and I could never really verify if he was a Christian or not. But none of that mattered. I loved him. Between a bunch of theater nerds who loved me for who I was, and a love deemed unclean by my faith community at large, I started to see the cracks. How could these people who loved me and were there for me be the terrible people my church perceived them to be? Clearly, they were not.

As I mentioned earlier, I was hungry for more spiritual knowledge, so I went looking for it. I started going to the adult Sunday school classes instead of my own. I also wandered to other youth groups, groping for something more than what my church had been spoon-feeding me my entire life. Eventually the leadership got wind that I was exploring and trying other churches. The youth pastor called me one evening to find out what was going on, and when I told him, he proceeded to yell at me for fifteen minutes. Every time I tried to interject to explain, he would talk over me. His wife did the same thing to me a few nights later, saying how her husband wasn't Billy Graham. All but one or two youth leaders abandoned me. When I shared my feelings with my church friends, many of them too deserted me. Another thing I noticed was their hypocrisy.

They preached all the time about love and looking out for the least, but they rarely ever did things with communities outside of the church body and missionaries. When a girl a few years older than I got pregnant out of wedlock, the church refused to host a baby shower for her because they "didn't want to condone her actions." She was left out in the cold.

They were strict about clothing for women too. One year they had a sexuality series in which the leaders said "ex" because they could not muster the strength to say "sex." They said that in the seven levels of physical contact, hugging was the closest thing to intercourse itself. There was a girl who wore clothing that fit her nicely, and they deemed it immodest because it *might* come up when she bent over. So, they had her change into the same outfit one size up, which looked frumpy on her, and they said this was the godly, modest thing to do.

They wouldn't let other students announce they were carpooling to an Acquire the Fire event because elders at the church would frown on them promoting an event with rock music. These are just a few cases where I figured out the church was far more invested in control, piety, self-righteousness, and image than [in] the spiritual lives of their congregants.

CHAPTER 7

The Lotus and the Mud:
The Sacred Wounds Healing Process

Where there is love there is life.
—Mahatma Gandhi

There is a Buddhist philosophy based on the lotus and mud. The lotus flower is a beautiful and bright symbol of life, but the lotus grows out of the mud in swamps. Just as there is no lotus without mud, so too there is no joy without suffering, and no transformation without grief.

This Buddhist imagery of the mud and the lotus remind us that in the dankest, darkest, most messy places is born one of the most beautiful flowers on earth. Without the mud, we cannot create a lotus; nature, yet again, is the teacher of humanity. Without pain, there is no growth and transformation. We wouldn't seek out the mud, but we need it to grow. The journey from hurt to healing looks like that—the blooming of a flower born from the messiest of places.

Hurt to Healing Explored

The following steps outline the process from religious and spiritual harm towards healing. Much of life transformation and personal evolution moves in a similar pattern, although we may take different side roads. A good portion of this book has included stories or "life parables" which model the process of religious hurt and healing. We are mining the information of the stories that will become tomorrow's scientific facts, measures, and methods. Join me as I delve into the patterns found in the data of the stories of religious and spiritual trauma.

1. **Recognize the hurt, inconsistencies, or wrongdoing in your spiritual/religious belief system—or with person[s] within that system.** This process can take a minute or a lifetime depending on the circumstances.

2. **Begin to question.** This can begin as an internal process. Depending on the strictness of your community group, it could be a completely secret endeavor or very public.

3. **Seek outside input.** This may include seeking out a therapist or another kind of discernment professional. It might entail reading books or finding mentors who are asking the same questions as you, and who are giving you the freedom to ask those questions and explore your ideas, belief, and feelings. It could also include finding Facebook or other online support groups of people seeking answers to similar questions, or who are in different phases of their hurt and healing process in faith contexts.

4. **Leave your spiritual home or faith of origin.** This may also include leaving family, friends, and lifelong community members. This phase is typically intensely emotional and includes many feelings of loss, confusion, and fear of the unknown on the other side of "knowing."

5. **Begin your own pilgrimage into the spiritual desert, or as I called it, my spiritual runaway phase.** This is the period in which you begin to explore what your world, beliefs, and community context might look like without your faith of origin. This is often a solitary part of the journey.

6. **Enter the anger stage of grief and loss, which can also be accompanied by some kind of spiritual or philosophical nihilism.** Like anyone who gets out of an unhealthy or abusive relationship and has time for the cloud of illusion to pass, as you move away from the community that hurt you, you will most likely become angry. Depending on the level of hurt, you might feel rage not only toward your own community group, but also toward any community, faith or otherwise. This can lead to a period of existential darkness or a kind of nihilism in which it feels as if nothing has meaning or value.

In the extreme presentation of this phase, you might fall into a major depression or even begin to feel suicidal. While it is not essential to be in a religious tradition to find peace, we all need something in our life to have meaning and a way to understand the world to find happiness. Without this, life is beyond lonely: it feels hopeless. This doesn't have to be forever, and if you are in this phase, know that it too will pass. If you are very depressed or suicidal, seek mental health counseling immediately. There is another way!

7. **Explore other ideas, beliefs, and opportunities.** We can call this period religion shopping or maybe spirituality speed dating. This is a step that not everyone takes, but many do, in which they begin to explore other faith traditions. You might choose to explore other sects of your original tradition or totally different traditions. A very common swap if you were hurt by a Western faith tradition is to begin exploring Eastern traditions because of their very different philosophies, spiritual languages, and practices. This also minimizes the chances for immediate triggers from your trauma, which would be harder to avoid if you stay in your own religious/spiritual group.

8. **Begin to reintegrate meaning, values, and beliefs in some way for yourself, whether that is a mix of different ideas, philosophies, and belief systems, or whether it is by joining a new community group or tradition.** During this time, you will begin to understand yourself and your ideals better. There is more clarity to who you are as an independent person. Because most people hurt by religion have felt stifled and without a voice, your initial set of beliefs may become a bit extreme in the opposite direction of your original system of belief, or even oppositional to and defiant toward these beliefs. Akin to starting a new spiritual kindergarten, this is normal. Because you are usually fighting back and finding empowerment after being silenced, your initial response can be very absolute, black-and-white thinking. With time and experience, this can soften— but it will take work. Be forewarned; you have to do the work, otherwise you might simply become the staunchly oppositional version of your previous self, or create a cycle of violence in which you become the absolutist you wanted to leave behind.

9. **Begin to trust in individual and communal relationships again.** Once you have begun to integrate your belief system and start to know yourself better, you find that authentic relationships form organically from that place. You begin to understand that while not everyone and every community is trustworthy, it is worth the risk to try because we grow and heal in community (religious or otherwise) and in relationships (intimate and friendships). This may mean you are hurt, but it also means you are able to have amazing moments of collaboration and partnership with others that help make you stronger by supporting and championing your authentic self, just the way you are.

THE WILDCARD: Anywhere along this process from hurt to healing, you can experience what I call the "wildcard." This is some hurt that unexpectedly intrudes on your healing path and can either stall you or set you back again a few steps. Since you now know from the outset of this journey that the "wildcard" will happen—that we are all hurt again, that this is the inherent risk in trust, openness and authenticity—you can prepare for it, expect it, and work to heal from it so it doesn't stagnate or permanently set back your healing process.

10. **Move toward a middle way, away from absolutes**. The full integration of your healing process will come when you are able to see what the eastern traditions call the "middle way" or "nondual consciousness" that mystics across traditions find in their contemplative mindset. This usually requires some kind of contemplative practice to take us out of action and rightness and to allow us to hold the tension between what we know, what we think we know, and what is "unknown." This means you no longer need to be right and can begin to understand that everything we can know from science or religion about the cosmos is a limited understanding of the ineffable. You can let go of black-and-white thinking, as well as what might remain of your hate and rage from your old wounds and find a way to transform your hurt into healing action and good work for and in the world.

11. **Enlightenment. Game Over. You Win!** OK, I am sort of kidding. But whatever comes after nondual consciousness might feel something like levitation, a state in which gravity no longer

applies to you. If you get anywhere close to step ten in a lifetime, be happy and know we all fall back sometimes into the earlier stages and places. We can't exist permanently in nondual consciousness. We simply get morsels of its goodness before our ego gets back in the way or hurt tramples on us again. Remember that what matters is the way we walk the path and not how far we get or how much we achieve. Walk your journey with awareness, hope, and openness to what is possible, and you will land where you fit in the world and be authentically you when you get there. Healing from religious injury and spiritual abuse is a long and arduous journey. Honor every improvement and moment of healing you experience on the journey and all your efforts and hard work. You deserve a moment to honor yourself, even if you never levitate!

***

Now that I have described a step-by-step process of the healing journey after religious trauma I want to explain how, even though I use the word *steps*, it is not a step-based system. We don't have very good language for a process of healing, growth, or transformation that moves deeper inward rather than upward, so I am stuck with this upward language to describe an inward deepening process. To get into the heart of a deepening process of healing transformation, I really need to bring in a new, non-dual concept of understanding healing, change, and growth.

When we have survived trauma, we know we can't just throw away experience. We can't eradicate memory or take away what has already happened. What we can do from a place of strength and empowerment is to evolve and transcend the hurt of our past and the ways of knowing that have kept us stuck in a limited way of understanding and incorporate our understanding from the past into our evolution in the present.

The images above symbolize a labyrinth and a spiral—which I am calling a healing spiral. If you look at it, though, it also could be just two different vantage points on the same symbol—one from above and one from the side. Both images illustrate an inward movement. On the left, the labyrinth spiral moves inward; on the right, the healing spiral move downward. This is the healing calling us to take with us what came before but without bringing with us all the emotional baggage, and to transcend, by which I mean to move deeper and deeper to the root of our true and authentic self, carrying with us into our deeper levels of truth the wisdom, the heart, and the soul of our experience and what we have learned through healing.

I say that simply but not flippantly. The process of healing is not easy. To transcend, we must forgive and release hurt. To transcend, we must let go enough to trust that our inward journey is taking us somewhere better, even and especially when it is uncomfortable to get there. Yet that does not mean we have to injure ourselves in order to heal. We have to take our time— and it may take considerable time. Transcendence of certain pains will take longer than others, but it is the pathway to healing.

While there is work to be done on the path from hurt to healing, I respect everyone's process in recovery from religious injury. In traumatic experience, a person's choice is taken away. We don't choose to be hurt and often, especially in institutional settings, there is little empowerment and control in the experience of being hurt. The choice to heal—or how much to heal, when to stop on the path, and when to move forward—is each person's choice to make. There is no right way or answer. There is only what is right for you. This is why I regularly say to my clients and trainees, "Don't poke the trauma bear." The traumatic experience is sufficiently painful and exposing as it is. There is no need to poke further into a person's pain. If you are the survivor, there is no need to push yourself too hard or too fast, or past your threshold for discomfort.

For you don't have to poke the trauma bear to get at the problem. You start with the first layer, the already exposed layer of trauma, and the triggers and symptoms that are already part of your present moment life experience. As you pull away the layers, or as you spiral inward, you go deeper into both the hurting experience and the healing and transformation of experience. Taking time in healing is critical. The process will go backwards at points, and that is OK. All our healing spiral journeys weave up and down—up to the surface and then down deeper—just like the rest of life. Take your process at your own speed. Likewise, if you are supporting someone in healing, let them choose if and when to move forward on their healing journey. Choice is something we can take back after traumatic experience and something we deserve to own in own lives.

LIFE PARABLES: The Healing Stories

ANONYMOUS: About four months ago, I commented to my husband that I felt I had discovered that the very bedrock of my life was turning out to be termite-laden, rotten wood. Thanks to his support, as well as the support and wisdom of my spiritual director (who also works in energy medicine), I've been able to face the layers of rubble, sit with the waves of pain, and begin to experience healing. I've discovered that what I thought was the foundation of my life was a façade, and beneath the facade is "What is real."

What *is* real?

Reality has turned out to be so much broader and more bountiful than I'd been led to believe. Because the tiny box of "acceptable spirituality" crumbled around me, I was able to see that the box itself was the problem, not all the "stuff outside" that I'd been told was so awful.

It's as though I was raised in a house of mirrors like one encounters at a carnival. Since that was all I knew, I didn't [realize that] the images before me were distortions. I've been gently, yet inexorably, lured toward the Light. There are times I've felt blinded by that Light. The wide-open vistas have been nauseatingly disorienting at first. It's been terrifying at times to look at a world without reflective, distorting walls. But while I've suffered and wept, I've been held securely. The gift of awareness of the Divine that was with me as a toddler has never wavered. I've been supported, comforted, and given solace through the process.

My soul is still very tender. I have to take care whom I listen to and whose stories I let into my heart. It takes very little to overwhelm me…for the moment. A friend of mine had open heart surgery a couple of months ago, and it has taken time for his strength to return. I believe I'm on the recovery side of my "open soul" surgery, but I know healing continues to be a process and a journey.

My dream is to somehow, someday, be able to be a midwife to others on their own healing journey. May it be so.

BILL: What I am clinging to is the idea that to see Jesus is to see what God is like, so I see this idea that Jesus is God incarnate. God moved into the neighborhood and showed us what God is like with the way he broke social norms and conventions in his value of people. I extrapolate that this is what God's character is really like. To those who can't be in community, God says you are welcome and loved, and God will reach out and touch you. That is what is keeping me sane. I am still healing from a lot of hurtful and psychologically devastating images of God. I am concerned about how sectarian religion is, that whole us versus them binary. So, one of the values is that religion can make you compassionate toward others, but in the United States it pushes you the other way. For me, I have the privilege of having access to technology that allows me to network and connect with people from different perspectives. I also have people in my life from communities I was once a part of, and a negotiation of relationship with people in communities I am no longer a part of is something that keeps me engaged outside of myself. One of the things I notice now, as someone in seminary, is that I never had any exposure to people of other religious traditions. I am thirty-one years old, and I just went to a Hindu temple and synagogue for the first time last weekend. As cosmopolitan as I like to think I am, I have not seen how these other traditions worship. A lot of my exposure to the world at large happens through social media and the internet and listening to where other folks are, around what Phyllis Tickle calls "the Great Emergence." I think we are all in emergence because we are in cultural or societal upheaval—even if you are a staunch Baptist and thinking of how to go deeper in that you are still part of that swirl of change. Through blogging and reading different people's perspectives, that is how I have begun to connect; we are all breathing the same air, no matter where we are religiously and philosophically.

I think the best question I ever learned to ask is, "Why?" In my own healing, asking why a situation is affecting me the way it does and why I am doing what I am doing was important. We need to explore all that we do on the surface and the deeper dynamic it reflects. Coming in touch with our own trauma and hurt and not discounting things, we can only move past hurt in the greater context of understanding it—and we need to take trauma in religious context seriously. Things we have been taught about God can be really damaging. My spiritual journey is about healing from trauma I have experienced in the church and my own life—I believe God wants to heal all things, and I can be a part of that story and experience that for myself. What do we think when we think about God? When those images are damaging, we need to take seriously those thoughts and community formed out of those negative thoughts and the trauma it can cause. We need to become serious about our healing from those things—not to discount it as not so bad or to just say we're going to move on without dealing with that trauma.

FAY: I have returned to the church several times, and I weep as I sing in worship because I deeply feel the words of the music and love music worship. But I am torn by the wonderful words and feelings and how different religion and the church really are from God. It is sad. I guess attending church is very connected with PTSD and the extreme feelings I experience when I attend. Maybe I will attend again in the future. I am a follower of the teachings of Jesus Christ, and I search for what that means in sorting out the religious corruption that I have seen throughout my life. I want to live my life in a way that others are drawn to a relationship with Jesus Christ and God, so there is lots of love. I cherish the stories and the scripture recognizing that the Bible is to be understood in the context of how and why it was written. I pray and talk to God and question. I favor social justice, love, acceptance, and peaceful responses to anger and hate. I am remarried to a wonderful man who loves me unconditionally and has taught me so much. We are opposites. I am Protestant, and he is Catholic. We were both divorced but do not believe in divorce unless the marriage is abusive. (We were both abused in our relationships.) I am pacifist; he was in the military for eighteen years. We love our children —my two daughters and his son—and we are a family committed to one another. We learn about God together, and we grow and change and heal. We are blessed to have found each other, but that is another story for another time. My spiritual journey is just that—a continuing journey. I miss the fellowship of others in the church and the community, and I support the memories of the good times that get mixed up in the memories of the trauma. Church picnics and always having a social place that was safe to see your friends can be a great social network for meeting others. I was privileged to grow up in a church where I heard the stories of the Bible and learned how much God loves us. Some people know nothing about God. That is sad. I would rather know about God and have some things that are messed up in the church's teaching than not to have been taught about Him at all.

HOPE: I believe that God is good all the time. . .and that he allowed the crazy stuff to happen to us to help us grow into the people He wanted us to be. He took us to places in our spiritual and emotional development we probably never would have gone if we had a more peaceful life. It's also made us very passionate about healthy church life, justice, and churches not spiritually abusing.

DEB: Religion is not for me until I can find a denomination that fits with my personal belief system. I'm aware that my system may be wrong, but I'm sitting here writing about Him, and I would not have done that a few years ago. I believe we are called to love, take care, and treat one another as Jesus would treat us today. I have a lot to work on in the way of forgiveness, and I am not Christ-like in any way, shape, or form; but, I am praying I continue my progress little by little. I speak of these things with my mother, who has become my spiritual adviser, even though we don't always agree with each other. And I have deep conversations with my agnostic fiancé who was raised Episcopalian (quite different from Pentecostal and Baptist churches!) and my atheist friend. I have one other person in my life who has the same questions and who believes in Jesus, and it's very refreshing. It's hard for me to talk to any other members of my family. I read progressive Christian blogs and Facebook pages, but I don't have the guts to strike up conversations.

MARG: When AIDS first started killing people, Christians said some unbelievably awful things. It was clear to me that some Christians were responsible for delaying the research that might have been able to save gay men from dying. This changed me. I started hating Christians. I didn't hate people just because they said they were Christian, but I hated Christians in general. I avoided individuals who identified as Christian, because they would often say hurtful things or behave in thoughtless or exclusionary ways. I isolated from them, and I hated them as a group.

Almost all lesbians who were active in the lesbian culture were extremely anti-Christian. It's hard to describe, but to say that many of us felt about Christians the way Jews felt about Nazis would not be much of an overstatement. To this day, there are lesbian and gay people, most of whom are over fifty, who still hate Christians and consider any LGBT person who identifies that way as delusional at best and a traitor at worst. But most LGBT people now know that some Christians are okay.

I got sober in the early 1990s when I was in my thirties. With my sobriety came clarity in the way I experienced the world. And with clarity came a longing for spiritual expression and experience. In the mid 1990s, I met some women who were Dianic Wiccans. This is a pagan, earth-based religion with a monotheistic, feminine divine presence (the Goddess), but [it] also allows for an understanding that the divine presence is expressed in a great variety of female deities spanning cultures and ages. There is no eschatology and no one specific creation story. There is an emphasis on ritual, peacemaking, feminist activism, doing no harm, care of the earth, and surrendering oneself to the Goddess in love. I found the spiritual practice of Dianic Wicca quite appealing, and it was so different than Christianity that I was able to approach it without fear or trepidation. As a result, I became aware of myself as a spiritual person again and began to see myself in a similar way to how I had understood myself for the first eighteen years of my life. It was as if I had been given back the key to my soul.

A few years after that, I sat in on a workshop presented by a therapist named Katherine Unthank. A psychologist, a born-again Christian, and a lesbian, she had a similar experience to mine, having found herself unwelcome in her own church after coming out. As a therapist, she was able to recognize what happened to her during and after this experience as trauma. She had developed a theory that what the church did to LGBT people was best understood as a form of spiritual power rape, and what happened to the LGBT people as a result had much in common with the PTSD experience of women who have been physically raped. She detailed symptoms one might develop after this experience, and in doing so, described the last fifteen years of my life. I sat stunned, hardly able to breathe or move, and for the first time I began to understand what I had lost when I told the youth minister I was gay. I had lost everything I knew or thought my life would be, the legacy of my grandmother and my mother, and the only safe place I had.

As the numbness of fifteen years started to wear off, I began to cry. For years I had hardly even let a tear run down my cheek, but now I cried for two days straight. Sobbing. Realizing, for the first time what had been unfairly taken, just because I happened to be a lesbian. Over time, I worked through my grief. Fortunately, I found a therapist who recognized the depth of this loss and helped me come to terms with it. I still didn't like Christianity, and I stayed afraid of Christians. But I began to heal. In 2002, by chance, I ended up being hired to do sound for a group called the Evangelical and Ecumenical Women's Caucus (EEWC). They were holding their conference in Indianapolis. I'm still a little shocked I took the gig, but I needed the money and figured I could lay low and live through a weekend with a bunch of church ladies.

I was shocked when I discovered [that] these women turned out to be no ordinary church ladies. [The] EEWC was a gender justice organization that had voted to support LGBT equality way back in 1986. Their founding members included Letha Dawson Scanzoni and Virginia Ramey Mollenkott, authors of one of the first books to make a biblical case supporting inclusion and welcome of LGBT people in Christianity, *Is the Homosexual My Neighbor?*

I spent that weekend watching and interacting with a group of feminist Christians, learning, worshipping, and sharing fellowship with one another. The lectures were the most stimulating I'd experienced since leaving school. Talking with lesbian Christian feminists was mind blowing. The last day there was a worship service. It was the first Christian worship service I had attended in years, and it affected me deeply. I sat at the soundboard, trying to do my job while holding back giant waves of emotion. I was taken back to the first eighteen years of my life, when this had been my weekly reality. I remembered how it felt. I cried, tried not to sob, and hoped no one was noticing. The women got up and moved forward to take Communion. One of the founders of the organization, Nancy Hardesty, saw me sitting in the back and noticed my tears. I think she knew exactly what I was feeling. As I tried to stop crying and become invisible, she casually walked right up to me, leaned over, and whispered in my ear, "You are always welcome at Her table." Then she turned and walked back to her seat. I didn't know what to think or feel. As I worked that afternoon, tearing down the system, I tried to talk to my partner about what had happened. But she couldn't understand, or I couldn't explain it. I tucked that weekend away but kept it close to my heart.

Four years later, the Indiana chapter of the organization called me out of the blue to see if I wanted to come to a meeting. I said yes, and thus began my involvement with EEWC. Thus, I began my journey back to Christianity. I have been active with EEWC ever since, becoming their office manager and web developer in 2012, and then their director of public information in 2013. It didn't matter to them that I wasn't able to refer to myself as a Christian. I think they knew my heart better than I did. For a very long time, saying I was a Christian felt like taking on the label of my perpetrator. I don't know what changed this year. I don't know why I started to be able to say it, but I think maybe it was that I stopped being afraid that some of my LGBT friends would hate me. Christian is still a dirty word to some LGBT people, because their wounds have never healed. I never let go of Jesus, but as long as I was afraid of those claiming to be His people, there was a separation.

I don't have a church anymore, and I don't think I ever will again. I'm still too triggered by being around groups of people and by the way church people often act. I'm hypervigilant and always looking for the judgment and exclusion to show itself. I can't imagine a time when I will feel safe in a church. But I have found my people, my tribe, and my faith community in the women and men of EEWC-Christian Feminism Today. They are my friends and mentors. They are my mothers, sisters, and brothers. And I am beginning to realize my heart is safe with them.

EMMA: I see a lot of healing on the brink right now, even the work I see my sister doing to push more intergenerational trauma and healing issues forward and get people trained to understand intergenerational/historical trauma. As they learn more about themselves, they are healing themselves. They can see the trauma others are going through too. A lot of times I felt really alone—it comes from my abandonment issues—and so I have to do self-talk to pull myself out of that. When I get a trigger, I can see where the trigger is coming from and talk myself out of it.

For me, spirituality is so huge in the work that I do that I don't know how to help people heal if they aren't connected with any sort of spirituality. I ask people I work with, "What do you believe in?" I always tell them that due to the way I grew up, I learned it is OK to believe in *all* ways (for me that includes Native and Christian spirituality), and I help them heal by calling their spirit back.

I see a lot of the healing work starting now because there is so much awareness around the intergenerational trauma issue in and out of faith communities. Currently there is more awareness of Native American people. We felt invisible, and society treated us that way. Now people are getting their voice and seeing how they can move toward healing. With social media, there are people who can see they are not alone and are learning about intergenerational trauma in [the] social media forum.

The people in social services and support programs are starting to come [to] the reservations [now], and they weren't before. Right now, my co-worker and I from the White Bison Mending Broken Hearts program (a healing program for intergenerational trauma) are working with Bishop John in the Episcopal Diocese of South Dakota to bring two more of our healing programs to South Dakota and the Lakota people who live there. Bishop John truly cares about helping people, and for me that is so heartwarming because I didn't feel that...from my church community [when I was growing up]. He understands about the intergenerational trauma and how important it is to do this work.

For me, to see that in South Dakota is unbelievable, to see [that] there is this bishop who cares. My hope is [that] I can help people to discard their old beliefs, hurts, and traumas instead of setting up blocks. When I moved toward healing, I had to let go of a lot of my old negative beliefs. My hope moving forward is that there can be many more programs like the ones we are working on now. I hope the church [can] work with the community to help it heal.

KISHA: At this time, I am not solid in my theology at all. I try to remain open. I believe there is a God simply because I believe it was Him who transcended and transformed my darkness on the day that would have been the last day of my life. No one else was present. No one else helped me. No one else could even reach me. It was just me, my darkness, and my plans to end it all until I experienced this luminous disruption. However, in spite of my belief in God and in Christ, I am very leery of Christian/Church culture. In my heart of hearts, I am not at all interested in church, though I am interested in community. However, I am very concerned about the hearts and souls who sit on church pews Sunday after Sunday, week after week, and get hurt, abused, misled, and misinformed. If we are going to have church, I would rather take the lead so I can know people are being cared for well. [However], I keep running into the same problem I had as a child; I don't fit into the church system, and I continue to be rejected. For some reason, I am a threat to the current equilibrium established within most church systems. [Therefore], the easiest thing to do is dismiss me, silence me, and push me out.

As a chaplain, I will have an alternative route [to] care for people spiritually. Instead of being pressured to be "on" all the time or to conform to the bullshit laced within church culture, I can merely go straight to the source, meet people where they are, and be a present help in the midst of their darkness. That is what I am excited about—presence, not performance.

In the meantime, I practice community with the local spoken word and open microphone artists in my area. I have learned there are some very common threads that run deep among poets, prophets, and preachers. Therefore, I make it my business to commune with such folks at least once or twice weekly. My loyalty to church attendance is not as significant. However, when there is something of interest happening at church, such as a book study I'm interested in, I attend. The United Methodist Church denomination seems to be a safe space for me during this particular season of my life.

Rage and Reconciliation: Reconciling on the Healing Journey

As a trauma therapist and survivor, I have personally and professionally spent much of my life mired in the sewage of abuses. This, however, is not the only thing that can come from trauma: we all have the potential to transform hate into love. Many times, though, we get stuck in the sludge of the hurt and get so entrenched that we can't find our way out to healing.

Throughout my time facilitating trauma therapy, I found three things inherent to healing: creative expression, spiritual and embodied practices, and relational experience. To articulate the depths of the sewage in which we can get mired in through our trauma, I used to show my clients a clip from *Shawshank Redemption*.

I'd begin the film near the end of the movie when the protagonist, Andy Dufresne, frees himself from the prison of his own rage, resentment, and guilt by chipping away, year after year, at the concrete walls of his cell until he reaches the path out. Andy's friend, Red narrates his escape path, saying, "Andy crawled to freedom through

500 yards of shit smelling foulness I can't even imagine, or maybe I just don't want to. Five hundred yards. That's the length of five football fields, just shy of half a mile."

The scene ends with him exiting the tunnel of crap, stripping bare his prison clothes, and standing in the midst of rain and lightning with his hands spread wide as he looks up to the sky, into the heavens.

The reason I'd show this clip is because the road out of trauma and suffering is like the hundreds of yards of waste that Andy Dufresne crawled through. The question of our lives is: Are we willing to crawl out of the crap and into freedom, or do we prefer to sit in the sludge or behind the prison walls of our pain forever? This is where the choice comes in. This is where we decide who we are in the mythology of our own lives.

Interestingly, the film is an adaptation of a novella written by Stephen King titled *Rita Hayworth and Shawshank Redemption*. I say "interesting" because Stephen King was a survivor of childhood trauma, a fact I learned in graduate school while reading a book by psychiatrist Lenore Terr about the impact of childhood trauma on the life and personal mythology of those who survive terrible things in their early lives. Terr believes we tell the stories of our pain in our lives, and our personal myths follow us. She explored the relationship between Stephen King's own childhood trauma and his experience of writing stories of horror and sometimes healing. To me, *Shawshank Redemption* is one of King's best stories of surmounting the horror to find freedom.

In the film, after Red recounts this story of escape from suffering, he closes by saying, "I remember thinking it would take a man six hundred years to tunnel under the wall with it [an old rock hammer]. Old Andy did it in less than twenty…Andy Dufresne, who crawled through a river of shit and came out clean on the other side."

We all have this potential. This is why I'd remind my clients of this story by showing the film to them as they moved through their own journey of trauma healing. We all have the ability to move through the crap of our suffering and come out clean on the other side. Or we can sit in rage and hate. Both are choices. We decide which way we go, but the transformation of healing is available to us when we crawl through the crap. We cannot control who hurts us, in and out of religion and spiritual contexts, but we can control how we respond. I have seen so many people live their lives in the tunnel of bile and sludge, and many who live inside the prison forever.

We cannot always control what happens to us, but we can control what we do with it.

Healing, Reconciliation, and Accountability

I have worked for years on personal reconciliation out of trauma and hurt with clients, but I think I have learned the most about the practice of meaningful reconciliation from my work with Indigenous communities on the topic of the Doctrine of Discovery with colleagues years ago who were working with a religious institution that was confronting its own complicity with the practice of Manifest Destiny through colonization and genocide of Native peoples in the Americas.

I have also at times engaged with people for whom this process doesn't work—when the harm-doing organization or institution is unwilling to make actual substantive change, bypasses any process of accountability, or engages in merely performative reconciliation with no actual accountability or change as the outcome. There is nothing we can do about those that don't want to change in this process. We also have no obligation to do the external work of repair or accountability for systems or organizations that have harmed us. We can choose our healing to be a personal process, one that maybe has support in a new and different community or is done with trusted and loving individuals with whom we are in relationship. But the victim has no requirement to have public-facing or direct contact with their abuser or those that harmed them or others.

This is something you can chose to do. You can see from the variety of mechanisms for reconciliation I articulate below that some are ones that can be done without interacting with the individuals or systems of harm. For instance, take someone who has been abused by a partner or a family member. Sometimes it is unsafe—emotionally, physically, or spiritually—to engage with that context again. In those cases, or if you chose non-engagement, then there is internal repair and reconciliation that can be done to heal your own heart and release what isn't serving you *without* needing to engage at all with the places/people of external harm.

Also, I have seen—particularly in instances in which an organization or a person has done serial harm (physically, emotionally, sexually) to many people who were or are in a certain community, the use of mass response and pressure from a collective voice visibilizing the harm done, as a way of not having to stand alone and for the public and personal pressure to be greater than single voice. For some people this can be an empowering process. Whether or not it results in change within that person or institution, it is nonetheless a way to be heard, to be visible, and possibly to prevent others in the future from being harmed in the same way by the same person/organization.

Ultimately, you chose how you engage with your own personal healing process. You decide what you let go and when. You decide into what processes of justice-seeking, accountability, and, sometimes, repair you want to put energy and into which you don't. As for organizations and institutions that have done harm, they have their own responsibilities in this equation. They may choose not to do that work; but even then, that is their responsibility.

The following are a few guidelines for internal and external processes of reconciliation and accountability with which you can choose to engage as you wish. You hold the roadmap to your own healing journey, and that includes reconciliation, inside and out.

1. **Healing and reconciliation can be a collaborative process.** To have whole person healing, you need to find a way to reconcile the hurts of the past. This does not mean forgetting it or ignoring the wrong, or avoiding seeking justice, but finding a way to heal internally from the hurts others have imposed on our lives. It doesn't have to mean forgiving a specific individual, but it does mean finding a way to move through the hurt to the other side of pain and pain alone. Otherwise, this power of the trauma and the abuser will always have more control over our lives than we do.

2. **No one is mandated to heal. It is a choice.** We have to respect that choice when it is made by others, and we have to be tender with ourselves if we are not yet ready to find internal reconciliation for our wounded experience.

3. **The healing and reconciliation path continues communally, even if some are not ready to make the journey.** This means that communities who have done harm have their own

obligation to be accountable to their participation in hurting others, even if the person(s) hurt never engage(s) with them or a process of reconciliation of the harm done. The community is accountable to do their own work and change their harmful practices, with or without the participation of their victims. It also means being open to external accountability systems and to the formal or informal engagement with systems of justice.

4. **Until we have found our own way to reconcile our hurts and let go of hatred and rage, we will carry that heavy part of our wound with us.** This may include personal and private practices of grieving, raging, and releasing. It can mean shared practices done with other victims of harm—to have community support through the process. This can mean healing practices and ancestral traditions of cleansing and clearing. Whatever the tools and methods of releasing the heavy energy (called *hucha* in Quechua) that are accessible to you and resonate with you, they can all be part of this practice of engaging with, honoring, and releasing the heavy energy.

5. **Education and justice are just as important as healing.** To have people who understand this hurt experience and to have protected spaces where people can tell their stories and find ways to organize around processes for justice and accountability is essential. Internal healing and collective justice-seeking can be a parallel process, and one may come before the other. You will find your own way in your own time. For some people, engaging with the public-facing accountability processes is too taxing or exposing, and that is OK, too.

6. **Heal in your own time and find your own path to inner peace.** We must honor our own journey, and others need to honor it too. We will find our path and our own rhythm in our own time.

As healing from religious and spiritual injury becomes more talked about, and formulas for both individual and communal healing and accountability are begun, there are many things we can learn from those who have gone through these processes before us. I begin with some of their practices.

A Cleansing Practice

This practice comes from the Q'ero Paqo tradition of healing, from the high mountains above Cusco, Peru, in the Kiko territory of the Q'ero tribal lands. It is passed on by the Apaza family lineage of the mountain Paqo lineage. They have offered this practice to the public. Whereas some practices of cleansing and healing are to be facilitated only by Paqos, this practice is shared freely for anyone to engage.

There are many ways in which the words *reconciliation* and *reconciling* apply in the healing process, but the most essential is release and clearing away that which doesn't serve us anymore. You release what you are able to release, knowing that sometimes there are parts of our own hurt which we are not yet ready to release. This is not a one-time process of letting go, but rather a continuing, ongoing practice, like an ongoing practice of tidying up or house cleaning, only in this case tidying and cleaning one's psyche.

There are many ways to cleanse and clear. This one is from one of my root spiritual and healing traditions and is grounded in the ancestral wisdom and practices of the Andes. It is rooted in the earth, for in Indigenous ways our spiritual and healing practices are connected with the earth, *Pachamama* (Mother Earth), and our natural relatives—those above, those below, and those that share this earth with us. This is part of the core principle of meaning-making for my tradition which we call *ayni*, meaning reciprocity. It refers to giving and receiving, like the cycle of the natural world where we give in equal measure to what we receive.

The disruption of this natural way of being and of this ethic of relating to everything around us is how we end up in the chaos and disruption that comes from humanity tipping the scales in its own favor, or from organizations and individual humans doing the same. The disruption to the natural world when we don't care for it in equal measure to what we take, the disruption from taking from others more than we give, the principles of what creates human harm and harm to the earth: these are all essentially the same.

The way to repair this is to repair the imbalance, for ourselves and for our communities, as well as for our natural world. In Quechua, the world of this imbalance includes the amassing of *hucha* (heavy energy), which comes from hurt, trauma, and emotional harm.

We collect this heavy energy even when we don't have traumatic experience. It is the detritus of daily living that we need to clear out periodically, like taking out the garbage or the recycling. Like recycling, *hucha* is energy that can be transformed. So, nothing is inherently bad energy, and we are not bad for the energy we hold, but we must release the heaviness so that it can be transformed or recycled into healthier energy—like cleansing oxygen—that can then be disbursed back into the atmosphere, transformed.

The practice below is one given to anyone in community to use for their own cleansing of their heavy energy. In my tradition, when someone needs further or deeper cleansing, they may go to a healer/Paqo for deeper work—much as we might go to a therapist if we have more than we can handle alone. This kind of energy healing can be done in many ways, but this practice is a baseline method that you can take and use in whatever way is useful to you.

Cleansing with Stones

Relax and meditate in a peaceful place and ask *Pachamama* (Mother Earth) to send you five stones for your cleansing. You can visualize what those stones might look like and where you will find them. We are connected to land that has meaning, is sacred, and brings us peace. For you this land might be a park or forest near you, a mountain or the land around a river, depending on the natural environments near you.

In the Q'ero Paqo tradition, we connect to the land through the four directions and the three planes of existence: the upper world or what some call the heavens or the wider cosmos; the middle world or earth; and the underworld, which is the place deep below the earth's crust in a place where cleansing and healing is done and where energy is recycled). We also connect to the land through the four animals of the four directions: the condor-upper world, the puma and the hummingbird-middle world, and the serpent-underworld. Each of those worlds has terrain that relates to them. So, for example, the serpent and undergoing cleansing practice is related to areas of water and the conduit for the serpent to enter the underworld with our heavy energy. To engage in this practice, bring into focus land that is grounding and peaceful for you and imagine finding your five stones in that natural place.

When you are ready, go outside into nature, to a place near to you and ideally with some meaning to you. I might be a park in which you like to walk, a river that calms you, a mountain or hillside that you connect with, but somewhere with some connection to you. Take your time to search out your five stones. If you don't have access to a natural place, then you can connect with stones in your home or backyard or garden. Collect stones that are small enough so that two or three of them can fit comfortably in your hand.

Take three of the five stones and put them in your right hand (*paña*) during the cleansing practice. They represent and work with Inca Huascar, who is a masculine energy conduit to the underworld and to the cleansing process. He was a warrior during the Incan times.

Leave the other two stones in your left hand (*lloque*) during the cleansing practice. They represent and work with Mama Sirena, known as the mermaid, who serves as the Queen of the underworld, which in Quechua is called *Ukju Pacha*.

Find a place in nature or in your own home that is peaceful and restful for you, a place where you won't be interrupted during your cleansing practice. With the stones in each hand, lift them up to your face and softly speak to them your intention for cleansing. What do you want to release? What is the *hucha* (heavy energy) that you want to let go of right now? Nature is our partner and relative in this practice and all practices. So, imagine the stones as your companions and support, listening and absorbing your intentions, and taking hold of what you want to release.

Like the sacred practice and principle of *ayni*—giving and receiving in equal measure—the stones are receiving your pain in this moment and are making it possible for you to release what you need to release. They are also the means or conduit for doing so. They will carry the heavy energies to the underworld (*Ukju Pacha*). They will work as a sponge, absorbing all the heavy energies from you. With gratitude, gently ask the stones for their help in this process of release and absorption. As you engage with this process of sharing your hurts, harms, and heaviness with the stones, be open: find forgiveness where you need it, apologize for any harms you might have done, and let go into the stones whatever it is you need to release. The strength of the cleansing, like any healing practice, is contingent upon your honesty and openheartedness.

When you feel you have said all you need to say to the stones and have found some lightness and release from letting go of what you are ready to release, then begin to rub your body with the stones in both hands, from the top of your head, down your midsection, arms, legs and to your toes, on both the front and back of your body. Sweep down your body as if you were sweeping away the remaining heavy energy that needs to be released to the earth beneath your feet and to *Ukju Pacha* beneath the earth. Do the sweeping action keeping in mind the intention of cleansing, strengthening, and energizing.

While cleansing/sweeping with the stones, repeat the word *Lluqsi* (pronounced: yuk-zi), which means "to clean." Say this three times in a row and then ask Inca Huascar and Mama Sirena (the two partners in protecting and facilitating access to *Ukju Pacha*) to help you in this cleansing. Ask the winds or *wayra* of *Ukju Pacha* to take this heavy energy away from you. The underworld will transform the heavy energy into light energy—recycling it back onto the earthly-middle world, known as *Kay Pacha*.

Everything serves a purpose, and even the energy that once weighed you down in its heaviness can be used for something new once it has been recycled and returned for its own new life. This, too, is the cyclical nature of *ayni*—giving and receiving in equal measure. The balance can be restored to the energy that once was so painful, and it, too, can be something new.

After you have completed this cleansing practice, throw the stones near a river, ocean, or lake, or bury them in your garden. If you don't have a garden, bury them outside, somewhere in the earth. This allows the stones themselves to be cleansed and restored from their labor, and they too will find new life. It is a way to honor their work and release them back to the nature from which they came—reciprocity and return.

For the Andean people who are descended from fifteenth-century Incas, stones are special. They are part of our *Apus* (mountain spirits). They are part of Mother Earth or *Pachamama*. To us, they are living and feeling beings who can hear us when we engage with them. In sacred practice, like all of nature, they can come to our aid and help us. The peoples of my ancestral cultures from the Andes communicated with the stones, an essential element of the mountains, and worked with them as part of spiritual and healing practices. The primary tool for healing and energy medicine practices in the Paqo healer's toolkit is the *mesa*, a set of stones we have collected from sacred places related to the four directions, the three planes of existence, and our own sacred experience of nature. This mesa we carry and work with throughout our lives as healers. This healing Andean practice is one that you and anyone can use, and this is shared with communities across the world to carry our people's wisdom into your life and to serve your healing needs.

This practice was shared with me by the Andean Q'eros Paqos and their ancestors, but I have expounded on the language, history, and terms to give you a full understanding of the practice. The following message is from the *Maestros* (teachers) of the Apaza lineage who shared the practice with you, with gratitude to them for their sacred wisdoms:

> *This is the time when everybody needs to learn how to rebalance their energy with their surroundings to avoid depression, stress, illness, and fear. We are all having a hard time that will bring new times of awakening for many, so we need to help to bring the ancient wisdom back.*

CHAPTER 8

Just for Today:

The 12 Steps, Community, and Recovery from Religious Injury and Spiritual Abuse

The wound is the place where the Light enters you.
—Rumi

In the fall of 2009, I moved from New Jersey to Southeast Florida. I landed in Delray Beach, Florida, unaware that it was the perfect spot in the universe for a trauma therapist to land. The addiction recovery industry, with the same desire for sunshine and summertime weather, had moved to Delray (and the surrounding Palm Beach County) decades previously and had created a large network of treatment centers, halfway houses, and an unusually lively addiction recovery community. Instead of one meeting in a church basement once a week, in Delray there was a meeting every hour, on the hour, if you were in the market for it. In truth, besides some of my few individual clients, I had little interaction with the addiction recovery community and the 12-Step methodology of Alcoholics Anonymous (A.A.) as a community dynamic. It was one of the greatest gifts to be immersed in it. Of course, like any group with tenets and doctrine, there are the fundamentalists in recovery. But what I found besides that was a caretaking community of young adults in their twenties and thirties, people who would have been anomalous and possibly outcasts in their home cities across the country where a twenty-something who avoids a glass or three of wine or a cocktail on a Friday night is considered strange, or even unwelcome. However, in Southeast Florida, people were willing to help their neighbors and even strangers; they held no judgment for people's past life errors, pains, or hurts; and, they offered unconditional acceptance. In many ways, they mirrored for me everything for which I had hoped in religious or spiritual communities on the best of days. Much like a system of belief, of course, there were the zealots, egomaniacs, fundamentalists, and condescending personalities. However, the system and doctrine as a whole offered something powerful that I thought was important to explore. In fact in Delray, if you met someone who was not in recovery, it was kind of unusual.

It felt incredible to connect to this unique subculture that had valuable wisdom to offer, not only to those in recovery but also to the wider community. Indeed, when we connect across different spiritual contexts and share our wisdom, we can be exposed to systems and communities that have much to offer us. The 12-Steps is one such system and community for which I am forever grateful. During that time, immersed in a community of recovery and studying the steps, I realized that we are all in recovery from something, not least are those of us healing from trauma and emotional wounds. The 12-Steps are a tool from which I think we can all benefit, and with that intent I share with you a spiritual trauma-conscious approach to the 12-Steps for your own journey or that of someone you are accompanying.

A 12-Step Path

Don't walk this path alone. In the traditional recovery model, this journey is meant to happen in community and, at the very least, in partnership with another person. This is for both support and accountability. To be this vulnerable, we need to have someone who says it is OK to do so, and that person will hold safe space and unconditional love for us throughout the process. If you have a group or community with whom you have been sharing your painful journey—especially other survivors—you might want to walk the steps together with them. If you have a mentor, therapist, or life partner, you might want to walk with them through these steps as a support.

If you are in a traditional addiction recovery, or recovery for codependence, an eating disorder, or sex addiction, or in some other 12-Step program, you might want to move through these trauma-conscious steps for religious and spiritual trauma with your existing sponsor or a new sponsor who might be better suited for this process. If you are in some kind of spiritual support program or working with a spiritual or emotional care provider, you could work with that person through the twelve steps. The key is to have support and companionship on the journey.

12 Steps for the Religious Injury and Spiritual Trauma Experience

1. **We admit we are being hurt by our human addictive nature manifesting as addictive/compulsive response to others and as our hurt and anger, and to unhealthy systems, communities, and leaders. We admit that our lives have become controlled by whatever we are holding onto addictively.** We all have inherent addiction and compulsions we follow, often to stop hurt, and sometimes to numb ourselves just to survive another day. I often say that smoking is a breathing exercise with consequences. Traumatic response is like that. Whether we self-medicate with drugs or alcohol, with emotional numbing or dissociation, or with panic attacks or rage, they are all coping skills with consequences. We become addicted to our feelings, to our hurt, and to our response to traumatic experience. Sometimes we are still nursing addiction to and the suffering caused by a system/leader who influenced us to rely on them to cope with life. Sometimes the system we were in is the addiction we are now trying to kick. Whatever it is, the addiction is just our human ego trying to find a place to act out its neuroses or narcissism. There is something or some things in our way of which we need to let go. Find what those are for you. See what it feels like to stop trying to get rid of it or them alone. For as a good friend reminds me, "We are wounded in isolation; we heal in community." First, we give up our assumption that we can control everything ourselves, and then we grow in a healthy version of community and/or mentorship to find a healthier way to live.

2. **We come to believe that a power outside of ourselves (God, the universe, the cosmos, that which can transform me) can restore us to wholeness and health.** Whatever it is that is greater than our own fear, anxiety, anger, or ambition can help us heal. For you, this power may be moral, religious, or philosophical. It could be something that a wisdom teacher or close friend is offering you. In any case, it is something greater than what we already know. This power will guide your growth and transformation. When we believe we are the ultimate source of all our answers, even if we believe that merely out of fear, we

can become like the institutions or false gurus of certitude we left behind. To avoid that, we all have to find reference points greater than us, and greater than what we know today, to guide us forward. Consider who, what, and where you can find those in your own current life.

3. **Make a decision to seek safe space, acceptance, and guidance from the Power outside of ourselves (God, the universe, the cosmos, that which can transform me), and that which manifests as this Power in the world (wisdom teachers, communities, helping professionals, and texts that expand our awareness of self and others, and help us find safety and healing).** Especially in early healing and recovery and even more so if we have been hurt by other people or people groups, our process of licking our wounds becomes private. This itself can lead to feelings of pain, guilt, depression, sadness, grief, loss, and anger, which bubble inside us without any vent or external resources to help us through the pain. It is essential to find a safe space or spaces with others, master teachers, therapists, or trusted friends who can help us see beyond the pain and find the beginning path to healing. Find that which feeds and provides you with unconditional love and acceptance, and nurture yourself while you heal in that space.

4. **Make a searching and fearless moral inventory of ourselves to see unhealthy actions, patterns, and behaviors and how they manifest in our own lives so that we are not doomed to repeat them.** In the early stages, we can be tempted to close ourselves off from others as a self-protection mechanism and not see beyond the pain of having been hurt. This doesn't help us move forward on a path toward healing, wholeness, and discovering our truest and most authentic self. Part of transformation entails having the introspection to see our own unhealthy patterns. Such patterns often arise from the trauma experience, from what an abuser said or imposed, and from whatever protective mechanisms we created that are no longer serving us. Seeing ourselves clearly and honestly is a key part to our own healing, growth, and development.

5. **Admit to the power outside of ourselves (God, the universe, the cosmos, anything that can transform me), to ourselves,**

and to another human being the exact nature of our hurt, broken places, trauma, regret, and moral indiscretions of the past, and how that has affected ourselves and others in our lives.** This admission can include telling our stories, but it is also more than just telling; it is telling in a way that is vulnerable, honest, humble, and transparent about our journey and hurting places in our life. It also means we have to see how our pain journey has affected others and ourselves. Part of any process of transformation, like any version of the twelve steps and in particular like this version created around the specific issues of religious injury and trauma, entails taking things at your own pace. Like all the rest, this step also brings its own sense of difficulty. Be kind to yourself. If you are not ready to admit the exact nature of your hurt—hold off. And remember that the greatest benefit of this entire 12-step process is that it is meant to be personal but also communal. Share the journey with someone—a therapist, teacher, or confidant. You don't have to walk into these difficult places alone.

6. **Become open to transforming ourselves with the help of the Power outside of ourselves (God, the universe, the cosmos, that which can transform me), and be willing to do the work to let go of whatever we are holding onto from our past that is holding us back or keeping us inside our pain and pain experience.** This step is a preparation for the work of the steps that follow. We have to be ready and willing to heal and let go of what is still hurting us about our past. That doesn't mean forgetting. It doesn't mean not speaking out. And it doesn't mean not seeking justice. It simply means that transformative speech, actions, justice, and living are most beneficial if they come from a healed and transformed heart. This means we have to be willing to do the work to let go of the pain, suffering, and anger of our past hurt to do better in our lives for ourselves and others. It will happen not all at once but in bits and pieces, one step at a time.

7. **With the support of others, our own intention, and the Power outside of ourselves (God, the universe, the cosmos, that which can transform me), work to remove from our minds, hearts, and spirits those things (listed earlier) that**

haven't served us, our lives, or others, and remove the heaviness on our conscience about these issues. **We give ourselves permission to forgive ourselves for anything we are holding onto about ourselves and our actions.** This is the next layer of willingness and preparation: to prepare our hearts, minds, and spirits to let go of past behaviors and feelings that aren't serving us, and to prepare ourselves to be able to offer forgiveness for the wrongs done to us, an action that is more for our benefit and healing than anything else, for to be unforgiving is a heavy load to carry.

8. **Make a list of all persons we have harmed and become willing to make amends to them all. Make a list of all persons who have harmed us and become willing to offer forgiveness to them.** Though this step merely entails writing the list, this in itself can be taxing. It is preparation for offering to make amends to people or, if you choose, forgiveness. Write the lists honestly and authentically and be gentle with yourself in the process.

9. **Make direct amends to such people whenever possible, except when to do so would injure them, others, or us (if it is currently not emotionally safe to do so in the present). Make a conscious effort to forgive those persons, communities, or institutions that are holding onto hate and unforgiveness. This does not mean they are not culpable; it just means we won't carry in our minds, hearts, and spirits the burden of their wrong deeds.** To make amends and to forgive are difficult things to do. Doing so may take time, and some people/actions on our lists may take time to address. With trauma, especially hurtful community trauma, this may or may not include an actual formal forgiveness to others. For some people that serves a purpose or is a public catharsis. For others, the forgiveness will be private and personal and may just happen in their hearts. Sometimes forgiving someone might include writing a letter that is never mailed to the person[s] you want to forgive. The forgiveness you get unburdens your heart; the forgiveness you give does the same. Regret and unforgiveness are heavy burdens to carry, and one of the hardest ingredients of whole person healing is the inner process of reconciliation.

10. **Continue to be aware of our actions and motives, and work to remove those things that hurt ourselves or others and are not serving us when we act from an unhealthy, angry, or wounded place. To keep ourselves honest and transparent about what we do and why we do it, we will also admit when we have acted from those unhealthy, angry, or wounded places.** To continue on the healing path, to stay humble, and to grow and transform, we have to be honest and authentic with others and with ourselves. If we don't, our process of healing and growth will stagnate, and we will become entrenched in one way of thinking about ourselves and acting in the world. Constant review of ourselves, our patterns, and behaviors is vital to a full and whole life.

11. **Employ contemplative methods and practices (mindfulness, meditation, contemplative prayer, etc.) to improve our awareness, consciousness, healing, and transformation as well as to connect with the Power outside of ourselves, whatever we call it (God, the universe, the cosmos, that which can transform me). Engage in these practices to increase insight and connect with our true and authentic self so that we continue to act out of that authentic place and not out of our hurts or anger.** Contemplative practice and mindfulness are essential pieces of a balanced life. That is why this practice was in the 12-step traditions from the start, why the contemplatives and mystics from every religious tradition around the world include long lineages of contemplative practice, and why even the contemporary mental health community is integrating mindfulness and contemplation in the treatment of mental health conditions from depression to anxiety to PTSD. How you practice contemplation in your life is up to you. It can include breathing exercises, mindful nature walks, contemplative prayer, or Eastern meditation practices, for example. Find the contemplative path that best fits you and your life, and engage with it deeply and regularly. It is a critical route to authenticity, transparency, and transformative healing.

12. **Having achieved spiritual insight and awakening, or some form of personal transformation as a result of these steps, we practice offering the message and practice of these steps**

to others healing from hurt and seeking personal transformation out of their own addiction (to self, others, hurt, unhealthy systems or feelings, etc.). We continue to practice the principles of these twelve steps in our daily lives, increasing our insight and becoming more aware of and connected to our authentic self as we move deeper into our healing. We are most whole when we can take what we have received and give it away in some fashion. Share these principles, your journey, and others' healing paths. Help others along the way with what you have learned so far; you would be amazed how much you can help. You are valuable, and someone else walking your same path needs your help. Reach out, build community, and be honest and vulnerable enough to help others in community and in companionship.

There is great wisdom in these principles. I have seen their content transform lives decimated by addiction and trauma. Like anything, these steps aren't a one-stop-shop for healing. Nor are they the only method useful for your healing journey. As we transform, we need a variety of things to meet us at each point in the road. But each of these methods can be a great tool for self-discovery when integrated into a healthy path of healing and recovery. You can also explore other methods of recovery online. There are meetings all across the country for a great variety of 12-step programs.

CHAPTER 9

The Voices Out of Darkness:

Messages from Survivors to Survivors and Spiritual and Religious Communities

He who sees all beings in his Self and his Self in all beings, he never suffers; because when he sees all creatures within his true Self, then jealousy, grief, and hatred vanish.

—The Upanishads

To make the voices of those who have been hurt and are now healing central to this book's narrative is not only powerful, but the most effective way I know to support those suffering from religious injury. Nor is anyone else better equipped both to speak to others in faith traditions who are suffering, and to build healthier spiritual communities. I hope this book has given such pivotal people the tools to create nurturing environments for wounded souls and hurt hearts.

In this section of the book, I once again foreground the voices of those who have been wounded speaking to others who are currently suffering sacred wounds. Through those voices, this section then speaks to those in religious and spiritual communities who wish to understand and nurture those who have been hurt, and who ardently want to do better in their own spaces and support those healing. In short, this chapter is from and to survivors and to communities who wish to support them.

TO SURVIVORS…

THE QUESTION ASKED: *What do you wish people who are being hurt by their spiritual or religious communities could know?*

HOPE: What I would like to tell people currently being hurt by their faith communities is two things: 1) God sees and knows, and *He will* avenge the wrong things done to them in His time. The truth will come out some day. And 2) Don't ever let go of God, even if people claiming to be his representatives are blowing it horridly. God is not to blame for the wrongdoing and the pain, and He can and will redeem it in our lives if we are patient.

I would like people to know that *they are worthy of finding a healthy church*. It took us a *long* time to wait for God to show us a healthy church (where we have been now for a long time), but it was worth the wait. When we stopped trying to be *members* in a denomination of our choice (the one we were in), we could focus on listening to God and watch what a healthy church looked like.

MELINDA: I wish [those being hurt] could know that people can be shitty. Shitty stuff happens. If the way you were treated is/was illegal, then the perpetrator should be prosecuted to the full extent of the law. I wish they could know that the strength to heal is inside them, and they are totally worth it.

KISHA: What I tell anyone who at any time feels unsafe in their faith community is two words: *Get out.* I am almost never that direct regarding anything else in life, and I am extremely evasive when it comes to giving people advice. However, people's safety is of *huge* concern to me, and I will *never* be silent when it comes to protecting someone else's safety and well-being. I have a zero-tolerance policy for other people's victimization to abuse and maltreatment.

DEANNA: Give yourself time. It's the worst prescription and the best one. Let yourself grieve whatever beliefs you are leaving, because it is not an easy transition. Let yourself just *be*. If you can't go to church today, that's okay. If you can't open your Bible today, that's okay too. Cling to those around you who make you feel safe and loved for exactly who you are. God is in the midst of those hugs and tears, and that laughter around the dinner table. Take time to examine yourself and your heart. What triggers you? What doesn't? Where does it hurt and why? The more you can articulate this—and it [can] sometimes… take years of work, so don't get frustrated with yourself when you can't pinpoint it overnight—the better you will be able to find a new path.

KATE: I think there is a deep need for communities of meaning. People need others they can count on. People need to be challenged to live out their values in an ever-wider circles of influence.

MARG: No one could have told me anything that would have helped for many years. But once I got sober, the best thing anyone could have said to me was what Katherine Unthank said in that workshop. In essence, "You have suffered a debilitating trauma, and your life has been forever changed by it." Almost as important…is what Nancy Hardesty [said] to me later, "You are always welcome at Her table."

BILL: For people hurt by faith, there are some terribly abusive situations, and people need to get out of those. If your faith is causing you pain in any way, you should pursue things that make you feel alive and whole, as long as it is healthy [and] not hurtful. Whatever that is, do it. When you find things that make you more whole, whatever it is, pursue that. If you are more despondent doing something, you need to be able to drop that thing. I think that applies [to] faith/tradition. I also understand that church/faith communities are human institutions and whatever community you find will have those same dynamics. You are going to have the same relational dynamics in your context. There will be disappointment, betrayal, and hurt anywhere. For anyone who has the courage to keep slogging through that to find a faith community, I think that is also a wonderful thing.

TO SPIRITUAL AND RELIGIOUS COMMUNITIES…

THE QUESTION ASKED: *What do you wish people in religion/spiritual culture could understand about how they treat people in general and those who are wounded? How do you think they should treat people who have been wounded?*

HOPE: I wish people would understand that a little love and patience goes a long way…In our case…the church [decided that] our son was "out of control." He was not, but he is on the autism spectrum, and it took him *much* longer to learn things, and it was much harder for him than it was for a neurotypical child. Had they tried to be more patient and understanding and had they been trustworthy and respectful, things would have been so different. We wanted to stay there. We deeply grieved being kicked out, and the pain, though healed in many ways by God after fifteen years, is *still* now there on some very deep levels; and, I think to some extent it will be until we get to heaven where God wipes away all tears. What I wish someone from that church had told me [is] that the church knew the truth and was going to stand on it. Instead, the people admitted to us that they were "confused" and that the "only thing we know to do is to submit." So they *knew* that something stunk but went along with it. I can't do that. If I think something stinks, I have to...take a stand, even if it costs me.

MELINDA: Listen better. Hear victims out. Listen more. Listen again. Listen until they are done telling the whole story. And then be the embodiment of empathy.

DAVID: My hope is not holding onto our scriptures rather than a person. My hope is for faith communities to be more open-minded, [to] have a bigger mindset, and [to] be able to break out of the old paradigms. I believe [that] thinking and feeling big can change the world. That is what I am hoping for and trying to contribute to—critiquing limiting styles in the church and helping people to be independent and interdependent. I think the mindset should be, "Out with the bad and in with the good."

KISHA: Ministry is as much about what God wants to do *in* you as it is about what He wants to do *through* you. Meanwhile, for those within religious systems who believe they can "fix" others, please stop. Physician, heal thyself! Love people where they are, receive grace for yourself, and then extend it to others. That's about all you are equipped to do, and in most unhealed circumstances, that is all that is needed: community.

FAY: Stop shooting their wounded! Listen before you speak! Be There! Cut out the clichéd answers and interpretations of scripture out of context to offer words of wisdom. I wish I had been told I was loved more than their fears and their own feelings and judgments. Rebuilding and forgiveness come from admitting wrongs.

DEANNA: One thing: If you care about the doctrine more than the person, you are doing it wrong. Countless times throughout the Gospels, Jesus violated the rules in order to take care of people. I think we need to treat one another like neighbors first. Religion and doctrine come later, not the other way around. There is too much false information about other faith groups, and it is breeding fear and hate, which lead to violence. We are all on this earth here together. We are here for one another, and we need to start acting like it. I remember talking to my mother about going on a trip with an organization that helps child soldiers in Uganda. The first thing out of her mouth was, "Are they a Christian organization?" I said I didn't know for sure, but that they were doing really great work. She said that there wasn't really a point in going if they didn't share this gospel. This is a really common viewpoint by many Christians, but it is a toxic one. It says that God does not care about the basic human needs of "unbelievers." That could not be further from the truth. The God I know cares less about your rightness of theology and more about not enslaving small children. He cares more about providing water for the residents of Detroit and pulling women out of human trafficking. To *ever* suggest otherwise is to blaspheme the heart of God. I don't often use the word "blasphemy," but I truly believe this. I don't know much, but I do know that.

DEB: When people are representing themselves as an authority on God and Christianity, they have a lot of responsibility to their followers to make sure they are getting the right message. I wish they would realize [that] they are playing a key part in influencing the faith of those [outside of that community] who may not know what it is…I have been told many times to give my pain to God. What is difficult about that is knowing that God is an all-knowing God. He knows my pain. He saw me go through it. If he wanted me to give him my pain, why would he allow me to have it in the first place? I think that communities need to realize there is true damage that can be done to someone's psyche, and the answer is not as simple as giving it up to God. Thankfully God allows us to be smart enough to have professionals who can help you on your healing journey, but mental health issues have always been dismissed as something that can be cured by having faith in God.

KATE: Well, I wish someone on the Plymouth staff had called to say goodbye instead of maintaining radio silence after I asked to be taken off their membership list. You'd think that twenty-five years of volunteering, financial support, leadership roles, etc., would merit a "Thank you; we're sorry to see you go." I think churches should be generous when members move on—they should find ways to express thanks and offer sincere good wishes. It hurt me when they let my husband leave without so much as a "see you around." It hurt me when they treated me the same way six months later.

JULIE: I've always been surprised [that] people in the church and especially leaders don't want to know why you left or changed your beliefs. They don't want to hear your story. They just want to tell you how wrong/sinful you are. But then some of the people who loved and really helped us were also Christian leaders. They were a blatant exception, but I'll always be really thankful for them.

MARG: How you treat the least of your fellow human beings defines the nature of your faith. Isolating from, attacking, and denigrating LGBTQ people ruins Jesus for us and devalues the Gospel. I don't think the result of anything, any policy, or any practice, should ever be something that ruins Jesus for anyone. What can faith communities do? Recognize that LGBT people suffer from deep spiritual wounds…almost every single one of us does. For many of us, well, I'm not sure those wounds will ever fully heal; they just become part of our story. Faith communities must intentionally validate our struggle, and conscientiously participate in the efforts to challenge the views and interpretations of scripture that enable this spiritual wounding to continue. To stand by and allow this attack on an entire group of people to continue unchallenged is implicitly to demean our humanity. Faith communities must admit the reality of the trauma we have suffered at the hands of Christian people. They must recognize this has left us with special issues regarding trust, fear, and the perception of how we are being treated. They must be patient and forgiving when these issues affect how we behave. Faith communities must recognize [that] these wounds do not heal themselves over time. They only fester. So, we must be encouraged to tell our stories when we are able to do so. People of faith must listen intently to the stories of the LGBT people in their midst. Christians must admit their own part in perpetrating the injury or allowing it to happen. LGBT people may even be able to respond with authentic words of forgiveness at times. These wounds we carry will simply not heal when they are closed up and left untended. The wounds we carry must be lovingly tended to with genuine compassion. Faith communities must strive to love LGBT people with abandon and appreciate the unique voice we bring to the table.

DAVE: Every single religion that believes in a God believes in a God who creates love and structure in their lives. So why would you ever want to confuse the kids walking into your church and make them think God is anything but love and acceptance? What is the purpose of [that]? Don't tarnish other people's beliefs and choices. What is the purpose of doing that? All organized religions need to understand [that] everyone may believe something a little different, and they, like us, are entitled to believe in that system. There are many disciples for many different traditions out there, and it doesn't mean one is wrong and one is right; so, why don't we just keep it that way? If I like chocolate milk, and someone likes vanilla; then, enjoy your milk, and I will enjoy mine. Now, strawberry milk makes me sick, but I don't go around knocking strawberry milk out of other people's hands. They are all milk, and they are all real. We can't say any one of them doesn't exist. I like religions that say, "These are my beliefs; they don't have to be your beliefs," and are welcoming. God is about acceptance because everyone is flawed and everyone sins, and when people make a mistake, you don't want to be made to feel you are going to hell over it. I think God accepts everyone, and I want to do the same.

BILL: In my age group and demographic, a lot of people are the "nones" [spiritual but not religious] and they are leaving church. So, I think whenever anyone shows up at a faith community, it should be seen as a great honor; and the community should offer hospitality rather than leaving someone to find their way. The community should have sensibilities about others. If I invited you over for dinner, and then I just sit down and start eating as you are standing there with your coat on, leaving you to figure it all out, that would not be hospitable. Or if I have a ritual at my dinner table, and I don't explain what is going to happen, that is not hospitable. I am responsible to help you land in my home. Faith communities I have been a part of have been like, "We are eating dinner and I may acknowledge you, but I'm doing my thing." For me it is all about hospitality and empathy. If you never saw football and went to the Super Bowl, your head would explode. It is all symbolic, and helping people learn the symbols and meanings is a faith community's responsibility.

CHAPTER 10

Extremism and the Religious Trauma that Touches Us All:

The Socio-Political-Religious Dynamics of the Rise of Christian Nationalism

This chapter is an unenviable addition to this second edition of *Sacred Wounds*. When I wrote the original book, the expression of spiritual and religious trauma most visible was the individually experienced incidents of trauma, mainly those from the inside of extremist and fundamentalist religious or spiritual contexts. In the intervening decade we have seen the rise of Christian Nationalism, which is inextricably linked to White Nationalism—something we can see play out in the dynamics of many of the stories of spiritual and religious trauma. The dynamics of power and privilege and how they express themselves in extremist religious and spiritual spaces against those with the least access to power is not a function of coincidence, but of intention. They are an invention with purpose by those at the top.

Though not surprising, it is still shocking a decade after this book's first publication to witness the national level (in the United States) and global expression (in many Western and authoritarian-leaning nations around the world) of this kind of extremism getting into the bloodstream of the social-political sphere and eventually the wider culture in dangerous ways. I realize that this is not without historical patterns and precedents. But as a trauma studies professional and not a political scientist or historian, I will reflect on this phenomenology through the framework of religious trauma, its mechanisms, and the impact of such extremism today.

The previous chapters focused on how the experience of religious and spiritual trauma affects the individual located within an extremist religious group. The ones most harmed are the ones close to the center, inside the community group. In the case of Christian nationalism and the violent and hateful leanings of its branches, that impact is not most expressed by the extremists on those inside the cult phenomenon but on those outside, in the wider culture.

Christian nationalism, which has merged with domestic terrorism, creates a dual membership to this cult of belief founded on white supremacy, homophobia, transphobia, and global isolationism, all to be attained by any means necessary, and with political extremism, along the lines of shared identity. The volatility of this specific cult hybrid has a ripple effect of collective religious traumatic impact on any bystander outside of it. Like being in the blast radius of religious dogma-driven zealotry, we are all knocked off our feet by the concussion blast. Consequently, we are in a period of collective religious trauma, one in which we carry the impact of the concussion blasts with us, resulting in a collective experience of exhaustion, anxiety, depression, and triggering.

This merging of political and religious extremism that at its worst becomes domestic terrorism is terrifying but certainly not incomprehensible. I spoke earlier of the false guru versus the wisdom teacher. While it is rare that someone ticks all the boxes in the false guru category, some of our most visible national and global figures of religious-political extremism and nationalism easily tick every single one. They are the caricature of the caricature of the false guru—and as a result are both calculatingly intentional in their actions and completely incapable of caring about how their actions affect others. This makes them the most dangerous form of false guru. Once people have been fully indoctrinated into this level of religious and political extremism, they are extremely difficult to deprogram.

So, the issue is not just the individual at the top, but the level of harm and trauma the many followers can cause. While the figure at the top understands he (and it's usually a he) is the man behind the curtain, all smoke and mirrors, his brainwashed disciples do not. Furthermore, when the core premise of all this person's teachings is hateful ideology, the man behind the curtain simply gives a permission structure for everyone to act out of their worst inclinations. It is a cult built on the philosophy that drove people in the movie aptly named, "The Purge." The point is destruction and, eventually, the doctrine or beliefs upon which the hate and destruction are built on is just window dressing for that hate.

This makes such a false guru particularly dangerous; whereas, the religious cult leader in isolation only does harm to its cult members and is often isolated from the wider world so as not to be vulnerable to its laws or consequences, the religious-political zealot doesn't fear the law, and does his work visibly. This makes him dangerous not just to his followers—who still risk expulsion, shame, or punishment if they go against the dictates of the leader—but dangerous to the wider public as well. Yet often first in the line of fire are those minorities at whom the leader primarily directs his vitriol.

Many of this book's anecdotes of spiritual and religious trauma were examples of people being harmed or denigrated within a particular religious or spiritual tradition because of their identity as a woman or marginalized gender, a queer or trans person, a person of color, or some other element of their identity that made them the other in the eyes of the community. In the religious-political cult anyone and everyone can be on that particular chopping block, and, again, not just those in the community, but anyone, anywhere, any time. This makes them a much wider threat.

Shortly after *Sacred Wounds* was first published, I was doing more work supporting trauma care for those in social movements. On August 11, 2017, early in the evening central time, I was in the middle of a workshop in Chicago for healers and activists/organizers. I was teaching my model of development and harm related to what I was defining as social movement trauma. Like me, many of the folks in the room worked with faith-rooted organizers as well as others in movements around the country, and had friends on the ground in Charlottesville, Virginia. The "Unite the Right" Rally for Confederate statue enthusiasts, centered around the removal of a statue of Robert E. Lee, was set for that Saturday, August 11, so most of us didn't expect anything unusual to happen on that Friday evening. The organizers of this rally were a mix of local and national White Supremacists and Christian nationalists, and they had decided to begin their festivities a day early with what is now an infamous and chillingly iconic tiki torch rally. Many people in the room in Chicago with friends on the ground in Charlottesville knew that people were gathering at a local church for speeches by faith leaders, the faith and secular organizers of the opposition to the rally, and a variety of other people from across the country who were planning to stand in opposition to the White Christian Nationalism marching through the town the next day.

Suddenly, people's phones around the room began to ping with text alerts. We began receiving social media feeds with videos and updates on what was happening at that moment in Charlottesville. The tiki torch Neo-Nazi collective was surrounding the church and the campus of University of Virginia. Out front student and local movement organizers were being surrounded by the torch-bearers as they chanted hateful rhetoric reminiscent of both the Nazis in Germany, the White nationalists, and Jim Crow enthusiasts of the Old American South. Here we were, a gathering of people working to support faith and civic social movements, and all we could do in that moment was sit together in that room in Chicago and wait for the next tweet. There are moments where you know viscerally that something is turning, shifting, and changing. Even hundreds of miles away from ground zero of this tectonic change, we could feel the ground beneath us move. It was reminiscent of pasts to which we didn't want to return, but it was also something frighteningly new. Something had shifted.

I remember a well-known faith leader saying to me, a couple of weeks later, when we ran across each other while speaking at a different gathering, "You know the difference from when I was a child? During the Civil Rights era, the Klan wore masks to hide their faces. They aren't even afraid to be seen now. That's what really scares me."

There was something particularly alarming about the public and visible nature of this movement that was arising and collectivizing. Like the false guru who isn't afraid of the law, members of this movement seemed to believe their actions were beyond repercussions, and they were stretching their arms, testing to see how for that autonomy reached. Like the raptors in Jurassic Park, they had evolved from their past iterations: they were testing the strength of the fences and finding the weak spots.

The next day in Charlottesville, Heather Heyer was murdered after a Unite the Right extremist drove through a group, and many others were injured physically and scarred emotionally. Colleagues of mine who were leading the faith movement organizing locally asked me to join them, and by Sunday I was on my way to Charlottesville. There is much to say about my time there—the pain and the fear I encountered, the division and fracturing under the pressure, and the heroics of those who were standing up against hate even when there was a new Klan, aligned with political and religious extremism. I spent a little less than a week there, and I remember continuing to feel as if something drastic was happening and something was coming to life in a new way that we hadn't seen before and didn't yet fully understand.

In the years since then, I have seen all the signs I once found only in secret and private places of religious extremism, fundamentalism, and spiritual cults now living loud and proud in public. Each season bringing greater ferocity, greater allegiance to the cause, less connection to a reality outside of the cult of misinformation, and increased hate, bigotry, and repression tethered to religious extremism. It has become a new thing—politics and religious fundamentalism as a hybrid doctrine, one that has torn down all the protective democratic fences.

I remember wondering when the rhetoric would come that would fully deify the political leaders and be completely direct about the line between politics and divine calling. I knew it was coming because it was the final step in the merger between two disparate things into a cohesive idolatry. When it happened, I was watching national news and a person came on, at a Trump rally, being interviewed about why they were a supporter. This person said, "Jesus came to save us and died on the cross for us. He is sacrificing himself and is showing us the way."

Period. Full stop. And the merger was complete.

Then those statements began to fall like a waterfall, in interview after interview—the divine in human form, the sacrifice of the Chosen One. It was all there: the religious cult blueprint fused with a political figure and social identity.

The great danger of this new strain of Christian nationalism in the United States is that if something is said to be ordained by God, among adherents this in itself is a permission structure for any action. Nothing is off the table. Because it is for God and of God, whatever the action, it is allegedly and inherently good and Godly. This kind of belief structure is why national terrorism is one of the greatest threats in the United States of America.

We simply must not underestimate the impact of this rising national and global phenomenon. We have to take time to study it more deeply, to mine our histories for examples of when it succeeded and when it failed, and envision an alternative that is bigger and more beautiful than hate ever can be.

Demystification and Education

As we watch this dangerous evolution in real time, as we observe the merging of two strains of equally virulent diseases—the extreme political movement and the extreme religious movement—there are a few things we—you, dear reader— can do to demystify and protect ourselves.

1. **Educate yourself and others on the false guru phenomenon.** Expose the man behind the curtain and the emperor with no clothes. Demystifying the phenomenon of the false guru means explaining what is actually happening behind the curtain. Facts, education, and knowledge are the starting place for true power.

2. **Don't live in a complete silo.** *Unless it is harmful to you*, have conversations across differences. Relationship is the greatest means of transformation—for ourselves and others. Being in relationship with someone with whom we fundamentally do not agree with can stretch us to look critically at ourselves and be more empathetic toward others. Being in relationship is a starting place to chip away at the edges of some of the brainwashing culture in our own midst. But avoid such relationships if they are likely to denigrate your own identity. For example: A heterosexual cisgendered man speaking to another heterosexual cisgender man who has a different opinion on global politics is speaking across difference. A heterosexual cisgender man who believes being queer/trans means you go to hell speaking to a queer or trans person may be emotionally or, in extreme cases, physically dangerous to that person. There are limits that we have to set for our own safety, and that is important and ok. Someone else for whom it is not dangerous can have that conversation.

3. **Believe beyond the limits of what we know is possible. Be an Ethnofuturist.** The practice of ethnofuturism, rooted in Afrofuturism, refers to building a world based on the strengths and wisdoms of our ancestors, with the forethought for what is needed for the future, and by beginning to live into that in the present. Sometimes, when the world feels bleak, we can lose our power to imagine beyond what already is and what we think is possible. Let go of what is and what is possible! Ask:

What is beyond what feels possible or accessible right now? What keys to life, thriving, and liberation did our ancestors give us that we have forgotten or lost along the way? What can we reclaim to bring us our own intergenerational resilience, healing, and innovation for tomorrow? How do we live into that as a possible future, today, one step at a time? Dream big and don't give up.

CHAPTER 11

Contigo, Conmigo: Moving Forward Together

Allyship and Accountability for Survivors of Spiritual/Religious Trauma

Spiritual and religious harm turns up in every tradition and spiritual lineage. That is just a fact. I know many people who were studying with teachers that they felt taught them powerful spiritual tools and helped them on their own spiritual journey—only to find out later that they had done harm to other people—more than once. Places that hurt can also teach—and that is heartbreaking, too. Moreover, we each have the potential to do harm, as a result of our ignorance, the limitations of our lived experience, or carelessness on our part. This happens every day. We want to do the best we can and exist in places without harm or blemish, but we live in a human world, and we can't guarantee any of those things. We are human beings and so we will mess up.

Our own imperfection and potential to do harm is the premise on which we have to begin any conversation about allyship, because it can't come from a place of spiritual or intellectual superiority. If we can start from the premise of imperfection—our own and that of our communities—then we are in a good place to begin the journey towards authentic allyship. It will require immense work and personal growth. Making ourselves the least harmful will demand critical analysis and asking hard questions of ourselves and our own communities.

One of my high school English teachers really brought my love of reading and writing alive in a new and grown-up way. He exposed us to young adult books with intense and complex themes, books outside the curriculum of my previous teachers. I thought he was so cool and countercultural for opening us up to a worldview and type of storytelling that was more expansive than anything I had experienced before. One of the books he gave us to read gave me the permission to write about deeply personal things and think about the world in new ways. It told the story of a complicated teen girl to whom I related better than any other character I had read before. I was so grateful to him. He made me think I might want to be an English teacher and offer others what he gave me.

Yet shortly after graduation, a classmate shared with me how this very teacher had been sexually inappropriate with her, flirting and touching her in an intimate manner that was deeply and understandably uncomfortable for her. Later, I found out after that she wasn't the first and she wasn't the last. Unfortunately, this wasn't the first or only teacher of mine who was sexually inappropriate with students. But this one broke my heart more than the others because he had meant something to me. His teaching and wisdom had deepened my life and my practice of reading and writing. At the age of seventeen, I had no idea how to hold the tension between someone who had deeply affected me for good and all the bad he had done.

I later learned that it is not unusual for people and also systems of belief both to be wise and to be capable of immense harm. Think of the relationship between Christianity and the Doctrine of Discovery, a relationship that "gave permission" for slavery and genocide through a distorted understanding of divine right. Does that mean that everything that has ever been done in Christianity is horrific and that it has changed no one for the good? No. Does it require atonement and accountability? Absolutely. It is important to understand the complexity in ourselves, in our systems of belief and spiritual understanding, and in the teachers within those traditions: we are human, and we can do harm. Sometimes, when a person allows themselves to be carried away by power or ego or their "shadow self," they can do great harm. This doesn't mean there isn't good in them as well.

The complexity of allyship begins with owning our humanity and, crucially, not being defensive or uncritical about our own wisdom traditions. By doing so, we can build healthier and more resilient communities and relationships between those who have been harmed and everyone else.

***

Many of the people who read the first edition of *Sacred Wounds* and invited me to speak or teach to their communities were leaders of spiritual or religious communities, chaplains, spiritual care providers of some kind, or mental health care providers. I intend the guidance throughout the book to support both those struggling through spiritual trauma and those who seek to support them. In this second edition of the book, I expand that goal by suggesting two important additional goals.

The first new goal and process creates equitable, accountable, and protective spaces for people to engage with spiritual or religious community. This applies to any community space, but it leaves room and a permission structure for those who have been harmed to show up and feel represented, heard and seen—and a process to address when harm might still happen. I often hear from leaders of progressive spiritual or religious communities who report that many people came to their spaces looking for safety after being in unhealthy and abusive religious contexts. But often even small harms would trigger the person's past, and the community leaders and members wouldn't know how to address their trauma. The person would leave, and the cycle would often repeat itself elsewhere. The "Practice of Protected Space" is an ethic I share as a way to stave off this pattern and repetition.

The second new goal and process addresses a community, organization's, or leader's serious, repeated harm in a way that addresses the harm at all levels: its current impact on the survivors, its future impact on survivors, its impact on the organization if harm continues to happen, and building capacity to stave off the possibility of future harm being done. This second process addressed repeated and/or serious harm that has been done—a level of harm determined by the person or persons harmed. Sometimes this process leads to creating healthier community. Sometimes, if done in a fully accountable way, if a system or community is not repairable, it may mean disbanding the organization in its existing form.

Creating Healthy Space and Accountability Processes in Community

To suggest that a person or an organization has done harm can understandably raise hackles. But let us be clear from the start: doing harm doesn't always mean intention to do harm. The preceding chapters have given us plenty of examples of instances in which great harm was done intentionally. But there are also instances in which harm occurs, whether the agent of harm intended it or not. Many experiences of harm occur in accidental and unintentional ways. However, intentionality and accountability and not tied together; even if you or your community didn't mean to do harm, it is still possible that you did it. And if you or your community or institution did, then being healthy means your or it must listen, accept responsibility, and engage in a process to make it less likely for harm to happen in the future.

Therapists and healers often, almost off-handedly, use the term "safe space" when we gather people together. We set the container of community assuming that we can offer safety in any space. This is impossible. Even with considerable training and skills, intuition and years of practice holding space and creating community, there is no way to *assure* safety. This doesn't mean we don't work hard create the best set of ethics, practices, and intentions to build space that is well-protected. It reminds us that safety is subjective and personal. It is also something that can be affected and distorted by past experiences of harm. Something one person can say or do, even without intention, can trigger someone else's past experiences of pain and trauma, no matter how careful we try to be.

So instead of "safe space," I follow a colleague in calling it protected space. I have built an ethic around creating protected space, what it means for me and to what we are collectively committing by creating shared protected space with and for ourselves and each other. To begin this conversation on accountability, I want to share with you this methodology of protected space.

The Practice of Protected Space: An Ethic and Collective Commitment

1. **We agree that safe space is a misnomer.** For we cannot prevent someone else from experiencing harm, intended or un-intended, in a collective space. We understand that we all have different experiences of past pain, trauma, and harm, and we that we can't always know what will harm or trigger someone else's hurt places.

2. **We acknowledge that protected space is different than safe space.** Knowing that we can't make space safe for everyone, we will shift from trying to practice perfection and instead build an ethic around the idea of protected space.
3. **We commit to a shared practice of protecting space for ourselves and others.** We will do our best to do no harm to anyone else: to listen to others, find empathy for different perspectives and lived experiences, not make assumptions about any one person based on factors of personality or identity, and give space for people to explain themselves when we don't understand what they are saying. We will do our best to hold each other accountable to these practices as a community and not be reactionary or defensive if someone brings to our attending some way in which we may not be being empathic and listening to others in shared space.
4. **We commit to taking care of ourselves and supporting others in engaging in the practices we need to protect ourselves in space when hurt places are touched on.** We will also commit to taking care and protecting ourselves. This may mean asking for conversations or practices to pause if we feel discomfort or uncertainty. It may mean taking a pause (time-out) for ourselves if we need to step away from a practice or conversation that is triggering us or bringing discomfort in some way. We will commit to engaging in our practices of self-support and care, and to ask for help and support when we need additional resources or feedback. We also commit as community members to support others if or when they are triggered or harmed within the community space, by listening to their experience of harm, its impact, and what they want to do to resolve it.
5. **We commit to addressing and working through harm done to others in this space, according to the comfort level of the person who has been harmed.** We agree to create a process and method suited to our community, which will address harm when it happens. This might entail talking through the harm when it happens, engaging with a learning and support process for those who have done harm, or having larger accountability measures that can be activated if a greater level of harm has been done.

6. **We commit to gentleness and generosity toward ourselves and others when harm is done.** For we understand that we all have the capacity to do harm, to have blindspots, not to understand someone else's experience and perspectives, and to honor ourselves as a work in progress every moment. We commit to addressing harm and working to learn from our experiences. But we also want not to fear engaging in community out of a fear of doing accidental harm or judging ourselves too harshly. Rather, we commit to doing the necessary work to act or react differently in the future. We understand that we can experience harm and triggering in a space. But we also commit to not judging ourselves when we are the ones triggered. There is no shame or blame in feeling our feelings and in feeling pain from our past arise in the present. We therefore commit to seeing it, moving through it, and caring for ourselves with gentleness and generosity when it happens. We will learn about ourselves and our reactions from the experience so that we have more tools to address such experiences if and when they arise in the future.

The Practice of Accountability for Leaders and Organizations

As I was beginning to write the first sentence of this chapter, a story aired on the news about a religious leader of a massive congregation who had just been reported for molesting a minor. This is not the first time this has happened during the book's writing and revision. I can recollect at least twenty such moments.

Clearly, this happens often and does great damage. To be an ally to those damaged by such behaviors and toxic dynamics within spiritual and religious communities, we must: be willing to do the work to address the harm; be accountable when we are part of that harm; hold organizations and leaders accountable when they do harm; and build an infrastructure that is more resilient and can diminish the capacity for harm in the future.

We also need processes of accountability and change-making within organizations, processes for leaders to use when harm is done. Here is one such process:

1. **We will engage in deep listening.** This means without defensiveness, explanations or excuses about why harm happened. The first step towards accountability and viable change is hearing from those who have been harmed. They are often the more marginalized, less visibilized, and least heard persons. We will listen in the ways that those harmed find most comfortable and safe. Such listening might include witnesses.
2. **We will invest in an outside and impartial review of the issue.** Because typically an insider's impulse is to minimize or obscure the issues and diminish the process of investigation, we need external, impartial reviewers. And we need to be prepared to pay them.
3. **Together with outside and impartial persons/organizations, we will facilitate a process for repair, reconciliation, and reparations for the harm done.** Please note that any attempt at reconciliation is entirely up to the victims. Repair of the harm is only the first process for effective accountability and change.
4. **We will restructure our systems, processes, and leadership, if that is integral to effective change, and will consider dissolving the organization and leadership structure if effective change is deemed impossible.** Change is uncomfortable, but it can be the only way to prevent harm in the future. Such change might include changing people in positions of power, removing people from the organization, and creating substantive checks on those in power.
5. **We will engage in public accountability. This includes honesty and transparency about the issues and our process of rectification, without provisos based on how it will impact our bottom line.** Since such process must allow victims' voices to be heard, nondisclosure agreements (NDAs) should be off limits.
6. **We will integrate any and all changes necessary to create an infrastructure which will protect against future harm.** If that is not possible, we will return to the question of the viability of continuing this community/organization/institution.

What does being a true ally entail? It means being intentional, authentic, and relational. It is hard work because changing and evolving as human beings is uncomfortable. Being an ally means making mistakes and not walking away after the first one, but being committed to repairing harm when it is done. It means finding the humility to stay in the discomfort and to build deeper relationship with ourselves and others out of those mistakes. It means doing our own healing so that we don't become persons who harm out of our hurt. We all have the capacity to be meaningful allies to each other. We can all change, and we can change our institutions. Let's get to work!

Epilogue

The Cracks are Where the Light Gets in: Woundedness and Transformation

Having begun this book and my story with an exploration of spiritual disillusionment in a Buddhist context doing yoga and meditation with a teacher who lacked boundaries, it seems fitting at the close to share one of the most spiritually healing experiences, which likewise occurred in a Buddhist context.

After graduate school I planned a month-long solo backpacking trip to Thailand and Laos, not least because of the ease of traversing this area of the world as a single female. As was customary for my body in transit, I managed to pick up a stubborn sinus infection during my trek. I had made my way from Bangkok to the northern city Chiang Mai and west to the Burmese border, and by the time I landed there, I was very sick. Boarding a plane headed for Luang Prabang, Laos, the feverish sweat poured off my brow. I felt drained by illness and the relentless monsoon season heat.

With a Brit and a Scot whom I had met on the plane, I made my way to a guesthouse made of misaligned plywood siding, just a block up the hill from the Mekong River. It was three dollars a day, and given my pounding headache, I was grateful for a mattress and a fan. The guesthouse was owned by *Mama*, or that is what she asked everyone to call her. I remember that she had a bag like Mary Poppins and it held everything from Band-Aids® to spare bananas, all to be offered to her guests for whatever needs they might have.

As my delirium escalated and the local pharmacy lacked the requisite antibiotics, Mama became increasingly concerned for my well-being.

Mama was a devout Buddhist and went to temple daily. On the day I left by plane for the Southern Thailand island of Ko Tao via Ko Samui, and for the cure that both antibiotics and beaches could offer, Mama came into my room to say goodbye and sat down on the mattress next to me. I had just finished packing my backpack for the flight ahead.

"This morning I go to temple," she said in hush.

Then she took my hand and placed into my open palm a bracelet made of black oblong beads and white skulls, a bracelet which she had taken to the monks for their blessing. She closed my hand and gave it a squeeze. With me so sick and so far from home, her subsequent hug filled me with a sweet mix of joy and sadness. It was sacred. It was sacramental.

Sitting on the plane an hour later, running my hand over my blessed bracelet, my eyes began to well with tears, which took me by surprise. I remember thinking, "Why am I so sad? Why is it so hard to leave this place and this woman I only just met?"

In life and on the spiritual journey, there are only a handful of moments as powerful for me as those few moments with Mama in that guesthouse in Luang Prabang. Her love was so implicit and sincere. Her generosity was so full and robust. She was an organic and innate wisdom teacher.

Such moments of love soften all the painful ones. They don't erase the hurts, but they do give us the courage to face them. We learn from the false gurus and the wisdom teachers. We learn from the humanity and imperfection that is in every bit of human experience.

Such moments revive my faith in humanity and the cosmos despite the hurtful and tedious evil that exists in the world. *That* is the image with which I leave you: Mama and me in a sacred moment one summer in Laos.

May you find your way through lonely nights.
May you find rest and calm and peace from sacred fights.
There are hard days and there are deep pains.
But tomorrow brings the possibility of hope, grace, love and healing on every new horizon.
Seek the healing you deserve. You are worth it.

Addendum

Finding a Mental Health Provider

to Support Your Healing from Religious Injury, Spiritual Abuse, and Church Hurt

How does one access the most effective and trained provider? How to find someone familiar with religious injury, someone who will understand the unique nature of this specific hurting experience?

The following are some basic tips to get you started on the road to finding a provider right for you.

1. **Make sure the provider is adequately credentialed and certified in counseling.** The provider should be master's level clinician or above in a field of therapy or counseling. The major fields of clinical therapy practice include psychology, psychiatry (although psychiatrists are usually medical doctors whose main function is to prescribe medication for mental health, a select few provide counseling), social work, marriage and family therapy, counseling psychology, and mental health counseling. Make sure the provider is licensed in the state in which they practice. You can check the record of every licensed professional in your state through the state's licensing website to make sure their licensure status is in good standing—meaning there are not any pending charges for issues related to client care.

2. **Check to see if the provider's *Psychology Today* profile and/or website lists trauma and PTSD as one of their areas of specialty.** This does not guarantee he or she is an expert in traumatology, but if it is referenced, there is a better chance he or she has a minimal working knowledge of trauma. Not everyone who mentions trauma in their biographical information is a trauma expert. Many have only a generalist's ability to treat trauma, and many will not have any direct practice with religious injury and spiritual abuse as an area of practice. This doesn't mean they are not a good fit for you; it just means it is important that you go into your consultation with a reason-

able expectation of the provider's abilities and knowledge about religious-oriented trauma.

3. **Imagine your first session with a provider as a job interview for that person.** You have no obligation to commit to a provider just because he or she has met with you. You are the person who decides what is best for your care. Trauma survivors tend to be yes-people as a means of self-protection. But you have the option of choice here. Have a list of questions you want to ask, questions such as: How much of your practice involves treating trauma and PTSD as the primary diagnosis? How many years have you been treating trauma? What therapeutic interventions do you use specifically for traumatic stress? Have you had any experience with religious trauma/injury specifically? If so, in what way? How do you treat religious injury and spiritual abuse? To your mind, are there any differences between treating this trauma and other traumas? How comfortable are you with addressing this issue in counseling?

4. **Consider finding resources outside of your local area.** While you might find a therapist who is a good fit in your area, it is possible that that therapist has little experience with religious injury or trauma. You can supplement that gap by accessing resources through books, websites, online religious hurt forums, and specialists.

5. **Consider sharing some of those resources with your chosen therapy provider.** If they are both adept and humble, they will be willing to learn along with you and process some of the elements unique to this kind of traumatic stress.

6. **Know that this field is growing.** Although trauma experts even those who also understand religious injury may be limited at present, it is encouraging to know that out of necessity both of these fields are growing in notice and practice.